LIBRARIANS AND INSTRUCTIONAL DESIGNERS

Collaboration and Innovation

JOE ESHLEMAN
RICHARD MONIZ
KAREN MANN
KRISTEN ESHLEMAN

CHICAGO 2016

ISBNs
978-0-8389-1455-7 (paper)
978-0-8389-1478-6 (PDF)
978-0-8389-1479-3 (ePub)
978-0-8389-1480-9 (Kindle)

Library of Congress Cataloging-in-Publication Data

Names: Eshleman, Joe, author. | Moniz, Richard, author. | Mann, Karen, 1971- author. | Eshleman, Kristen, author.
Title: Librarians and instructional designers : collaboration and innovation / Joe Eshleman, Richard Moniz, Karen Mann, Kristen Eshleman.
Description: Chicago : ALA Editions, an imprint of the American Library Association, 2016. | Includes bibliographical references and index.
Identifiers: LCCN 2016014823 | ISBN 9780838914557 (print : alk. paper) | ISBN 9780838914793 (epub) | ISBN 9780838914786 (PDF) | ISBN 9780838914809 (Kindle)
Subjects: LCSH: Academic libraries—Relations with faculty and curriculum. | Academic librarians—Effect of technological innovations on. | Academic librarians—Professional relationships. | Instructional systems—Design. | Education, Higher—Effect of technological innovations on.
Classification: LCC Z675.U5 E77 2016 | DDC 027.7—dc23 LC record available at https://lccn.loc.gov/2016014823

Cover design by Alejandra Diaz. Imagery © Shutterstock, Inc.

Text composition by Dianne M. Rooney in the Chaparral, Gotham, and Bell Gothic typefaces.

∞ This paper meets the requirements of ANSI/NISO Z39.48-1992 (Permanence of Paper).

Printed in the United States of America

20 19 18 17 16   5 4 3 2 1

Contents

Acknowledgments

We would like to thank the following who were instrumental in helping us complete this book: George Siemens, Joshua Kim, Allison Dulin Salisbury, Suzanne Churchill, Mark Sample, Jennifer Hunter, Karen Tercho, and Amy Knauer. We would like to offer a special thanks to Jamie Santoro, our editor at the American Library Association, who believed in our project from the beginning and encouraged us every step of the way.

Introduction

Learning in the digital age is a networked and participatory process. Therefore, supporting faculty members' and students' ability to master digital methods and tools increasingly requires thoughtful partnerships between librarians and instructional designers. As technology continues to influence the direction of higher education, each of these fields faces both challenges and opportunities. Those individuals who are able to keep up with the consistent change are at an advantage. More importantly, those who are open to collaborative opportunities become more valuable to their institutions as they build networks of relationships and shared skill sets. Due to the increased importance and influence of digital technologies and the move toward design thinking as a way to offer strategies and solutions, it is time for librarians and instructional designers to team up to show their value to their institutions.

It is the combined interest in design along with a deep understanding of information creation and use with a focus on technology that is so important here. The intent is not to develop a magic bullet that somehow solves all of the woes of higher education. It is instead the desire to bring together human resources with unique and helpful knowledge (and skill sets). They can become valuable assets in the move to the newer technology-driven types of teaching and learning that current and future students need. Note that although technology continues to influence education, our focus here is on the people (librarians, instructional designers, students) and the collaborative opportunities available to them. While awareness and understanding of how to use the tools offered by today's technology are of utmost importance, they do not supersede the need for relationship building.

Certain day-to-day realities, as we all know, have the potential to make good intentions fall by the wayside. "How can I begin working with a librarian or an instructional designer when that is not part of my job?" In some cases, the position of instructional designer may not even exist in a given workplace.

"Yes, this is a good idea, but what does it look like in reality on my campus?" These are good questions to ask as we search for creative but practical solutions. Creating a concrete plan for moving from a basic project in which a designer and a librarian work together to one that involves a team that influences and impacts campus decisions is a justified goal. Hopefully, in addition to the examples we provide, this book will also generate conversations that help to add new and improved strategies to our ideas.

To be clear, this book is a combined effort between librarians and instructional designers and in some ways does more to represent the goals within it than what has actually been written. Furthermore, within our own various institutions, we continue to work toward its loftier goals. That is to say that although we work in tandem with our own instructional designers and librarians (as the case may be), we have not yet been able to achieve the kind of interest or influence on our own campuses for which we strive. As a type of enthusiastic exhortation rather than an extensive review or an exhaustive reference, this book is meant to inspire librarians and instructional designers to get to know one another and then to work collaboratively. The group foundation of this effort (two librarians and two instructional designers/technologists) supports this notion. The main goal is to spark ideas for collaboration among those who have not yet done so and to open up avenues of opportunity for those who cannot find them in their environments.

Once more, in the implementation of these ideas, another common question is likely to arise: "How does a concrete collaborative relationship between librarians and instructional designers that influences administration on my campus work and what form would it take?" While we provide numerous examples of what has already been done, we also put forth theories and conjecture to encourage creative solutions on the part of readers. The goal at this point is not to give that question one distinct answer but, rather, to inspire more people to ask the question and to come up with answers that make sense for them and their institutions.

A renewed focus on the building of academic networks that can create strong bonds on campus needs to be discussed to improve higher education's capability to move forward. As a way to think about how librarians are affected, Keith Webster, in a recent presentation titled "Leading the Library of the Future: W(h)ither Technical Services?," points out:

- We operate in a networked world—local collections in themselves make learning and research incomplete.
- We should no longer focus on acquiring the products of scholarship; we must be embedded within scholarship.
- New methods of research—open science, digital humanities, etc.—reshape researchers' needs and demands.
- How do we get there?[1]

One way to get there is to change the way we think about what librarians do and how our institutions think about librarians. We must also come to the realization that we cannot get there alone. Looking for those on campus to work with has frequently led us to view faculty as good partners, and this has provided for many fruitful collaborations. Still, such relationships have not created the elevated reputation or integration for librarians that we desire. We have much to offer our institutions that remains hidden below the surface. Although many partnerships with teaching faculty work well, there may be even more opportunities and situations in which librarians and instructional designers are better matched as peers. There are numerous cases where librarians and instructional designers have worked together in the past, yet the opportunity for more cross-pollination between these two campus roles has yet to be fully realized. This book recommends exploring those opportunities that may yield collaborations on campus. It places emphasis on making the effort to work with those in technology and design positions because these areas will continue to both impact and define higher education. Additionally, a focus on design allows us to reinvent roles and helps us to be prepared when considering ourselves as campus leaders.

Librarians can sometimes react negatively to joining (or even collaborating) with technologists on campus. Such efforts can be met with divided positions along the academia/technology line. It is not the goal of this book to take a position or to adhere to an agenda but merely to point out that technology and design thinking will continue to influence how teaching and learning take place. And it is imperative for librarians to move with the tide. Within this is the opportunity to learn, grow, and build relationships.

There continues to be a great deal of discussion about the future of higher education and how it is being impacted by technology. Educational technology, commonly shortened to edtech, has had an interesting relationship with academia, one that seems to be both altruistic and antagonistic at times. As a librarian, it is interesting to observe how libraries earlier went through a similar experience that is currently occurring within the broader arena of higher education. The questioning of value and the subsequent need to prove worth continue to occur. Whether technology (including educational technology) will be a partner or an imminent threat (or a mix of these) moving forward is a topic that is continually raised.

Librarians by now are well aware of how they are frequently viewed as obsolete and have grown accustomed to "value questioning" fatigue and the numerous countdowns to their demise. Yet they still remain generally optimistic. Many view this as a time for opportunity rather than buying into an end-time mentality. To move forward, there needs to be less attention given to the academia/technology divide and a greater effort toward combining skill sets to gain greater leverage and advantage. Often, librarians feel as though they need to develop all of these technology skills themselves and overlook potential campus partners as a way to develop collaborative relationships and exchange ideas.

As libraries begin to move away from their legacy systems and branch out in many different directions and in creative ways, they are sending a message to their schools. The message is that there is value in the librarian's attentiveness to emerging trends and technologies, independent agency in openness, and freedom in flexibility. The collaborative initiatives that have occurred on our campuses span the entire spectrum, from informal discussions about new software to deep teaching partnerships within numerous learning spaces and in MOOCs (massive open online courses).

Although there is a history of departmental association with the campus information technology (generally referred to as IT) group, in this case, the authors desire to view the instructional designer and technologist as more separate entities connected to the library. There is a history of examination that strongly associates the role of instructional technologist with the campus IT department when collaborating with the library, and while there is no need to erase that history, a new perspective is needed.[2] Just as librarians have begun to focus more on teaching and learning, so have instructional designers been drawn to topics within librarianship. In fact, one of the main observations made when researching and writing this book is how these roles are influencing each other and slowly blending in interesting ways. A fervent goal of this book is also to inspire the recognition of the value of design thinking in any endeavor and to place focus on the ways in which design affects instruction.

An interesting parallel that affects both instructional technology and libraries is a minor predicament related to definitions, in particular on the library side with respect to library instruction. The term *information literacy* is now generally understood and accepted in higher education yet often needs to be further defined when mentioned to students or outside academia. In a similar way, *instructional technology and design* has grappled with defining itself. An excellent chronological summation of instructional technology's problem can be found in Robert A. Reiser's chapter "What Field Did You Say You Were In? Defining and Naming Our Field" in the textbook *Trends and Issues in Instructional Design and Technology*.[3] Reiser points out that the definition of instructional technology has historically moved from one focused on media to one concerned with process. He suggests that *instructional design and technology* would be a more precise and inclusive term, and his desire to add design here fits in well with our thought process (see the sidebar for a discussion of terms used in this book).

An interesting examination of the two roles discussed in this book is "Identity Crisis: Librarian or Instructional Technologist?" by Ryan L. Sittler, which corresponds to a conclusion that was made by our group.[4] *Instructional technology* has various definitions, and this has led to confusion about what it actually means, particularly in relation to librarianship. Although it is easy to

AN INSTRUCTIONAL DESIGNER BY ANY NAME IS STILL . . . WHAT?

As the pace of technology affects how words are invented, used, and changed, it can be difficult to settle on an appropriate term and feel comfortable knowing that the term is accurate and inclusive and will continue to refer to its original meaning in the future. Beginning work on this book as a team, we became confused about what consistent terms to use to describe the roles and positions to which we continually referred. We settled on using *instructional designer* as our most consistent term because one theme of this book is the importance of design. In some cases we used *instructional technologist* and just the title *designer* as well as others, but we felt as though the term *instructional designer* mapped most completely to our ideas. As an incomplete but hopefully clarifying way to help with this situation at the beginning of the book, here is a glossary with some additional references that may help readers to understand some of the terms we use.

blended librarian: "A position that combines the traditional aspects of librarianship with the technology skills of an information technologist; someone skilled with software and hardware. . . . To this mix, the Blended Librarian adds the instructional or educational technologist's skills for curriculum design and the application of technology for student-centered learning."[a]

instruction librarian: "(Associated with) instructional programs designed to teach library users how to locate the information they need quickly and effectively."[b] Also, "any librarian with instruction responsibilities."[c]

instructional design/designer: "The process by which instruction is improved through the analysis of learning needs and systematic development of learning materials. Instructional designers often use technology and multimedia as tools to enhance instruction."[d] Also, "a process for systematically designing effective instructional materials and learning opportunities."[e]

instructional technology: "[T]he theory and practice of design, development, utilization, management, and evaluation of processes and resources for learning."[f]

---

a. Steven J. Bell and John D. Shank, *Academic Librarianship by Design: A Blended Librarian's Guide to the Tools and Techniques* (Chicago: American Library Association, 2007).

b. Joan M. Reitz, *Dictionary for Library and Information Science* (Westport, CT: Libraries Unlimited, 2004), 71.

c. Association of College and Research Libraries (ACRL), *Standards for Proficiencies for Instruction Librarians and Coordinators: A Practical Guide* (Chicago: American Library Association, 2008), 3, www.ala.org/acrl/sites/ala.org.acrl/files/content/standards/profstandards.pdf.

d. Richard Culatta, "Instructional Design," InstructionalDesign.org, accessed February 1, 2016, www.instructionaldesign.org.

e. Association of College and Research Libraries, "Instructional Design for Librarians: The What, Why, and How of ID," accessed February 1, 2016, www.ala.org/acrl/conferences/instructionaldesign.

f. Barbara B. Seels and Rita C. Richey, *Instructional Technology: The Definition and Domains of the Field* (Washington, DC: Association for Educational Communications and Technology, 1994), 24.

get hung up on and confused about these titles, and there may even be cases within this book where the terms seem to be interchangeable, it is imperative for readers to recognize that strict adherence to one title or another may not occur consistently. This situation should not create pause. It is important to prioritize the exchange of ideas and develop a collaborative outlook as having greater significance than the unswerving use of a title. As stated by Shonn Haren in the comments section of the soul-searching article "Librarianship Doesn't Need Professionals," "I have had outlandishly dressed coworkers who were the soul of professionalism, and conservatively dressed coworkers who were utterly unprofessional and immature in the way they worked. In the end, the way we act and treat each other, not the way we look, determines what makes us professionals."[5] In the same way, the way we work together should take precedence over what we are titled.

Chapter 1 of this book points out that as changes to higher education occur, there are opportunities for librarians and instructional designers to lead through their unique positions on campus. As professionals who work with faculty, students, and staff and who have a wide knowledge of curriculum and personnel, the people in these departments can offer distinctive services and perspectives on campus. They can offer even more when working together. The importance of the timing for these collaborations sets the tone and purpose for this book.

In chapter 2, we review instructional designer–librarian collaborations with an introduction to some of the history of their cooperative endeavors. Most importantly, we ground the discussion within the context of the overarching philosophies and goals that have historically influenced professionals in these fields.

In chapter 3, our focus is on potential best practices and opportunities for instructional designer–librarian collaborations. This section of the book also reviews in a general sense many of the emerging issues that are affecting higher education and, therefore, these two departments or areas. Topics such as combined meetings and messaging, cooperative workshops, assisting parent institutions with intellectual management and copyright issues, supporting faculty research, assisting with digital scholarship, and others are discussed.

Chapter 4 primarily focuses on the conceptual nature of how to collaborate and presents strategies for developing a collaborative mindset. It begins to point out ways to create an environment for collective action.

Chapter 5 offers an introduction to current topics affecting library instruction, particularly the relatively new *Framework for Information Literacy for Higher Education* from the Association of College and Research Libraries (ACRL) and its associated threshold concepts.[6] The movement toward more online library instruction taught by instruction librarians and how it can be supported with good instructional design and help from instructional designers is a focus here.

An introduction to digital humanities and an outline of the foundations of the field appear in chapter 6. This chapter surveys opportunities within the digital humanities that invite collaboration among faculty, librarians, academic technologists, and, often, students. Following a detailed description of the roles of librarians and academic designers is a case study in collaboration at Davidson College. This case study outlines the work of each collaborator in relation to an evolving digital project that mirrors changes in technology and collaboration over more than a decade. Chapter 6 also explores MOOCs that continue to morph into related online learning models. Attempting to find a solid and consistent role in relation to MOOCs is a difficult task for librarians. Collaborating with instructional designers allows librarians to gain a better understanding of MOOC construction, design, goals, and responsibilities. A brief look at human-centered design closes this chapter.

Chapter 7 explores how digital media have helped to create a partnership between librarians and instructional designers due to the abundance of digital resources and tools available to faculty today. Whether professors are providing instruction in the digitally enhanced classroom or through online resources, such as a learning management system, they are able to seamlessly integrate media into the curriculum to enhance the student experience and increase learning. This chapter examines how librarians and instructional designers can work together to encourage, inform, train, and support both faculty and students in the use of available digital resources and equipment. Types of media discussed in this chapter include digital media, media databases, online media, public domain resources, and streaming media tools. Other topics mentioned include the embedded librarian, equipment, and copyright issues.

Chapter 8 puts forth the idea that librarians and instructional designers are natural allies in the effort to support the most ideal learning environments within the institutional learning management system (LMS). The LMS is generally the central purview of the instructional designer. This individual often has primary responsibility for preparing faculty to make the most of the multitude of features—everything from facilitating better online discussions to validating tests and quizzes. The librarian, however, often interfaces with the LMS from the perspective of providing research support. Librarians now have significant experience in this role through the implementation of embedded librarian programs and/or personal librarian programs. While both librarians and instructional designers often help the faculty individually, a more focused partnership could allow them to further assist instructors by linking to appropriate resources and designing those links in the most impactful ways. A number of creative opportunities exist for the collaborative development and presentation of tutorials, learning objects, and workshops for students and faculty as well as team-based interventions personalized for a given instructor.

Finally, chapter 9 concludes the book by attempting to answer this question: "What's next for librarians and instructional designers?" This short chapter briefly explores the new roles that are developing from the intersection of librarianship and technology, for example, the instructional design librarian.

The EDUCAUSE Learning Initiative (ELI) series "7 Things You Should Know About . . ." came out with "7 Things You Should Know About Leading Academic Transformation" in November 2015.[7] One of the questions asked in the document is, "What moves academic transformation forward?" And one of the answers given is, "Cross-Functional Teamwork." The report states:

> A hallmark of transformation is cross-functional teams. CIOs [chief information officers] need to be in conversation with CFOs [chief financial officers], provosts, presidents, faculty, instructional designers, enrollment, and financial aid. The conversations are often surprising and empowering, creating greater awareness of abilities to support one another. Effective leaders devote time and attention to making sure that cross-functional relationships are healthy and productive, and they prioritize the work of those teams.[8]

Note the importance of conversation and the inclusion of instructional designers in this suggestion and, unfortunately, the exclusion of librarians (they are not mentioned in the entire document).

On a more positive note, the New Media Consortium (NMC) teamed up with ELI to publish the *NMC Horizon Report: 2016 Higher Education Edition* in February 2016.[9] In it, "18 topics carefully selected by the 2016 Horizon Project Higher Education Expert Panel related to the educational applications of technology are examined, all of them areas very likely to impact technology planning and decision-making over the next five years (2016–2020)."[10] Libraries and librarians are mentioned here several times. The paragraph titled Leadership, under "Significant Challenges Impeding Technology Adoption in Higher Education," makes a particularly important point:

> Again, while all the identified challenges have leadership implications that are discussed in the following pages, two pose roadblocks to employing effective vision and leadership. There is a pressing but solvable need to improve digital literacy at institutions across the world. Fortunately, the presence of academic libraries on campus is opening up channels for students to gain confidence in using technologies for the express purpose of learning. The Association of College & Research Libraries' Framework for Information Literacy for Higher Education has established a set of interconnected core concepts to help campuses better organize ideas about information, research, and scholarship into a comprehensive whole.[11]

Once again, the driving force behind this librarian–instructional designer effort is to present ways to work together and to force a reconsideration of how these campus roles can provide much more for their institutions. Each has so much to offer the other, and at times it seems as if the only thing preventing them from sharing is ingrained culture. Initiating these relationships begins the same way all collaborative efforts do: "One of the most important steps information technologists and librarians can take is to learn more about the nature of each unit's work."[12] And most importantly, "librarians, instructional technologists, faculty, and students should not plod onward in isolation."[13]

NOTES

1. Keith Webster, "Leading the Library of the Future: W(h)ither Technical Services?" (presentation at the ALCTS President's Symposium, ALA Midwinter meeting, Boston, MA, January 8, 2016), www.slideshare.net/KeithWebster2/leading-the-library-of-the-future-whither-technical-services.
2. Marvel Maring, "Webmasters Are from Mars, Instruction Librarians Are from Venus: Developing Effective and Productive Communication between Information Technology Departments and Reference/Instruction Librarians: How Instructional Design Collaborations Can Succeed," in *Brick and Click Libraries: Proceedings of an Academic Library Symposium*, eds. Frank Baudino, Connie Jo Ury, and Sarah G. Park (Maryville, OH: Northwest Missouri State University, 2008), 70–76.
3. Robert A. Reiser, "What Field Did You Say You Were In? Defining and Naming Our Field," in *Trends and Issues in Instructional Design and Technology*, eds. Robert A. Reiser and John V. Dempsey (Boston: Pearson, 2012), 1–7.
4. Ryan L. Sittler, "Identity Crisis: Librarian or Instructional Technologist?" *Indiana Libraries* 30, no. 1 (2011): 8–14.
5. Madison Sullivan, "Librarianship Doesn't Need Professionals," *ACRLog*, January 19, 2016, http://acrlog.org/2016/01/19/professionalism.
6. Association of College and Research Libraries, *Framework for Information Literacy for Higher Education* (Chicago: American Library Association, 2016), www.ala.org/acrl/sites/ala.org.acrl/files/content/issues/infolit/Framework-ILHE.pdf.
7. EDUCAUSE Learning Initiative, "7 Things You Should Know About Leading Academic Transformation," November 4, 2015, https://library.educause.edu/~/media/files/library/2015/11/eli7126-pdf.pdf.
8. Ibid., 2.
9. L. Johnson, S. Adams Becker, M. Cummins, V. Estrada, A. Freeman, and C. Hall, *NMC Horizon Report: 2016 Higher Education Edition* (Austin, TX:

The New Media Consortium, 2016), http://cdn.nmc.org/media/2016-nmc-horizon-report-he-EN.pdf.

10. Ibid., 3.
11. Ibid., 20.
12. Maring, "Webmasters Are from Mars," 72.
13. Bonnie W. Oldham and Diane Skorina, "Librarians and Instructional Technologists Collaborate," *College and Research Libraries News* 70, no. 11 (2009): 634–37, http://crln.acrl.org/content/70/11/634.full.

JOE ESHLEMAN AND
KRISTEN ESHLEMAN

1
The Changing Environment of Higher Education

Changes within and outside higher education continue to occur, and these lead to new opportunities to address them. In a similar fashion to numerous industries, sectors, and services preceding it, higher education is in the midst of external pressures. Technological change is driving the need to adapt. As higher education moves to a more digital focus, this creates a situation in which added resources are needed in those areas that directly support digital initiatives. Because they have unique experience in this regard, librarians and instructional designers should be considered as valuable institutional resources to help guide this transformation.

HOW HIGHER EDUCATION IS CHANGING

In their report *Preparing for the Digital University: A Review of the History and Current State of Distance, Blended, and Online Learning*, George Siemens, Dragan Gašević, and Shane Dawson point out, "Higher education is changing. Central to this change is the transition from a physically based learning model to one that makes greater use of digital technologies."[1] What do we mean when we say that education is going digital? In an interesting response to this question, Clay Shirky, in his article "The Digital Revolution in Higher Education Has Already Happened. No One Noticed," begins:

> In the fall of 2012, the most recent semester with complete data in the U.S., four million undergraduates took at least one course online, out of sixteen million total, with growth up since then. Those numbers mean that more students now take a class online than attend a college with varsity football. More than twice as many now take a class online as live on campus. There are more undergraduates enrolled in an online class than there are graduate students enrolled in all Masters and Ph.D. programs combined. At the current rate of growth, half the country's undergraduates will have at least one online class on their transcripts by the end of the decade. This is the new normal.[2]

This "new normal," Shirky goes on to say, is defined by a higher education landscape that is composed of a much wider variety of students. They are taking more online classes than previous students had. Relaying the information from the study *Online College Students 2014: Comprehensive Data on Demands and Preferences*,[3] Shirky highlights the demographics of online students: "[H]alf are married, compared with fewer than one in five undergrads generally. Half also have children. (Student mothers outnumber student fathers 2 to 1.) Two in three work; two in five work full time. A third live in rural areas, a far bigger proportion than the general population. Four out of five are 25 or older."[4] He concludes that a disconnect needs to be bridged between this group of students and antiquated ideas held by higher education administration. Shirky's focus on who is using these digital technologies as they apply to online learning does not fully address the transitional view of Siemens, Gašević, and Dawson. But it does help to emphasize that the design of learning technologies needs to take into account this new and different user. This move to digital and a diverse set of students needs design thinkers to help craft ways in which an "old guard" higher education can reinvent itself and appeal to a broad range of people. The capabilities that instructional designers and librarians bring to this issue should be considered by leaders in higher education. Collaborative efforts by instructional designers and librarians could lead to positive solutions.

To reiterate, one critical point is not just the shift of focus on the digital but also the need for higher education to be more open and inclusive. Additionally, leaders within higher education need to reflect on the realization that the communities they serve consist of a wide mix of demographic backgrounds and cannot be considered to be of a certain type. Interestingly, libraries have been at the forefront of some of these issues. Most notably, they have dealt with the self-questioning of value and a renewed focus on community (that they serve and of which they are a part). Under scrutiny for their continued purpose in a world where everything that was formerly on bookshelves is now considered to be at one's fingertips and faced with budgetary cuts and pressures, academic libraries (and librarians) have been questioned about their value for some time. As stated in the *Association of Research Libraries/Columbia University/Cornell University/University of Toronto Pilot Library Liaison Institute Final Report*, "Higher education and academic research libraries are changing with unprecedented speed. New methods of conducting and disseminating research, new pedagogies, increased public scrutiny, and financial pressure call for accountability and value-added impact."[5] Responding (or not responding) in different ways to these challenges, academic librarians had been confronted earlier with some of these same questions with which higher education currently grapples. And these inquires will continue, led primarily by the leading question, "What is the value of libraries/higher education?" and closely followed by the introspective (and potentially stress-inducing) question, "What is the future of libraries/higher education?"

Understanding the community that they serve has been a consistent concern for librarians for quite some time. Although commonly associated with the public library mission, academic libraries have also seen value in understanding their community in its many forms (although perhaps never so adroitly as they do today). As stated in the Libraries' Strengths section of "Part 5: The Present and Future of Libraries" in the *Library Services in the Digital Age* Pew Research Center report, "One common theme was libraries' role as a community center, and their connection to patrons and other local institutions."[6] In a broader sense, academic librarians see their community as students foremost, yet faculty and staff are also part of the group they serve. Additionally, the library community of which they are part is now being evaluated more stringently (by librarians, especially in the efforts of critical librarianship), and a greater focus than ever before has been placed on having the library community reflect a broad mix of constituents in the same way in which Shirky points out that higher education needs to better reflect diverse populations. All of this reflection is timely and can ideally add purpose and value to larger communities.

As part of this self-evaluation of their own community and attempts to reach out to a vaster group of patrons, academic librarians are also realizing that they must physically "get out of the library" and connect to the many community partners available to them. This effort means that more libraries are seeing the value in cross-departmental and institutional collaboration. Keith Webster, in his presentation "Leading the Library of the Future: W(h)ither Technical Services?," lays out five generations of library focus: in the first generation, libraries were collection centric; they moved on to become client focused, then experience centered, and recently have been interested in the connected learning experience; now, in the current generation, libraries think about collaborative knowledge, media, and fabrication facilities—what he refers to as the fifth generation.[7] Although the focus of his presentation is on technical services, Webster also includes "Bold Assertions" from Anne R. Kenney's presentation about collaboration between libraries ("Approaching An Entity Crisis: Reconceiving Research Libraries in a Multi-institutional Context").[8] In a series of slides from her presentation, Kenney first states, "Our history of collaboration may ironically make it more difficult to do radical collaboration,"[9] which could mean that venturing away from previously comfortable joint ventures may be difficult. (See chapter 4 for some discussion about radical collaboration.) Finally, she shows that an area ripe for collaboration is "The Power of Many."[10] The power-of-many concept as envisioned here could involve supporting library enterprises that are concerned with promoting inclusion (critical librarianship) and cooperative ventures (cross-collaborative library initiatives).

When considered as potential agents of change on campus, it is the uncommon college or university that has librarians and instructional designers at the top of their lists. Reasons for this are given throughout this book. The primary one appears to be that librarians and instructional designers do little to position themselves as strong contributors to the direction that higher education must take (even in reference to their own expertise). Although it may at first sound difficult or not aligned to their general responsibilities, librarians and instructional designers need to consider themselves today as leaders on campus and act accordingly. Librarian staff and faculty in these roles have expertise dealing with digital networks and information use. In many cases, the reaction to this call for action is that day-to-day tasks or current institutional obligations do not allow for this type of leadership work. Yet, at minimum, shouldn't daily discussions of the higher education situation take place as a first step? And these conversations between instructional designers and librarians need to begin now as a way to lead to collaboration, influence, and leadership.

This is not to say that there are no larger discussions around these points. The American Library Association (ALA) offers a "Library Leadership Training Resources" list on its website,[11] and articles such as "It Takes a University to Build a Library" by Dane Ward point out, "The world of libraries is changing rapidly, and those who lead them need to realize that they need the expertise of others on campus."[12] The key point is that even more of this needs to occur, and quickly.

It is the rare librarian or instructional designer who would draw attention to the idea that he or she could be a leader in this arena. Despite this, it would appear that a college or university with administrative leaders who understand the continued importance of information use in the workplace would consider those on campus who work with information as valuable resources. Additionally, those who have experience designing instruction, especially those with an awareness of how to design online learning effectively, should be sought-after sources for understanding how to move forward. Campus leaders would be making an insightful and prescient decision to use these human resources more efficiently. If we do live in a world that continues to value technological awareness, skillful use of information, and intuitive design talent, shouldn't more higher education leaders recognize the value of librarians and instructional designers for their students' futures (and even as allies in the evolution of the future of higher education)? Shouldn't those positions on campus that present themselves as information experts (librarians) and as possessing deep knowledge into the design of education (instructional designers) be those who are consulted on how to move forward? Or are we overestimating the worth and capability of these two positions?

Perhaps another way to view the positions (and roles) here is to take them out of the equation. It is possible that the roles and positions actually hinder the ability to consider librarians and instructional designers as primary resources for solutions to some of the problems plaguing higher education. Preconceived notions of what people in these positions do (and, even more, what they are interested in) can continue to keep librarians and instructional designers in subservient positions. It can be the case that decision makers on campus do not have a great awareness of what instructional designers do and they may harken back to their own collegiate experiences in the library or their own subjective understanding of the role of the librarian. Experienced instructional designers surely know how little the majority of those on their campus (including librarians) know about instructional design. These limited assessments may be responsible for a type of self-fulfilling environment for instructional designers and librarians, and it is up to them to break these systemic preconceptions by taking the initiative. There are numerous ways to do so outlined in this book, and one that continues to gain momentum is holding collaborative workshops with centers for teaching and learning on campus. In thinking about moving beyond preassigned positions, such aptitudes as enthusiasm, openness, and the desire to be forward thinking may be better criteria for considering whom to collaborate with than institutional roles. It may not always be the case that a title or job description can be changed easily, but changing one's mindset about seeking out whom to work with and looking beyond potential institutional limitations can be accomplished.

Connected to the idea of changing how to think about what librarians and instructional designers do is a consideration of the ways in which they are perceived. Although this concept may seem to initially present itself as a conundrum because the overall view of libraries is generally positive, librarians have a great deal of difficulty changing the stereotypes applied to them. Many of these appear innocuous at first but prove to be more damaging when examined closely. Chapters 4 and 6 provide a more detailed review of how librarians are perceived, but for now, it is worth noting that librarians are highly invested in moving toward becoming more illustrative of the changing student dynamic that Shirky illuminates.[13] One example of this self-reflection that is indicative of the forward thinking associated with critical librarianship is the current interest in devoting efforts to grappling with the pervasiveness of the "whiteness" of librarians and, in conjunction, pushing for a greater representation within librarianship that aligns with those who use the library.[14] One aspect of critical librarianship is evaluating how libraries operate and focusing on analyzing how closely librarians are aligned to their stated values. Associated with this are efforts to give opportunities to librarians who are underrepresented, and this can be bolstered by hiring a more representative spectrum of librarians. This type of work could help to spread a better and more wide-ranging conception of what librarians do and what they are capable of doing because more representative and wider connections can take place, inside and outside of the library. Another pertinent issue in librarianship for quite some time has been how the profession is aging and losing touch with current ideas, although this can be somewhat of a sore spot within the profession. In a post about embracing "next-gen librarianship" from the blog *Library Lost and Found*, Ashley Maynor makes the case that stereotyping librarians by generations does not help and that, "[n]ot defined by birth year, next-generation is about a mindset, a disposition, and an outlook."[15] (See chapter 4 for more on the importance of dispositions and mindsets.) All of this examination of roles and perceptions may appear to be off topic or impractical, yet it is crucial to understanding how one is viewed as an authentic librarian or as a potential collaborator or leader. Although instructional technologists do not openly grapple with these issues as often, these predicaments still apply to them in reference to leadership.

In the book *Transforming Our Image, Building Our Brand: The Education Advantage*, Valerie Gross conveys the idea that the educational role of librarians needs to be prominent in library mission statements.[16] Although her book is primarily intended to encourage public libraries to consider "replacing typical library terms and phrases with bold, compelling, and descriptive terminology that commands value and *that people understand*,"[17] this type of reinvention can also reinvigorate the perception of academic librarians. In a related case, in chapter 2 of *Proactive Marketing for the New and Experienced Library Director: Going beyond the Gate Count* by Dr. Melissa Goldsmith and Dr. Anthony Fonseca, titled "The Academic Library as an Educational System," they offer this observation: "Currently administrators and academic library directors alike fail to recognize that the library is a unit much like other units on any campus, where teaching, learning, and life experiences occur, rather than a place where books (and their ideas) go to die."[18] As mentioned previously, there is a great deal of emphasis on moving forward to recognize the importance of the librarian as educator and as a type of instructional designer. Yet, it would seem as if placing *all* of our chips in the "education basket" could limit academic librarians to some extent. This idea is addressed in detail in chapter 5 when considering the importance that academic libraries place on information literacy and library instruction.

How then should librarians and instructional designers present or position themselves in order to be considered prominent resources on campus for help with the issues more broadly affecting all of higher education? Noted writer/speaker and former president of ACRL Steven Bell can provide some insight on this issue. Bell points out that the nomenclature "library science" is both limiting and perhaps a misnomer for the degree librarians often achieve (Master of Library and Information Science). Shifting to the more apt "Master of Library Design" would be more applicable as librarians are currently much more focused on the design elements of the profession. As Bell states, "I've personally observed a growing trend in the library profession over the past few years that recognizes the value of design across many functional areas of librarianship, whether it's instruction, signage, programming, assessment, or any number of services we offer our communities."[19] Design is certainly "having a moment" in the library world, and it is interesting to think about the reasons for this. At its core, design is focused on helping to create products, experiences, and events (among many other creations) that appeal to a wide range of people and are useful and valuable to them. That is, design makes all of these things better. Similarly, Bell posits that the answer to what librarians do is related to people, not the production of things. He continues, "We make everyone else better. Whether it's providing computer access in neighborhoods afflicted by the digital divide, providing education for children whose school library closed long ago, helping the unemployed find jobs, or enabling the illiterate to change their lives, librarians make things better."[20] While it may be a stretch to say that librarians design people, those who are more conscious about design thinking might be willing to put it that way. This is one reason why thinking strictly in terms of education may be limiting. Awareness of design principles and elements helps one to both step back and evaluate and also allows for renewed re-creation, which is particularly important in a world of ever-changing technologies. Contemplating that one aspect of design is that it considers multiple perspectives, and that this in turn can help with community and collaboration, Bell emphasizes this with his many examples. Bell concludes, "Design may be the right path to a future where we get better and make the world a better place,"[21] thus inviting us to focus on this loftier angle and more inclusive goal.

WHY LIBRARIANS AND INSTRUCTIONAL DESIGNERS SHOULD COLLABORATE

While the mainstream mission of higher education has been affected by technological and societal changes and one reaction to these upheavals has been collaboration in various forms, there remains *specific* value in getting librarians and instructional designers to work together. The question can be asked, "Why these two?" Could not librarians collaborate with anthropologists, information technologists, faculty, or other staff on campus (or off campus)? Certainly any (or all) of these connections can be beneficial, and it is important to remember that if there is no one on campus with the title *instructional designer*, then these ideas are hopefully not voided. In fact, in many cases (including ours), the instructional technologist is the person with whom a librarian would be most likely to work with on any given campus. As mentioned previously, the skill sets, dispositions, and opportunities for relationships supersede any formal titles, and we decided to opt for the title *instructional designer* even if it may not apply to every situation. The reason behind this choice is to continue to reemphasize design, teaching, and learning.

The primary reason why a library–instructional designer partnership is an especially good fit for the benefit of campus communities is that the twofold aspects of digital technology and design are both topical and relevant for the future. Likewise, from the instructional designer's perspective, working with a librarian offers the ability to gain a better understanding of how information is developed, presented, and used. Instructional designers often work with numerous people on campus yet mainly help faculty. Academic librarians often have a great deal of interdisciplinary experience or exposure. Jeffrey A. Knapp, in "Plugging the 'Whole': Librarians as Interdisciplinary Facilitators," urges librarians "to promote the 'whole' of knowledge and give the growing interdisciplinary research movement the support that it deserves. Librarians are uniquely qualified to play a central role as 'connectors' in this movement."[22] Laura MacLeod Mulligan and Dr. Adam J. Kuban at Ball State University worked together on the curriculum and capstone for journalism students and eventually a project about the practical consideration of interdisciplinary collaboration. They note that "as educators, we recognize the globalization of society and the overlapping nature of most occupations, and we want our students to have diverse, interdisciplinary experiences—thus it seems prudent to adopt a similar mindset for our own scholarly endeavors. We should set an example for our students, valuing efforts to 'reach across the aisle' and emphasizing interdisciplinary opportunities."[23] Instructional designers also have the insight that comes with working with many different disciplines on campus and thus understand the advantage of this cross connection too.

Steven Bell, as previously mentioned, has a unique and forward-thinking perspective on library issues. His idea (along with that of noted author John Shank) of the blended librarian could be considered to be exemplary of the collaborative message of this book. Whereas Bell generally offers the path for librarians to move forward using and improving their own technology and design skills, the collaborative nature of working with instructional designers is a greater focus for us here. Occasionally, there is pushback from instructional designers at the idea of librarians "encroaching on their turf," and Bell is excellent at addressing this. For example, in response to a comment from a designer on a blog post about librarians not being in a good position to be designers, Bell responds, "It's really important for all library staff to have a role in designing the UX [user experience] because it's the front line staff, not a UI specialist who designs the home page, that will ultimately have to deliver on the experience."[24] This awareness of how design applies to libraries is another reason for librarians to improve their design aptitude. As a reminder, the emphasis on design influence as it relates to education must always be bolstered by an open disposition, that is, being inclusive and holding on to the understanding that new communities are continually inhabiting our actual or virtual campus(es). For example, each year greets a fresh class of first-year students who are new to campus and any initiatives that will help them to succeed should take precedence. Fortunately, design thinking has the potential to open pathways to empathy and inclusivity.

Another way to consider changing roles in the digital age is to think about how librarians deliver content in places like MOOCs, digital archives, digital humanities projects, and other online learning areas. Numerous intellectual property and security issues crop up as this delivery occurs. An entire section of the book *Network Reshapes the Library: Lorcan Dempsey on Libraries, Services, and Networks* is composed of selected posts focusing on data and metadata, as opposed to the systems designed to store or manage them.[25] Dempsey asks, "What are libraries doing with data, and what untapped sources are there?"[26] This question goes directly to a difficult place for librarians who are concerned with protecting library data that is connected to students and continuing to earn student trust. One of the conversations around this topic is the development of personal application programming interfaces (APIs), which looks to be a helpful solution.

Personal application programming interfaces, or personal APIs, are a way for someone to gain control over the data they access and share while doing research. Related to schools offering students (and others) personal web spaces for their work (as begun by University of Mary Washington's Domain of One's Own project in 2013[27]), personal APIs take this idea as an opportunity to educate students on how online identities and data work. Connected to the personal domain, Brigham Young University allows for advanced data choice, control, and capabilities for students: "[T]hey'll be able to install applications that allow their data to talk to other programs, such as a learning management system. From their domain site, users will have the option to publish work and share data with different spaces, including social media and class sites, and control privacy settings to decide which other sites can access their information."[28] What makes this type of project relevant is that librarians are involved with technologists on it, but this is not solely due to the research element involved. Concerned with how student research data is being used by library vendors, librarians spoke up about this issue, for example, in Trina J. Magi's article, "A Content Analysis of Library Vendor Privacy Policies: Do They Meet Our Standards?"[29] This ongoing conversation has helped to propel personal API discussion. A case like this helps us to see the possibility of retaining long-held librarian values while moving forward with technological gain. A related topic here is the continued and ever-expanding use of students' data to provide assessment of them. In the article "In the Library in the Gym, Big Brother Is Coming to Universities," Harriet Swain references the report *From Bricks to Clicks: The Potential of Data and Analytics in Higher Education* and expresses concern over how student data is used in several ways.[30] Parallel to the design of personal APIs, Swain states, "One option, the report will suggest, is for institutions to make it compulsory for students to agree to a core set of data being collected but should allow them to opt in or out of anything more."[31]

Returning to the educational support role, academic librarians have a part that is often overlooked outside (and even within) the library. The role of library liaison is one that has historically been buried due to its insufficient definition, unfocused goals, and lack of formal assessment. But in typical fashion, it is one that while being unnoticed and sometimes disregarded may be more important and impactful than other librarian duties and roles that get more attention. Rarely is the word *liaison* used in a librarian's title, and focus on library liaisonship is usually not prioritized in library school programs. These shortcomings need to be addressed as a way to spotlight collaboration. As a springboard, librarians need to improve upon their ability to liaise with learning technologists.

A brief detour here is beneficial because the history of library liaisons has traditionally been focused on relationships with faculty and been associated with the library-focused duties of reference, instruction, and collection development. Yet, this is changing. In a 2013 report, *New Roles for New Times: Transforming Liaison Roles in Research Libraries,* Janice M. Jaguszewski and Karen Williams point out a shift from these concerns to a change that puts more emphasis on user needs and suggest a move from "subject or discipline specialists" to "functional specialists."[32] This renewed way of looking at the liaison role again reinforces how to move away from titles (or, in some cases, subject specialties) to competencies and other connectors (such as librarian expertise in technology or intellectual property) that can bridge departments. The *Pilot Library Liaison Institute Final Report*, referenced earlier in this chapter and completed in December 2015, was a combined effort by three universities to define and shape the role of the library liaison. One of the observations made by this library liaison institute was the effect of the "[p]erception that institutional rewards for advancement (i.e., promotion and tenure) and systems of assessment encourage liaisons to focus on what they do rather than on the impact they make on academic goals and objectives."[33] As mentioned earlier, the idea that librarians need to be thought of as crucial sources for understanding the current information landscape (and its importance in relation to future jobs for current students), as well as professionals with numerous interdisciplinary experiences, should position them well to make an impact on specific institutional academic goals and objectives.

There is an active subset of librarians who are forward thinking and will not be confined by old labels and preconceived limitations. They see moving past some of the legacy services and traditional roles as a way to show leadership within the library and, therefore, outside the library. Opportunities are available to those who wish to reinvent themselves, but there needs to be more daily discussion about the role of the librarian on the college campus and within higher education. A consistent strain of "invisibility" has classified librarians as second-rate citizens within their institutions, and this continually downplays their potential leadership impact. But, as with most perceptions, there is an element of truth here and, of course, there are reasons.

In many cases, the reality is that academic libraries and librarians do not "message" well outside the library. This does appear to hold some truth, especially as it pertains to messaging to faculty and administration, although there are certainly efforts being made to correct this in many cases. For every administrator or faculty member on campus who has a comprehensive and up-to-date understanding of the capabilities and current work activities of the campus librarians, there are many more who do not. There are cases where very few administrators, staff, and faculty frequent or even visit one of the places on campus where students continually do academic work. To the librarian, who is helping students accomplish academic work daily, this seems odd. The situation can be compounded by continued and successful campus exhortations directed to faculty and staff to attend and support students at athletic and social events. That is to say, it would follow that campus leaders interested in academic success would show the same type of effort to implore faculty to go see their students completing academic achievements in the library.

Efforts to incorporate more emphasis on digital projects and to embed design thinking into librarians' jobs may be one way to model its importance for higher education. Ideally, this would then translate into administrators noticing that worth. What other attributes must staff possess so that institutions of higher education can continue to thrive (or even just survive) moving forward? This type of thought experiment requires a broad and insightful understanding of the higher education landscape, which, of course, cannot be so easily characterized in any simple way. Joshua Kim's "The 3 Things I'll Say about EdTech in 2016" includes these observations: "A Liberal Arts Education Is the Most Valuable Type of Postsecondary Education"; "Learning Is a Relationship"; and "Increased Competition Demands Greater Investment and Experimentation in Learning."[34] He points out, like Clay Shirky, that online learning is expanding, adding that online learning has

> brought with it new methods, thinking, and skills to our residential campuses. Prior to the rise of online learning we had few instructional designers and not much talk about Bloom's Taxonomy on our campuses. The methods necessary to create a quality online program work just as well for quality residential programs. Backwards course design, an identification of learning objectives, and a focus on active learning techniques are as essential for a blended residential class as they are for a fully online program. Applying research (SOTL [Scholarship of Teaching and Learning]) on how people learn best is of equal value in residential as it is in online courses. Open online education (MOOCs) [has] accelerated the push to investment in residential teaching and learning, as free online classes have raised the bar for expensive residential offerings. The improvements in learning are great for students, but they pose real challenges for our colleges and universities.[35]

These trials can be addressed with help from librarians and instructional designers who are ready for the challenge.

WHY DESIGN THINKING IS IMPORTANT

A constant theme that leads discussion about how to address changes to higher education is the belief that the effect of technology on teaching and learning is so pervasive that looking back toward historic ways to educate is futile. One solution offered time and again is to begin rethinking and redesigning education, from the physical setting in the classroom to pedagogical tactics. Surely there is still much that can be gleaned from the past, and there are many who question if there is real change or just duplicated methods with a technology twist. However, for librarians, beginning to think in a way that puts priority on design (over other factors such as the quantity of resources and historical antecedents) helps to shine light on decision making and can open up opportunities for empathy and collaboration.

In the article "Using Design Thinking in Higher Education," Holly Morris and Greg Warman contend, "Design thinking focuses on users and their needs, encourages brainstorming and prototyping, and rewards out-of-the-box thinking that takes 'wild ideas' and transforms them into real-world solutions."[36] The writers note that creating a mindset for applying design thinking does not require huge changes. These ideas allow for the ability to apply design principles:

- Introduce the user perspective into the conversation whenever you can. Think about the person or people buying your product or service and what they would want.
- Use the brainstorming rules. And brainstorm. Integrate the practice of bringing forward multiple ideas as much as you can.

- Seek inspiration through analogs. Look outside your department and outside higher education for successful innovations and think about how they might apply in your context.[37]

Note that the last suggestion points to the way for collaboration. One result of using design thinking is an increase in "looking outside" instead of continually within and a renewed focus on following these steps: frame the problem, brainstorm, and create a prototype.[38]

Often aligned in libraries with UX (user experience) design, design thinking lays at the core of how information is used. Because information use is a great concern for librarians, job titles such as *user experience librarian* continue to gain momentum. In their book *Useful, Usable, Desirable: Applying User Experience Design to Your Library*, Aaron Schmidt and Amanda Etches lay out eight principles of library UX design:

- You are not your user.
- The user is not broken.
- A good user experience requires research.
- Building a good user experience requires empathy.
- A good user experience must be easy before it can be interesting.
- Good user experience design is universal.
- Good user experience design is intentional.
- Good user experience design is holistic.[39]

The authors go on to examine how librarians can use these principles when designing physical space, service points, policies and customer service, signage and wayfinding, online presence, and student use of the library space. They conclude, "Every decision we make affects how people experience the library. Let's make sure we are creating improvements."[40] Design thinking allows for a type of "opening up" to new ideas and new ways to do things, which can lead to innovation.

INNOVATION—NEW WAYS

Education research in general is not a new field, but over the past five to seven years, a new field called learning analytics has emerged. As noted on the EDUCAUSE website, the *NMC Horizon Report: 2013 Higher Education Edition* describes learning analytics as the "field associated with deciphering trends and patterns from educational big data, or huge sets of student-related data, to further the advancement of a personalized, supportive system of higher education."[41] This section of the EDUCAUSE website points to more resources about this topic. Organizations and programs such as Carnegie Mellon's Open Learning Initiative (OLI; http://oli.cmu.edu), Georgetown's Formation by Design (FxD; http://futures.georgetown.edu/formation), the

University of Texas–Arlington's Digital Learning Research Network (dLRN; http://linkresearchlab.org/dlrn), and the Online Learning Consortium (OLC; http://onlinelearningconsortium.org) are doing the more thoughtful research in learning analytics, and their findings are beginning to shape the direction of edtech more broadly, and that's a good thing. There is a higher commitment than ever to learning about learning.

One of the pressures that is affecting change in higher education is the need to shape the personalization of learning due to some of the aforementioned concepts, one of which is an increased number of online students. This, again, includes the ability to understand diverse demographics and needs as well as the continued importance of advising systems and digital courseware. Understanding and including diverse groups is one of the goals of critical librarianship. Another pressure on higher education is the labor market and how that will affect future employment. The impact of technology on work is just one factor here. Librarians are also concerned about this factor, especially with reference to lifelong learning as it relates to a continuing need to update skills. For example, Project Information Literacy's most recent report (*Staying Smart: How Today's Graduates Continue to Learn Once They Complete College*), which was published at the start of 2016, addresses this idea in its fourth recommendation for academic libraries: "Make strategies for lifelong learning as part of information literacy curriculum."[42] Additionally, these factors continue the discussion of how higher education curriculum is in the process of being "unbundled." That is, the former model of the four-year college experience leading to a traditional degree is moving toward different designs, such as MOOCs, focused boot camps, and microcredentials.

As higher education goes ever more digital, many on the outside and inside are beginning to question the assumptions about the value of institutes of higher education. We are in a time of uncertainty. It's difficult to know for sure what higher education will look like in the future, so where should we be placing our efforts and energy? Organizations within and outside of higher education are already working to address these questions. Librarians and instructional designers need to be full participants in these efforts and look to industry for models that we can adapt. One widely accepted model for tackling an uncertain future is referred to as the "three horizons of growth." As featured in the book *The Alchemy for Growth: Practical Insights for Building the Enduring Enterprise*, this model provides a framework for concurrently managing the immediate needs and future opportunities that sustain any core business.[43]

Horizon one is concerned with the here and now, with an emphasis on extending and defending the core business and the bulk of revenue that it generates. The main focus here is on sustaining current success. Horizon two looks at emerging opportunities for improvement in the areas of efficiency and effectiveness, while remaining focused on the existing value network and customers. In some ways, this horizon could be said to be aligned with certain aspects of design thinking, although horizon three also could be associated with design. Horizon three is a look further down the road at new ventures and experimentation that usually take the form of research projects or pilot programs. These are the big, disruptive innovations and typically involve units that sit outside of the regular business model. Looking outside for opportunity once more is key.[44]

How are businesses planning for the important need to maintain what is crucial to their daily activities and also allocating resources to the three horizons as a percentage of internal expenditures? According to a 2014 survey of business leaders across a range of industries, this was the average breakdown: 85 percent on day-to-day operations in horizon one; 5 percent on incremental improvements and 5 percent on sustaining innovations in horizon two; and finally, 5 percent on the big, disruptive innovations in horizon three.[45] Thinking about how these ratios map to libraries can shine light on this approach. When those same leaders were asked what would be a better allocation, their response was this: 75 percent should go to day-to-day operations, 5 percent to improvement in operational efficiency, 10 percent to sustaining innovations, and 10 percent to disrupting innovations.[46] That's potentially a 10 percent shift in funding toward innovation in an ideal scenario. How would education and library leaders or instructional designers divvy up these numbers?

Most higher education innovation efforts fall squarely in horizon two. If we aim to serve higher education optimally in a time of change, we need to be more intentional about horizon three and engage in the disrupting innovations that go directly to our core business of teaching and learning. We can either shape this direction responsibly or be shaped by it. For higher education leaders, borrowing this framework can be particularly useful in times of uncertainty. An investment in horizon three ensures a focus on a sustainable future, one that cannot be easily driven out by the urgency of business needs in horizon one. So, how might we begin to map these horizons for higher education? For most of us, the essential question is this: "How might we be more intentional about horizon three?" It is important to remember that disruption can occur in such a way that some of the original ideas and principles can be maintained.

George Siemens aptly states, "The best strategy in a time of uncertainty is not to seek or force the way forward, but to enter into a cycle of experimentation."[47] As examples, the Institute for the Science of Teaching and Learning at Arizona State University (https://istl.asu.edu) and the University Innovation Alliance (www.theuia.org) take the work of experimentation and innovation seriously. Digital learning, which could be considered by many to be in an experimental stage, means learning in networked communities, understanding and creating multimodal projects, developing digital identities, and reckoning with the ethical issues that arise from technology use in and outside the classroom. This combination of innovation with the need to respect ethics should be appealing to librarians and instructional designers alike. The research connected to digital learning plays a significant role in a time of change. The systematic study and application of new models, methods, and processes highlight our value assumptions while deepening our understanding of learning in the digital age. As higher education continues to go digital, employing new methods of experimentation and research can help us articulate (with evidence) the value of education. Design, or putting research findings into broader practice, is equally important.

Here are some initiatives in which librarians can play a key role as levers of institutional change, now and into the future:

Digital humanities. Librarians can bookend this process: they lead in the beginning, around research and discovery; they cycle in and out in the development of scholarship; and finally, they lead in the preservation of scholarship over time.

Open access. A core value of the library supports the notion that the public good is better served when everyone has access to the knowledge created through research.

Tor Project for relay configuration. For those unfamiliar with this effort, the Tor Project (www.torproject.org) provides free software for anonymous communication. Libraries are democratic public spaces that protect our intellectual freedom and privacy and provide unfettered access to information. It's natural that they would take a leading role in protecting patrons from government and corporate surveillance of the use of library resources.

Makerspaces. Where libraries have traditionally showcased content, makerspaces represent an opportunity to showcase the knowledge creation process and the role of librarianship in that creative endeavor.

Here are some leadership strategies for librarians:

Focus outward. Most leaders and educators associated with higher education have a tendency to focus inward, on internal politics, departmental needs, and tending to the immediate day-to-day operations. Libraries in particular have traditionally been the space people came to, so there was less need to go out. Be intentional about an external focus—on new kinds of collaborations and on bigger-picture change pressures.

Empower people. To participate fully in innovation, openly question the degree of verticality in your division, department, or team. The science of social physics tells us that the best ideas emerge in egalitarian, flat structures. Create these spaces that enable the optimal flow of ideas.

Build networks. Continuing on these themes, make a concerted effort to look beyond job titles and hierarchies. People with the best ideas can be anywhere in the organization. Don't assume your leaders are the best suited for this kind of research and development. As revealed in studies conducted by Alex Pentland and the MIT Media Lab, "It's not simply the brightest who have the best ideas; it is those who are best at harvesting ideas from others."[48]

Engage publicly. Position the library as an authority in public discourse. Consider presenting at conferences beyond those offered by ALA and ACRL so that others will see the need for librarians in these conversations.

THE "COLIBRARIAN"

As a way to both form deep and meaningful alliances and elevate their role on campus, academic librarians should be having daily conversations about their ability to increase both their ROI (which in this case stands for return on influence) and also their ROE (return on effort). These new ways to look at two common abbreviations also invite a new way to think about the collaborative librarian. In the same way in which someone is considered to be a "cowriter," "coteacher," "coworker," or "cofounder," there should be some consideration of the term *colibrarian*. Although the term may not be the best fit, conceptually there needs to be a collaborative mantra set in place. The prefix *co-* is "[t]aken in English from the 17c. as a living prefix meaning 'together, mutually, in common,' and used promiscuously with native words and Latin-derived words not beginning with vowels, sometimes even with words already having it (e.g., co-conspirator)."[49] As a playful way to use the term, it should be thought of in a different sense than "someone doing librarian-type work in common"; rather, one might apply the sense of the word as coming *from* the perspective of the librarian and thus more closely associated with *co*operating and *co*llaborating with others.

As a practical way to also link this concept, the new phenomenon and growth of coworking spaces should be considered as options for collaborative work. In the same way that it is beneficial to "get out" of the library, instructional designers and librarians could perhaps profit from "getting out" of their institutions of higher learning and connecting at these creative team learning spaces. Coworking is "a style of work that involves a shared working environment, yet independent activity. Unlike the typical office environment, a coworking space is generally shared by individuals from different organizations and professions."[50] Begun in Europe and modeled in some public libraries, coworking spaces are designed to improve collaboration and bring together different viewpoints. Some libraries have also begun to view and promote their spaces as coworking environments.

A much bigger question than whether librarians are up to the task of taking on the challenges that will continue to be confronted by higher education is whether institutions of higher learning see this as a campus role for librarians. It is the rare college campus that considers the ideas, knowledge, experience, talents, and skill sets of its librarians as resources to be consulted on broader issues. Another avenue of exploration is how other campus agents are able to influence the university's decision-making process related to preparing itself for the future. Are there examples of universities or colleges that see librarians as those who could be used in this manner? The information landscape is constantly changing, and who are the people who can make sense of it? Although many institutions do not recognize this, information architects/designers and librarians have a part to play here, as open access to information will continue to evolve and grow. Hopefully, higher education will open the way for librarians and instructional designers to help. In the next chapter, we contemplate the driving motivations behind both professions. We also consider how the background of each profession might foster collaborative efforts in which each both creatively complements and supplements what the other has to offer.

NOTES

1. George Siemens, Dragon Gašević, and Shane Dawson, *Preparing for the Digital University: A Review of the History and Current State of Distance, Blended, and Online Learning* (Athabasca, AB: Athabasca University, 2015), http://linkresearchlab.org/PreparingDigitalUniversity.pdf.
2. Clay Shirky, "The Digital Revolution in Higher Education Has Already Happened. No One Noticed." *Medium* (blog), November 6, 2015, https://medium.com/@cshirky/the-digital-revolution-in-higher-education-has-already-happened-no-one-noticed-78ec0fec16c7#.wlrh1pdlk.
3. David L. Clinefelter and Carol B. Aslanian, *Online College Students 2014: Comprehensive Data on Demands and Preferences* (Louisville, KY: The Learning House, 2014), www.learninghouse.com/wp-content/uploads/2014/06/2014-Online-College-Students-Final.pdf.
4. Shirky, "The Digital Revolution in Higher Education."
5. Barbara Rockenbach, Judy Ruttenberg, Kornelia Tancheva, and Rita Vine, *Association of Research Libraries/Columbia University/Cornell University/University of Toronto Pilot Library Liaison Institute Final Report* (Washington, DC: Association of Research Libraries, 2015), 9, www.arl.org/storage/documents/publications/library-liaison-institute-final-report-dec2015.pdf.
6. Kathryn Zickuhr, Lee Rainie, and Kristen Purcell, *Library Services in the Digital Age* (Washington, DC: Pew Research Center, Internet and American Life Project, 2013), 67, http://libraries.pewinternet.org/files/legacy-pdf/PIP_Library%20services_Report.pdf.

7. Keith Webster, "Leading the Library of the Future: W(h)ither Technical Services?" (presentation at the ALCTS President's Symposium, ALA Midwinter meeting, Boston, MA, January 8, 2016), www.slideshare.net/KeithWebster2/leading-the-library-of-the-future-whither-technical-services.
8. Anne R. Kenney, "Approaching an Entity Crisis: Reconceiving Research Libraries in a Multi-institutional Context" (presentation at the Distinguished Seminar Series, OCLC Research, September 23, 2009), www.oclc.org/content/dam/research/events/dss/ppt/dss_kenney.pdf.
9. Ibid., slide 2.
10. Ibid., slide 28.
11. American Library Association, "Library Leadership Training Resources," accessed January 23, 2016, www.ala.org/offices/hrdr/abouthrdr/hrdrliaisoncomm/otld/leadershiptraining.
12. Dane Ward, "It Takes a University to Build a Library," *Inside Higher Ed*, April 21, 2015, www.insidehighered.com/views/2015/04/21/essay-calls-librarians-seek-more-involvement-their-campuses-developing-future.
13. Shirky, "Digital Revolution in Higher Education."
14. April Hathcock, "White Librarianship in Blackface: Diversity Initiatives in LIS," *In the Library with the Lead Pipe* (blog), October 7, 2015, www.inthelibrarywiththeleadpipe.org/2015/lis-diversity; Jennifer Vinopal, "The Quest for Diversity in Library Staffing: From Awareness to Action," *In the Library with the Lead Pipe* (blog), January 13, 2016, www.inthelibrarywiththeleadpipe.org/2016/quest-for-diversity.
15. Ashley R. Maynor, "Technophobia and Generational Stigma: Embracing and Supporting Next-Gen Librarianship," *Library Lost and Found* (blog), December 22, 2015, http://librarylostfound.com/author/amaynor.
16. Valerie J. Gross, *Transforming Our Image, Building Our Brand: The Education Advantage* (Santa Barbara, CA: Libraries Unlimited, 2013).
17. Ibid., xi.
18. Melissa U. Goldsmith and Anthony Fonseca, "The Academic Library as an Educational System," in *Proactive Marketing for the New and Experienced Library Director: Going beyond the Gate Count* (Amsterdam: Chandos, 2014), 18.
19. Steven Bell, "MLD: Masters in Library Design, Not Science," Opinion: From the Bell Tower, *Library Journal*, November 19, 2014, http://lj.libraryjournal.com/2014/11/opinion/steven-bell/mld-masters-in-library-design-not-science-from-the-bell-tower/#_.
20. Ibid.
21. Ibid.
22. Jeffrey A. Knapp, "Plugging the 'Whole': Librarians as Interdisciplinary Facilitators," *Library Review 61*, no. 3 (2012): 212.
23. Laura MacLeod Mulligan and Adam J. Kuban, "A Conceptual Model for Interdisciplinary Collaboration," *ACRLog*, May 14, 2015, http://acrlog.org/2015/05/14/a-conceptual-model-for-interdisciplinary-collaboration.

24. Bell, "MLD: Masters in Library Design."
25. Lorcan Dempsey, *Network Reshapes the Library: Lorcan Dempsey on Libraries, Services, and Networks*, ed. Kenneth J. Varnum (Chicago: American Library Association, 2014).
26. Ibid.
27. University of Mary Washington, "A Domain of One's Own," accessed March 31, 2016, http://umw.domains.
28. Marguerite McNeal, "BYU's Bold Plan to Give Students Control of Their Data," *EdSurge News*, December 18, 2015, www.edsurge.com/news/2015-12-18-byu-s-bold-plan-to-give-students-control-of-their-data.
29. Trina J. Magi, "A Content Analysis of Library Vendor Privacy Policies: Do They Meet Our Standards?" *College and Research Libraries News* 71, no. 3 (2010): 254–272.
30. Harriet Swain, "In the Library in the Gym, Big Brother Is Coming to Universities," *The Guardian*, Higher Education, January 19, 2016, www.theguardian.com/education/2016/jan/19/big-brother-universities-data-higher-education-students; Xanthe Shacklock, *From Bricks to Clicks: The Potential of Data and Analytics in Higher Education* (London: Higher Education Commission, 2016), www.policyconnect.org.uk/hec/sites/site_hec/files/report/419/fieldreportdownload/frombrickstoclicks-hecreportforweb.pdf.
31. Swain, "In the Library in the Gym."
32. Janice M. Jaguszewski and Karen Williams, *New Roles for New Times: Transforming Liaison Roles in Research Libraries* (Washington, DC: Association of Research Libraries, 2013), www.arl.org/storage/documents/publications/nrnt-liaison-roles-revised.pdf.
33. Rockenbach et al., *Pilot Library Liaison Institute Final Report*, 6.
34. Joshua Kim, "The 3 Things I'll Say about EdTech in 2016," *Inside Higher Ed*, January 3, 2016, www.insidehighered.com/blogs/technology-and-learning/3-things-i'll-say-about-edtech-2016.
35. Ibid.
36. Holly E. Morris and Greg Warman, "Using Design Thinking in Higher Education," *EDUCAUSE Review*, January 12, 2015, http://er.educause.edu/articles/2015/1/using-design-thinking-in-higher-education.
37. Ibid.
38. Ibid.
39. Aaron Schmidt and Amanda Etches, *Useful, Usable, Desirable: Applying User Experience Design to Your Library* (Chicago: ALA Editions, 2014), 4–7.
40. Ibid., 158.
41. EDUCAUSE, "Learning Analytics," accessed January 30, 2016, https://library.educause.edu/topics/teaching-and-learning/learning-analytics (quoted definition no longer posted); see instead L. Johnson, S. Adams Becker, M. Cummins, V. Estrada, A. Freeman, and H. Ludgate, *NMC Horizon Report: 2013 Higher Education Edition* (Austin, TX: The New Media Consortium, 2013), 5, www.nmc.org/pdf/2013-horizon-report-HE.pdf.

42. Alison J. Head, *Staying Smart: How Today's Graduates Continue to Learn Once They Complete College* (Seattle, WA: University of Washington Information School, Project Information Literacy, 2016), 65, http://projectinfolit.org/images/pdfs/2016_lifelonglearning_fullreport.pdf.
43. Mehrdad Baghai, Stephen Coley, and David White, *The Alchemy of Growth: Practical Insights for Building the Enduring Enterprise* (New York: Perseus, 1999).
44. Ibid.
45. Brad Power and Steve Stanton, "How to Prioritize Your Innovation Budget," *Harvard Business Review*, September 24, 2014, https://hbr.org/2014/09/how-to-prioritize-your-innovation-budget.
46. Ibid.
47. George Siemens, "White House: Innovation in Higher Education," *Elearnspace* (blog), August 3, 2015, www.elearnspace.org/blog/2015/08/03/white-house-innovation-in-higher-education.
48. Cited in Geoff Colvin, "How to Build the Perfect Workplace," *Fortune*, March 5, 2015, http://fortune.com/2015/03/05/perfect-workplace.
49. Dictionary.com, "Word Origin and History for Co," accessed January 28, 2016, http://dictionary.reference.com/browse/co.
50. Hera Hub, "What Is Coworking?," accessed January 25, 2016, http://herahub.com/about/what-is-coworking (no longer available).

BIBLIOGRAPHY

American Library Association. "Library Leadership Training Resources." Accessed January 23, 2016. www.ala.org/offices/hrdr/abouthrdr/hrdrliaisoncomm/otld/leadershiptraining.

Baghai, Mehrdad, Stephen Coley, and David White. *The Alchemy of Growth: Practical Insights for Building the Enduring Enterprise*. New York: Perseus, 1999.

Bell, Steven. "MLD: Masters in Library Design, Not Science," Opinion: From the Bell Tower. *Library Journal*, November 19, 2014. http://lj.libraryjournal.com/2014/11/opinion/steven-bell/mld-masters-in-library-design-not-science-from-the-bell-tower/#_.

Clinefelter, David L., and Carol B. Aslanian. *Online College Students 2014: Comprehensive Data on Demands and Preferences*. Louisville, KY: The Learning House, 2014. www.learninghouse.com/wp-content/uploads/2014/06/2014-Online-College-Students-Final.pdf.

Dempsey, Lorcan. *Network Reshapes the Library: Lorcan Dempsey on Libraries, Services, and Networks*. Edited by Kenneth J. Varnum. Chicago: American Library Association, 2014.

Goldsmith, Melissa U., and Anthony J. Fonseca. "The Academic Library as an Educational System." In *Proactive Marketing for the New and Experienced Library Director: Going beyond the Gate Count*, 17–27. Amsterdam: Chandos, 2014.

Head, Alison J. *Staying Smart: How Today's Graduates Continue to Learn Once They Complete College*. Seattle, WA: University of Washington Information School,

Project Information Literacy, 2016. http://projectinfolit.org/images/pdfs/2016_lifelonglearning_fullreport.pdf.

Hera Hub. "What Is Coworking?" Accessed January 25, 2016. http://herahub.com/about/what-is-coworking (no longer available).

Kenney, Anne R. "Approaching an Entity Crisis: Reconceiving Research Libraries in a Multi-institutional Context." Presentation, Distinguished Seminar Series, OCLC Research, September 23, 2009. www.oclc.org/content/dam/research/events/dss/ppt/dss_kenney.pdf.

Kim, Joshua. "The 3 Things I'll Say about EdTech in 2016." *Inside Higher Ed*, January 3, 2016. www.insidehighered.com/blogs/technology-and-learning/3-things-i'll-say-about-edtech-2016.

Knapp, Jeffrey A. "Plugging the 'Whole': Librarians as Interdisciplinary Facilitators." *Library Review* 61, no. 3 (2012): 199–214.

Maynor, Ashley R. "Technophobia and Generational Stigma: Embracing and Supporting Next-Gen Librarianship." *Library Lost and Found* (blog), December 22, 2015. http://librarylostfound.com/author/amaynor.

McNeal, Marguerite. "BYU's Bold Plan to Give Students Control of Their Data." *EdSurge News*, December 18, 2015. www.edsurge.com/news/2015-12-18-byu-s-bold-plan-to-give-students-control-of-their-data.

Morris, Holly E., and Greg Warman. "Using Design Thinking in Higher Education." *EDUCAUSE Review*, January 12, 2015. http://er.educause.edu/articles/2015/1/using-design-thinking-in-higher-education.

Mulligan, Laura MacLeod, and Adam J. Kuban. "A Conceptual Model for Interdisciplinary Collaboration." *ACRLog*, May 14, 2015. http://acrlog.org/2015/05/14/a-conceptual-model-for-interdisciplinary-collaboration.

Power, Brad, and Steve Stanton. "How to Prioritize Your Innovation Budget." *Harvard Business Review*, September 24, 2014. https://hbr.org/2014/09/how-to-prioritize-your-innovation-budget.

Rochenbach, Barbara, Judy Ruttenberg, Kornelia Tancheva, and Rita Vine. *Association of Research Libraries/Columbia University/Cornell University/University of Toronto Pilot Library Liaison Institute Final Report*. Washington, DC: Association of Research Libraries, 2015. www.arl.org/storage/documents/publications/library-liaison-institute-final-report-dec2015.pdf.

Schmidt, Aaron, and Amanda Etches. *Useful, Usable, Desirable: Applying User Experience Design to Your Library*. Chicago: ALA Editions, 2014.

Shirky, Clay. "The Digital Revolution in Higher Education Has Already Happened. No One Noticed." *Medium* (blog), November 6, 2015. https://medium.com/@cshirky/the-digital-revolution-in-higher-education-has-already-happened-no-one-noticed-78ec0fec16c7#.wlrh1pdlk.

Siemens, George. "White House: Innovation in Higher Education." *Elearnspace* (blog), August 3, 2015. www.elearnspace.org/blog/2015/08/03/white-house-innovation-in-higher-education.

Siemens, George, Dragon Gašević, and Shane Dawson. *Preparing for the Digital University: A Review of the History and Current State of Distance, Blended, and Online Learning*. Athabasca, AB: Athabasca University, 2015. http://linkresearchlab.org/PreparingDigitalUniversity.pdf.

Swain, Harriet. "In the Library in the Gym, Big Brother Is Coming to Universities." *The Guardian*, Higher Education, January 19, 2016. www.theguardian.com/education/2016/jan/19/big-brother-universities-data-higher-education-students.

Ward, Dane. "It Takes a University to Build a Library." *Inside Higher Ed*, April 21, 2015. www.insidehighered.com/views/2015/04/21/essay-calls-librarians-seek-more-involvement-their-campuses-developing-future.

Zickuhr, Kathyrn, Lee Rainie, and Kristen Purcell. *Library Services in the Digital Age*. Washington, DC: Pew Research Center, Internet and American Life Project, 2013.

RICHARD MONIZ

2

Comparisons and Collaborations between the Professions

The interesting mix of similarities and differences between instructional designers and librarians suggests the key points at which collaboration may most effectively and creatively improve services provided by both professions. While this book is intended to provide a practical and hands-on approach to partnerships and collaborations between librarians and instructional designers, we felt it would also be important to lay the groundwork for this by exploring some of the foundational principles within each profession, some of the differences between the two professions, some of the challenges or obstacles we may face in collaborating, and some early examples of such partnerships. As described in the introduction to this text, a key assumption is that while examples and ideas may be culled from K–12 or corporate training and education, our focus is mostly on higher education. As a result, documents and professional guidelines as espoused through such organizations as EDUCAUSE and the Association of College and Research Libraries are paramount in our exploration of the topic here.

SIMILARITIES AND DIFFERENCES

So, where do the similarities begin? Librarianship is fundamentally a service-oriented profession. According to Deborah Hicks, "The professional identity of librarians can be exposed by studying the language resources, or interpretive repertoires, librarians use when they speak about their profession."[1] She goes on to state, after an extensive study of the profession:

> The service repertoire was found in the text and speech of librarians throughout the data set. Service, broadly defined, was often considered to be the essence of librarianship. Service included activities such as public services (for instance, reference, instruction, and reader's advisory), technology services (from helping people with e-readers to providing public-access computers), the organization of information (from cataloguing to knowing how information on the Web is organized), provision of access to information (books, journals, DVDs, specialized databases, and the Internet), and professional service (such as publishing in journals, association membership and participation, and mentoring of other professionals). Service was described as a core value, the ethos and purpose of librarianship.[2]

Clearly, when speaking to just about any librarian, especially those who have most recently graduated with an MLIS (Master's in Library and Information Science), service is a key value and reason why they have chosen the profession. Interestingly, Hicks went on to discover that "[l]ibrarians used the service repertoire to position themselves as technology experts in relation to users."[3] In fact, when she suggests that librarians could make up a meaningful component within the context of cross-functional teams, we can sense the very possibility that we wish to address through this text.

While a description of the academic librarian as a professional obviously includes a wide array of duties and outlooks, the instructional designer is even harder to pin down. According to Cammy Bean, author of *The Accidental Instructional Designer*, "In practice Instructional Designer is an umbrella term that covers a whole slew of people and jobs."[4] In fact, when we look further into the differences between librarians and instructional designers, one of the things we will see is that, as librarianship is more historically established, the qualifications for becoming a librarian are much more clear-cut (i.e., usually, possession of an MLIS from an ALA-accredited institution). Some authors, it should be noted, have traced the origins of instructional design as far back as the 1920s and have explored the varying definitions that have come along as technology has changed and become more ubiquitous.[5] Others have placed its origins more recently connected to the development of computers.[6] Most of these older ways of defining the profession seem to fall flat, however, as the profession has taken on a much greater role and focus in the twenty-first century. While instructional design programs seem to be growing by leaps and bounds, many in the profession come to it from other areas (a prominent one being librarianship). In the end, however, service is as central a value to instructional designers as it is to librarians, if sometimes more removed from the front lines, so to speak. According to Bean, "The most successful e-learning initiatives . . . have a clear vision of what the audience needs to learn and how best to achieve that outcome; a creative design that looks enticing, creates interest and sustains attention; the right technology that stands up to the delivery needs; and a solid connection back to the overall goals and objectives of the organization."[7] Perhaps the most detailed description of the profession, one that covers the idea of service but stretches far beyond, comes from Reiser and Dempsey:

> The field of instructional design and technology encompasses the analysis of learning and performance problems, and the design, development, implementation, evaluation, and management of instructional and non-instructional processes and resources intended to improve learning and performance in a variety of settings, particularly educational institutions and the workplace.
>
> Professionals in the field of instructional design and technology often use systematic instructional design procedures and employ a variety of instructional media to accomplish their goals. Moreover, in recent years, they have paid increasing attention to non-instructional solutions to some performance problems. Research and theory related to each of the aforementioned areas is also an important part of the field.[8]

Again, the connection to service is obvious. The difference may lie in that librarians have historically focused more on issues related to accessing information as a part of the learning process, whereas instructional designers have a greater focus on the arrangement of knowledge or skill building for the associated learner. Both professions also seem to recognize that an iterative process involving research, reflection, and assessment is critical to the vitality of their ongoing initiatives.

These combined issues of assessment and embracing new ways of thinking are important to dwell on for a bit since academic librarianship has been in the crux of change for the past two decades (or more) regarding its focus on providing access to information and teaching information literacy skills. While bibliographic instruction has been a mainstay of the profession since its inception, it had very much the feel of being a means to an end. That is, the goal was related really to the information itself. The role of "protecting" books or serving as a warehouse of print materials has been rapidly fading, partially due to the transformations occurring in digital scholarship (which is addressed in much greater detail later in this text) and more so because of an emphasis on teaching and learning information literacy–related skills.

With its adoption of the *Information Literacy Competency Standards for Higher Education* in 2000, the ACRL began what some might deem a profound shift in direction. At the outset, this document states, "The uncertain quality and expanding quantity of information pose large challenges for society. The sheer abundance of information will not in itself create a more informed citizenry without a complementary cluster of abilities necessary to use information effectively."[9] Indeed, the adoption of these standards changed the way librarians operate. The integration of information literacy–related learning outcomes went from a luxury to a mandate as each of the regional accrediting bodies within the United States adopted some language necessitating their incorporation. This shift has more recently culminated in the adoption of ACRL's *Framework for Information Literacy in Higher Education*. This profound document seeks to break the ties of the past by firmly grounding librarianship within the context of higher-order learning. The introduction to this document begins with this statement: "This *Framework for Information Literacy for Higher Education* (*Framework*) grows out of a belief that information literacy as an educational reform movement will realize its potential only through a richer, more complex set of core ideas."[10] It continues:

> Because this *Framework* envisions information literacy as extending the arc of learning throughout students' academic careers and as converging with other academic and social learning goals, an expanded definition of information literacy is offered here to emphasize dynamism, flexibility, individual growth, and community learning:
>
>> Information literacy is the set of integrated abilities encompassing the reflective discovery of information, the understanding of how information is produced and valued, and the use of information in creating new knowledge and participating ethically in communities of learning.[11]

The emphasis on learning is critical here and is addressed in great detail in chapter 5. Librarianship has thus evolved from fundamentally a service profession to one that could be seen as now having a central focus on the facilitation of teaching and learning (albeit within the context of information literacy). As such, there is a natural affinity with a profession such as that inhabited by instructional designers which focuses also on the learner. The connection is palpable and overlapping, as authors such as Angiah Davis have written about the application of instructional design principles and values to the profession of academic librarianship, especially when it comes to instruction. Davis notes that while ADDIE, for example, with its emphasis on analysis, design, development, implementation, and evaluation, may be a systematic approach to teaching and learning well known by the typical instructional designer, it is relatively new to the typical librarian.[12] According to Brandeis University's Graduate Professional Studies webpage:

> Instructional design and technology encompasses the creation of dynamic learning content for online delivery. Instructional designers analyze learning outcomes and design, develop, implement, evaluate and manage instructional processes and resources intended to improve learning and performance in a variety of settings. The field is growing rapidly in private, governmental and nonprofit settings alike as organizations seek to optimize and adapt their learning content to online and mobile platforms.[13]

Other instructional design programs state similar goals. Again, there is an obvious connection here between the deliberate and purposeful intent embedded within instructional design and the now more focused efforts of academic librarians to carefully craft student learning.

While much of the previous discussion may be obvious to both librarians and instructional designers, our contention in this book is that we have yet to really tap the potential synergy that could result from further binding our efforts. Certainly, this isn't the case in every instance, but in many, an invisible wall exists between the two professions. The American Library Association should be applauded for offering courses such as "Introduction to Instructional Design for Librarians."[14] Such efforts as these have the potential for breaking down barriers and creating a greater appreciation and understanding across what really should not be such a big divide. High attendance in such minicourses as the one sponsored by ALA also seems to indicate a significant desire on the part of librarians to better understand the work being done by instructional designers both to incorporate new and improved methods on their own and to gain a greater awareness of points at which the two professions might collaborate and support each other for the benefit of learners.

When considering similarities, another very obvious connection between librarians and instructional designers that has the potential for synergy is the direct role that instructional designers and librarians play in supporting faculty. In this sense, both librarians and instructional designers move slightly aside from direct interaction with the learner (keeping our focus on students—we are all, of course, learners as well) but with the intent of providing those who are in direct contact (i.e., the faculty) with the tools and resources necessary to be more effective. Much has been written about the role academic librarians play as liaisons to faculty. The traditional emphasis has been on subject specialization. Thus, a librarian was expected to assist faculty by staying in tune, so to speak, with the way information and research have been organized and produced or communicated in a given area or discipline.[15] One of the more interesting recent developments in liaisonship, however, has been how some institutions have begun to emphasize function specialization instead. Thus, a given librarian might be the "go to" person on any number of issues, such as digital scholarship, open access, intellectual property, copyright, or other areas (many of which are addressed more specifically later in this book). This approach has best been explored by guru of liaisonship and author of the blog *This Liaison Life* (https://liaisonlife.wordpress.com) Steve Cramer. He has been at the forefront, especially in North Carolina, on the debates and discussions considering the changing nature of liaisonship. One can see where this new functional approach could even more readily connect with the focus of instructional designers. Oftentimes instructional designers target specific faculty needs, whether it be assisting with grading through their LMS or developing an effective online quiz. In this sense, librarian liaisons can take on a very similar, targeted role for a faculty member, assisting with not just subject area resources but functional activities related, again, to issues such as copyright, digital scholarship, and so forth. Furthermore, as is outlined later, the service ethos that evolved to incorporate these kinds of targeted needs of faculty hints at some intriguing possibilities whereby instructional designers and librarians could form a team (perhaps even in conjunction with other areas as well) for supporting improved learning in the classroom and beyond.

When considering the professions of instructional design and librarianship, certainly service and a focus on helping others to learn rise to the top, but we might also consider what motivates someone in the first place to choose either of these professions. Library science students as well as librarians tend to be some of the most inquisitive people in academia. Due to the nature of the profession, despite any particular specializations that they may have, librarians have a significant need to be generalists and models of the "lifelong learning" that institutions of higher education seek to instill within their student populations. Many librarians, albeit not all, also tend to have an affinity for organizing information or understanding how it is organized. Likewise, instructional designers seem to relish the opportunity to learn new pedagogy and technology (ideally merging the two), and they thrive on adapting a very deliberate approach to the design of effective instruction whether directly or, as mentioned earlier, by educating and training faculty. These are not insignificant points of comparison when considering the nature of those whom both groups tend to assist, students and faculty. Undergraduates in particular typically have not developed the metacognitive ability to view their learning in an organized or systematic way. Likewise, many faculty are so focused on their content areas that they may also have deficiencies when it comes to pedagogy associated with teaching and learning as well as in navigating the rapidly changing information landscape. So, while librarians and instructional designers regularly interact with people who are fundamentally interested in the process of education, they each possess a contextual view that may not be as readily available to those they assist. Yet again, this is thus an area wherein librarians and instructional designers could strengthen the quality of instruction and learning at their respective institutions. How can we work together to not just spread concrete skills, such as how to manage intellectual property or how to create an online quiz, but also help learners (primarily faculty but students as well) gain at least some understanding of the kinds of global changes and issues that we know will impact the future with regard to lifelong learning? Again, librarians and instructional designers may not be alone in this and could find other relevant partners on campus as well, but they are uniquely positioned to lead the charge (as duly noted in chapter 1).

What else then does this highlight for both librarians and instructional designers? Change. Change. Change. And yet more change. Our respective areas are rapidly changing and evolving. One of the shared burdens in this regard is stress. According to Cain, "These days, librarians and technologists must both contend with rapid change. I first heard the term 'technostress' applied to library employees, yet it applies equally well to IT staffers. Do you think they don't get tired of a constantly shifting landscape? Think again."[16] Once again, on a concrete level, librarians are ever racing to stay on top of modifications to databases, the development of discovery services, the rapid expansion of e-books and streaming videos, and numerous other changes. While the profession is an established one, it has seen radical change in recent years that is likely to occur even faster as we move into the future. Likewise, among many other issues that instructional designers frequently must be aware of, institutions sometimes change their LMS or implement a steady stream of changes, updates, or upgrades to an established LMS. There is a sense in each profession that change is a constant and that translating that change to their constituents is a fundamentally important component of their jobs.

While much of the emphasis here has been on similarities, we should also consider the differences between the professions. Again, the argument that we make is that the similarities are greater but the differences are also intriguing because they suggest the very points at which collaboration makes sense and can improve services provided by both professions. One way to explore the differences is to consider some of the content associated with the professional conferences each is more likely to attend. For example, EDUCAUSE's 2015 preconference agenda included program titles such as these:

- Building Your Interpersonal Toolbox: The Human Side of Supporting Technology
- Building an Emerging Technology and Futures Capacity in Your Organization
- Becoming a Successful Technology Manager
- Six Secrets for Evaluating Online Teaching[17]

The emphasis is clearly on technology in terms of supporting the needs of the organization and its constituents and strategic long-range planning associated with the institution's technology infrastructure. Most of the presenters appear to be other instructional designers but also include consultants, managers of teaching and learning or faculty development centers, and librarians.

On this latter note, it's clear that an overlap seems already to exist, albeit piecemeal, as librarians seek to integrate with instructional designers and better understand their culture and concerns.

In once again examining professional development associated with the profession of librarianship, this sample of preconference titles from the ACRL 2015 biannual conference is telling as well:

- Developing Research Questions, Methods, and Habits of Mind: A Workshop for Innovative and Sustainable Research
- Getting Down to Brass Tacks: Practical Approaches for Developing Data Management Services
- Creating a Culture of Assessment: Norming Rubrics to Nurture IL Instructional Practice
- Tutorials Toolkit: Creating Sustainable Library Instruction[18]

The overlap between the two professions is clearly demonstrated by these two sets of workshop titles. Both have an emphasis on teaching and learning and at least some connection to technology. Both also have an emphasis on service to appropriate constituencies. Obviously, however, the EDUCAUSE workshops lean more heavily toward technology and planning campus infrastructure. The ACRL topics seem to relate to technology more exclusively, as they may be associated with the management of data and information, although they are not entirely removed from directly employing technology for teaching purposes. The description for the last ACRL program in the previous list is as follows:

> Through a variety of interactive activities, attendees will develop the concepts, framework, and skills needed to create a cohesive and sustainable suite of online video tutorials. Participants will be guided through the process by a team of librarians and the Creative Director of a professional video company with whom the librarians partnered on a two year grant project. Attendees will leave the workshop with a toolkit to craft their own collection of information literacy tutorials.[19]

This is an especially poignant example relative to our discussion for a number of reasons. Again, most obviously, there is a connection between technology and teaching and learning to which both professions can relate. One difference between the EDUCAUSE sample and the ACRL sample, however, is that the ACRL workshops are almost exclusively done by librarians as opposed to the greater variety of backgrounds seen with the EDUCAUSE presenters. That said, in the previous example, librarians have reached out to a creative director of a video company. Clearly, while the profession of librarianship seems a bit more "closed off," there is a willingness to reach out and learn from beyond the profession.

Another way that we could explore the similarities and differences between librarians and instructional designers is to look at advertisements for positions within each area. At the outset it's important to recognize how murky this could get. Librarians themselves obviously can be hired into very different roles, as can instructional designers, based on individual institutional culture, need, structure, mission, and so forth. That said, it is worth exploring. Following are some recent samples of job summaries for the position of *instructional designer* or *instructional technologist* from *The Chronicle of Higher Education* and EDUCAUSE's website:

> The Instructional Designer will work in a collaborative team to design distance learning courses that are under revision, or newly developed, for online delivery. In partnership with College faculty and staff, the Instructional Designer will use learning methodologies appropriate to adult learner needs, select learning-oriented technologies and media, and facilitate the course development and revision process.[20]

■ ■ ■

> This position is responsible for assessment, planning, training, design, and other activities associated with the integration of new technologies into instructional programs. Work requires analysis of curriculum and instructional methodologies and the evaluation and application of hardware and software for instructional purposes. Responsibilities include faculty/staff technical training and the development of information and plans that will influence technology implementation. Requires interaction on a one-to-one basis and with a variety of groups across the service area.[21]

■ ■ ■

> In a highly collaborative environment, design elearning and face-to-face courses and activities as part of a design team. Use a variety of instructional design strategies that ensure achievement of learning goals and objectives. This work includes management of the content development process, ensuring that deliverables are timely and meet quality standards for a diverse group of adult learners.[22]

■ ■ ■

> The Instructional Designer will report to the Associate Director for Instructional Design & Development and will be part of the Instructional Design team within Instructional Innovation Services. The Instructional Design team provides leadership in the area of research-based instructional design, including the creation of engaging and effective learning materials and activities, the development of assessment techniques, and the pedagogical design of learning technology solutions. The team provides consultation and course creation services to the University as a whole as well as within DELTA itself. The production environment for this position is collaborative and team-oriented, with each ID team member working closely with members of both the Project

> Coordination and New Media teams to develop courses and learning tools that build on effective practices as well as the unique needs of each project.23

It should immediately be noted that this type of search brings up some librarian positions as well, as some institutions have deliberately sought to build hybrid positions in this regard (more on this later). Clearly the emphasis is on technology-related planning, assistance with curriculum development, and assistance one on one and with groups in utilizing technology to continuously improve teaching and learning.

Now, let's take a look at a few recent representative ads for librarians posted in *The Chronicle of Higher Education*. Despite the potential bias in doing so, the following examples come from searching for *instruction librarians* or *library liaisons* (understanding that these may be more closely related to instructional designers or instructional technologists than would other library positions):

> The Instruction and Online Learning Librarian teaches library workshops, participates in the design and assessment of online learning modules and tutorials, and is a member of the library instruction team under the leadership of the Instruction Coordinator.[24]

■ ■ ■

> Reporting to the Director of the Irvin Department, the Reference and Instruction Librarian will work a regular shift at the reference desk and will fill the majority of requests for library instruction. The Reference and Instruction Librarian will share in the collection development, outreach, digitization, and exhibit responsibilities with the other Department staff.[25]

■ ■ ■

> The Humanities Librarian will serve as subject specialist supporting the teaching and research endeavors of departments in the College of Arts and Letters (CAL) by providing research, reference and instructional services. Subject knowledge and development of instructional materials are integral to the position. Additionally, the successful candidate will develop collections appropriate to the pedagogical and research needs of the university and will work closely with other liaison librarians and departmental faculty to understand and integrate research and curricular needs with the libraries' collections and services. Partnering with other humanities-based librarians, this librarian will work to create and sustain strong relationships with the Collections Department (in particular Special Collections and Digital Collections), the Center for Instructional Technology and other campus organizations to support evolving digital humanities campus initiatives. We welcome applicants

> with a demonstrated interest in exploring how libraries can support research related to digital humanities. The successful candidate will serve as humanities liaison, but will support all disciplines, including General Education, through reference work. The successful candidate must demonstrate a strong commitment to service and collaboration and an interest in supporting undergraduate as well as graduate students.[26]

One qualification that seems to jump out in all of these descriptions is the need to collaborate and build a variety of connections across the campus. Indeed, this is the main purpose of our text, to highlight the need to do so! The previous descriptions of library roles include some of the traditional duties one would expect of a librarian, such as reference work and collection development. Such tasks don't really overlap much with the assigned duties of a typical instructional design or technology staff member. The descriptions also hint at some of the differences that may exist in reporting relationships, which can vary widely. The ads do, however, point out a couple of crucial similarities that have already been touched on. They show that librarians, much like instructional designers, are focused on creating or designing meaningful learning experiences for students (at least with regard to information literacy). They also demonstrate the importance of building relationships in support of faculty. The support, however, instead of focusing on bringing faculty up to speed on tools and pedagogy tends to emphasize more the need to connect faculty to information resources. Again, this is not a surprise, but it's worth consideration as we ask an important question: "How can these two professions work together in order to more holistically support faculty goals and efforts?"

Before moving on, it is worth examining at least one representative hybrid position recently posted on the American Library Association's website. The following ad appears in its near entirety to provide the best possible example of what is being sought, in this case, at Nevada State College:

> **Instructional Design Librarian**
>
> Nevada State College invites applications for an Instructional Design Librarian. This position reports to the Director of Library Services and will join the College during an exciting period of growth and development.
>
> The Instructional Design Librarian provides leadership for the integration of scalable and sustainable information literacy initiatives into the curriculum.
>
> The ideal candidate will be inspired by:
>
> - The chance to work at an institution that has a laser-like focus on creating successful outcomes for students from largely underserved, first-generation, and non-traditional backgrounds.

- The opportunity to work in an environment that embraces innovation and experimentation.
- The prospect of working in an environment in which assessment and evidence drive institutional improvement and innovation.

Responsibilities

- Consults and collaborates with full-time and part-time teaching faculty to integrate information literacy learning outcomes, assignments, learning activities, and learning assessments into in-person, hybrid and online courses. (30%)
- Works collaboratively with campus stakeholders to integrate library resources, services, and other tools into the curriculum. (20%)
- Creates and maintains a repository of reusable learning objects. (20%)
- Provides library instruction for students in designated subject areas. (10%)
- Creates scholarly products; actively participates in committees, professional engagement or service; and meets other NSC requirements for promotion and tenure. (20%)[27]

Aside from being exceptionally well written, this ad is telling in a number of ways. It describes an instructional design position, but one that really still has strong roots in the library. Reporting to the library director is one obvious way this is laid out. The emphasis on library instruction and information literacy is also something you wouldn't typically see in a job description for an instructional designer. That said, one would not expect many library positions to refer to "reusable learning objects." Also, the language used to describe the environment (e.g., "laser-like focus on creating successful outcomes for students," "an environment that embraces innovation and experimentation") seems a bit out of character for a typical library posting—but extremely refreshing to see! This is clearly an attempt to directly embed the experience and values of the instructional designer within the library. It is an interesting model. It seems likely that the possibility for doing more of this within larger-sized college and university libraries is great. That said, it doesn't negate our purpose here, which is to consider collaboration and partnership across areas. Even in the previous example, presumably, some form of instructional design experience or personnel exists outside the library and is worth partnering with.

We now come to the issue of what has been done already to bridge the gaps that may exist between librarians and instructional designers. In particular, what efforts have librarians and instructional designers already made to collaborate, and what challenges may have already been recognized in this regard? While this book covers this topic as a whole (and is itself an exploration of the topic as opposed to an exhaustive listing), it is worth beginning by looking at a handful of early examples.

EARLY EFFORTS AND COLLABORATIONS: CHALLENGES AND POSSIBILITIES

In an article written for *New World Library* in 2002, Joyce Latham writes, "If a librarian, technologist and information scientist go out in a boat, who is going to steer? Navigate? Propel the boat forward? Can anyone do all three? Can any three do one well?"[28] While we may not always frame things in such nautical terms, the spirit of these very same questions still remains poignant today. By very briefly exploring some early efforts to navigate obstacles and ways in which librarians and instructional designers have cooperated and may cooperate in the future, we can begin our search for answers.

Among others, Joan Lippincott has reported on some of the earliest efforts to build collaborations in the 1990s. Aside from a few stray samples, however, she notes that "collaborative projects do not necessarily proceed smoothly on campuses, and many higher education institutions have not even attempted such relationships."[29] One of the challenges she mentions was the perceived competition and confusion over areas of responsibility between the two professions. She describes an initiative begun in 1994 under the directive of the Coalition for Networked Information (CNI) that led to a series of "Working Together" professional development workshops attended by librarians and instructional designers from various institutions. Reporting on the results of these workshops, Lippincott indicates that projects were begun on many campuses: "Such collaborative projects have involved the development of facilities, creation of policies, implementation of networked information resources, and teaching and learning. Other efforts have focused on the development of joint service points, technology workshops, and faculty training programs."[30]

In 1999, Merri Beth Lavagnino reported on interviews with chief technology officers on six different campuses, some of whom were directly associated with the library and some of whom were not. While she doesn't describe much by way of specific projects, her early observations based on her discussions are very telling. She describes possibilities yet to be realized on most campuses even today. In short, the individuals interviewed pointed to the sharing of resources such that technology and research support could coexist in the same space (and they seemed to have been greatly influenced by the move many academic libraries were first making at the time toward a 24/7 service model).[31] Similar reports exist of attempts to connect librarians and instructional designers by having them share space, such as the detailed description of such efforts at Southern Illinois University.[32] According to Lavagnino's report, in addition to the sharing of space, ideally, cross training would occur so that librarians and IT staff could at least have greater awareness, understanding, and appreciation of each other's roles. The librarians seemed to have a better reputation for service in general, and so the thinking was that they could positively impact IT staff in this regard. Meanwhile, librarians could benefit from the tech-savvy IT staff who were not afraid of new technologies and emerging computing trends. Both had a direct connection to teaching and learning, and there was recognized overlap in that regard.[33]

Another notable early effort to bring librarians and instructional designers together occurred in 2000–2002 with the support of a grant from the Andrew W. Mellon Foundation. This project, Talking toward Techno-Pedagogy: A Collaboration across Colleges and Constituencies, brought together librarians and instructional designers/information technologists from Bryn Mawr, Haverford, Swarthmore, Vassar, Amherst, Mount Holyoke, Hampshire, Smith, Hamilton, and the University of Massachusetts at Amherst.[34] The participants discussed a number of important questions at the time, considering in particular how technology was affecting teaching and learning at their various institutions. They found that there was a need for more discussion and collaboration in general. One report on the project refers to "yawning gaps in our institutional structures" and further notes that "a collaboration such as this model proposes, embodies, and requires entails a culture change at our colleges."[35] A similar report from 2007 on the situation regarding potential collaboration notes this regarding the two groups: "They usually have limited understanding of one another's skills and knowledge and how they apply them."[36] One result of participation in the aforementioned program sponsored by the Andrew W. Mellon Foundation was stated as follows: "Librarians and information technologists learned that the integration of their knowledge and expertise into the shaping and teaching of a course sharpens their own focus in providing useful and successful service."[37]

Another report on the Talking toward Techno-Pedagogy project raises additional salient points and also hints at conceptual challenges that perhaps still exist as a roadblock toward more collaboration. According to Jonathan T. Church, "Perhaps one of the most immediate effects of the proliferation of information technologies across college campuses is how these technologies have transgressed boundaries of authority and expertise associated with professional identities."[38] This is perhaps a central issue even today as we struggle with defining the roles of both the instructional designer and the librarian in nonthreatening and collaborative as opposed to potentially competitive ways. Another central issue identified by Church is how both librarians and instructional designers view time. In a nutshell, they see it as a very limited resource and thus a pretty big hurdle toward developing collaborative projects that can also take into account the rapid progression of technology.[39]

Bonnie W. Oldham and Diane Skorina presented some interesting collaborations in 2009 and showed how collaboration might differ across institutions of different sizes.[40] For example, a smaller institution created an "i-frame" that was embedded into all courses through Blackboard. This frame provided students with quick and prominent access to library resources. Over time, the librarians and instructional designers at this smaller institution also created a first-year library orientation within Blackboard that addressed issues such as plagiarism (much more is shared on collaborating through the LMS in chapter 8). At a larger-sized institution, Oldham and Skorina report, collaborative efforts seemed a bit more structured, with shared committee interactions. This in turn led to a project for which the librarians and instructional designers worked together to convert quiz and testing materials for a computing and information literacy course into electronic format so that students could complete the work through their Angel LMS. An academic integrity tutorial was also developed within this collaborative environment. These examples in many ways touch on some of the more obvious areas where collaboration can occur. Utilization of the LMS and connecting it to library resources appear to be very ripe areas for working together. Another collaborative area exists in introducing or connecting students to critical information literacy concepts, such as those related to academic integrity and plagiarism.

As we move through this text, many more areas of partnership and collaboration are discussed, in addition to the few early examples briefly touched on here. As stated by Eleta Exline, author of one of the early reviews on the topic of partnerships between instructional designers and librarians:

> Although achieving the ideal conditions for collaboration sounds like a daunting task, successful models for working together do exist and typically incorporate deliberate efforts to start out on the right path. Collaborators participate in activities and exercises intended to encourage teamwork, create group identity, nurture trust, foster mutual understanding, eliminate stereotypes, encourage creativity, and develop a shared sense [of] purpose. Aligning projects with broad goals of the institution and formally establishing clear expectations can make it easier to initiate partnerships, gain the support of upper-level administrators, and sustain a cooperative spirit long term.[41]

It is also hoped that while we have tried to cover much ground, you as the reader will be inspired to consider your own creative and innovative ideas, test them out at your institutions, and share them with others. Local collaboration projects are great, but they are made even better if we can share them as models for our librarian and instructional designer colleagues! Let us look at the key connection points laid out here showing the similarities and differences between the two professions and use them as a catalyst for effective innovation!

NOTES

1. Deborah Hicks, "The Construction of Librarians' Professional Identities: A Discourse Analysis," *Canadian Journal of Information and Library Sciences* 38, no. 4 (2014): 252.
2. Ibid., 258.
3. Ibid., 260.
4. Cammy Bean, *The Accidental Instructional Designer* (Alexandria, VA: ASTD Press, 2014), 5.
5. Robert A. Reiser and John V. Dempsey, *Trends and Issues in Instructional Design and Technology* (Upper Saddle River, NJ: Prentice Hall, 2011), 6–10.
6. Mark Cain, "The Two Cultures? Librarians and Technologists," *The Journal of Academic Librarianship* 29, no. 3 (2003): 177.
7. Bean, *The Accidental Instructional Designer*, 15.
8. Reiser and Dempsey, *Trends and Issues in Instructional Design*, 12.
9. Association of College and Research Libraries, *Information Literacy Competency Standards for Higher Education* (Chicago: American Library Association, 2000), www.ala.org/acrl/sites/ala.org.acrl/files/content/standards/standards.pdf.
10. Association of College and Research Libraries, *Framework for Information Literacy for Higher Education* (Chicago: American Library Association, 2016), www.ala.org/acrl/sites/ala.org.acrl/files/content/issues/infolit/Framework-ILHE.pdf.
11. Ibid.
12. Angiah Davis, "Using Instructional Design Principles to Develop Effective Information Literacy Instruction: The ADDIE Model," *College and Research Libraries News* 74, no. 4 (2013): 205–7.
13. Brandeis University, Graduate Professional Studies, "Master of Science in Instructional Design and Technology," accessed April 4, 2016, www.brandeis.edu/gps/future-students/learn-about-our-programs/instructional-design.html.
14. American Library Association, "ALA Online Learning," accessed April 5, 2016, www.classes.ala.org.
15. Richard Moniz, Joe Eshleman, and Jo Henry, *Fundamentals for the Academic Liaison* (Chicago: ALA Neal-Schuman, 2014).
16. Cain, "The Two Cultures?," 180.
17. EDUCAUSE, "Annual Conference Face-to-Face Agenda" (October 27–30, 2015, Indianapolis, IN, and online), accessed May 9, 2016, www.educause.edu/annual-conference/agenda-and-program/indianapolis-preconference-seminars.
18. Association of College and Research Libraries, "ACRL 2015 Pre-Conferences," accessed October 6, 2015, http://conference.acrl.org/preconferences-pages-267.php (no longer available).
19. Ibid.

20. Vitae (a service of *The Chronicle of Higher Education*), "Instructional Designer (Job #2425): Excelsior College," accessed April 5, 2016, https://chroniclevitae.com/jobs/132709-2109098271.
21. Ibid., "Instructional Technologist—Winter Haven (150043): Polk State College," accessed April 5, 2016, https://chroniclevitae.com/jobs/0000884518-01.
22. Ibid., "Instructional Designer: The Joint Commission," accessed April 5, 2016, https://chroniclevitae.com/jobs/0000880858-01.
23. EDUCAUSE, "EDUCAUSE Career Center," accessed April 5, 2016, http://jobs.educause.edu/jobs/7181513/instructional-designer.
24. Vitae (a service of *The Chronicle of Higher Education*), "Instruction and Online Learning Librarian: Dominican University," accessed April 5, 2016, https://chroniclevitae.com/jobs/0000885874-01.
25. Ibid., "Reference and Instruction Librarian: University of South Carolina," accessed April 6, 2016, https://chroniclevitae.com/jobs/0000885491-01.
26. Ibid., "Humanities Librarian—0406667: James Madison University," accessed April 6, 2016, https://chroniclevitae.com/jobs/0000882620-01.
27. American Library Association, "ALA Job List," accessed October 6, 2015, http://joblist.ala.org/modules/jobseeker/Instructional-Design-Librarian/29606.cfm (via personal account).
28. Joyce Latham, "A Librarian, an Information Technologist, and an information Scientist Are Out in a Boat . . . ," *New World Library* 103, no. 10 (2002): 393.
29. Joan Lippincott, "Working Together: Building Collaboration between Librarians and Information Technologists," *Information Technology and Libraries* 17, no. 2 (1998): 84.
30. Ibid., 85.
31. Merri Beth Lavagnino, "Librarians and Information Technologists: More Alike than Different? Interviews with CIOs," *Library Hi Tech* 17, no. 1 (1999): 114–20.
32. Carolyn A. Snyder, Howard Carter, and Mickey Soltys, "Building Bridges: A Research Library Model for Technology-Based Partnerships," *Resource Sharing and Information Networks* 18, no. 1/2 (2005): 13–23.
33. Lavagnino, "Librarians and Information Technologists."
34. Talking toward Techno-Pedagogy: A Collaboration across Colleges and Constituencies, last updated May 13, 2002, http://serendip.brynmawr.edu/talking.
35. Elliott Shore, "Liberal Arts Education in the New Millennium: Beyond Information Literacy and Instructional Technology," *Moveable Type* (newsletter of the Mark O. Hatfield Library, Willamette University), Fall 2001, 2, http://serendip.brynmawr.edu/talking/liberalarts.pdf.
36. Liz Orna, "Collaboration between Library and Information Science and Information Design Disciplines: On What? Why? Potential Benefits?," *Information Research* 12 (October 2007): under Why They Don't Collaborate.

37. Shore, "Liberal Arts Education in the New Millennium," 2.
38. Jonathan T. Church, "Reimagining Professional Identities: A Reflection on Collaboration and Techno-Pedagogy" (paper published on the Talking toward Techno-Pedagogy website, June 16, 2000), 2, http://serendip.brynmawr.edu/talking.
39. Ibid., 7–8.
40. Bonnie W. Oldham and Diane Skorina, "Librarians and Instructional Technologists Collaborate: Working Together for Student Success," *College and Research Libraries News* 70, no. 11 (2009): 634–37.
41. Eleta Exline, "Working Together: A Literature Review of Campus Information Technology Partnerships," *Journal of Archival Organization* 7 (2009): 21.

BIBLIOGRAPHY

Association of College and Research Libraries. "About ACRL." Accessed April 5, 2016. www.ala.org/acrl/aboutacrl.

———. *Framework for Information Literacy for Higher Education*. Chicago: American Library Association, 2016. www.ala.org/acrl/sites/ala.org.acrl/files/content/issues/infolit/Framework-ILHE.pdf.

———. *Information Literacy Competency Standards for Higher Education*. Chicago: American Library Association, 2000. www.ala.org/acrl/sites/ala.org.acrl/files/content/standards/standards.pdf.

American Library Association. "ALA Job List." Accessed April 5, 2016. http://joblist.ala.org.

———. "ALA Online Learning." Accessed April 5, 2016. www.classes.ala.org.

Bean, Cammy. *The Accidental Instructional Designer: Learning Design for the Digital Age*. Alexandria, VA: ASTD Press, 2014.

Brandeis University, Graduate Professional Studies. "Master of Science in Instructional Design and Technology." Accessed April 4, 2016. www.brandeis.edu/gps/future-students/learn-about-our-programs/instructional-design.html.

Cain, Mark. "The Two Cultures? Librarians and Technologists." *The Journal of Academic Librarianship* 29, no. 3 (2003): 177–81.

Church, Jonathan T. "Reimagining Professional Identities: A Reflection on Collaboration and Techno-Pedagogy." Paper published on the Talking toward Techno-Pedagogy website, June 16, 2000. http://serendip.brynmawr.edu/talking.

Cramer, Steve. *This Liaison Life* (blog). Accessed April 6, 2016. https://liaisonlife.wordpress.com.

Davis, Angiah. "Using Instructional Design Principles to Develop Effective Information Literacy Instruction: The ADDIE Model." *College and Research Libraries News* 74, no. 4 (2013): 205–7.

EDUCAUSE. "Annual Conference Face-to-Face Agenda" (October 27–30, 2015, Indianapolis, IN, and online). Accessed May 9, 2016. www.educause.edu/annual-conference/agenda-and-program/indianapolis-preconference-seminars.

———. "EDUCAUSE Career Center." Accessed April 5, 2016. http://jobs.educause.edu/jobs.

———. "Mission and Organization." Accessed April 5, 2016. www.educause.edu/about/mission-and-organization.

Exline, Eleta. "Working Together: A Literature Review of Campus Information Technology Partnerships." *Journal of Archival Organization* 7 (2009): 16–23.

Hicks, Deborah. "The Construction of Librarians' Professional Identities: A Discourse Analysis." *Canadian Journal of Information and Library Sciences* 38, no. 4 (2014): 251–70.

Latham, Joyce. "A Librarian, an Information Technologist, and an Information Scientist Are Out in a Boat . . . ," *New World Library* 103, no. 10 (2002): 393–98.

Lavagnino, Merri Beth. "Librarians and Information Technologists: More Alike than Different? Interviews with CIOs." *Library Hi Tech* 17, no. 1 (1999): 114–20.

Lippincott, Joan. "Working Together: Building Collaboration between Librarians and Information Technologists." *Information Technology and Libraries* 17, no. 2 (1998): 83–86.

Moniz, Richard, Joe Eshleman, and Jo Henry. *Fundamentals for the Academic Liaison.* Chicago: ALA Neal-Schuman, 2014.

Oldham, Bonnie W., and Diane Skorina. "Librarians and Instructional Technologists Collaborate: Working Together for Student Success." *College and Research Libraries News* 70, no. 11 (2009): 634–37.

Orna, Liz. "Collaboration between Library and Information Science and Information Design Disciplines: On What? Why? Potential Benefits?" *Information Research* 12 (October 2007): 1–32.

Reiser, Robert A., and John V. Dempsey. *Trends and Issues in Instructional Design and Technology.* Upper Saddle River, NJ: Prentice Hall, 2011.

Shore, Elliott. "Liberal Arts Education in the New Millennium: Beyond Information Literacy and Instructional Technology." *Moveable Type* (newsletter of the Mark O. Hatfield Library, Willamette University), Fall 2001. http://serendip.brynmawr.edu/talking/liberalarts.pdf.

Snyder, Carolyn A., Howard Carter, and Mickey Soltys. "Building Bridges: A Research Library Model for Technology-Based Partnerships." *Resource Sharing and Information Networks* 18, no. 1/2 (2005): 13–23.

Talking toward Techno-Pedagogy: A Collaboration across Colleges and Constituencies. Last updated May 13, 2002. http://serendip.brynmawr.edu/talking.

Vitae (a service of *The Chronicle of Higher Education*). "Find Jobs." Accessed April 5, 2016. https://chroniclevitae.com/job_search/new.

RICHARD MONIZ

3
Best Practices and Opportunities for Collaboration

Building a culture of collaboration requires that we exit our comfort zone at times, explore new ideas, consider best practices, and seek out meaningful opportunities to enhance partnership and understanding. It may seem premature to explore best practices in brief since, in some sense, this whole book is about best practices. That said, we felt that it would benefit the reader to have one chapter that at least touches on many of the best practices that have already been discovered through our research and highlight key areas of potential synergy moving forward. Other areas were also identified that, while already representing ongoing collaborations at many institutions, remain significant opportunities for the future. Each is addressed in turn below.

BEST PRACTICES

In every area within higher education, one can find a multitude of best practices, whether for teaching pedagogy, incorporating technology in the classroom, or any other area pertinent to teaching and learning. Best practices with regard to instructional designers and librarians are really just emerging.

It is not our intention here to encapsulate *all* best practices. In fact, we hope that you, the reader, will come up with many more as you read and reflect on what we have written here! Rather, the following is, in a sense, our sample of some of the items we view as best practices in this regard. One thing also to remember with best practices is that we all work within unique institutional contexts. Just because something works well in one context does not mean it will in another. We encourage you to consider our text as it may (or may not) apply to your specific institutional circumstances.

Regular and Combined Meetings

One regular occurrence in academia that often gets eyes rolling or glossing over is the need to attend meetings. All campuses have some meetings that are more productive than others. For our purposes, what is being referred to is inclusive of meaningful meetings that involve some form of representation from both the library and the instructional design. These meetings could be exclusive to those groups or they could be bigger, including other key faculty or departments on campus.

While this may seem fairly pedestrian, it is worth noting some critical elements of good meetings (especially because we all attend some that are not at times). Some basic tips can be taken from Sharon Lippincott's *Meetings: Do's, Don'ts and Donuts*. Her first principle is "be discerning about the need for meetings."[1] Too often, we simply schedule meetings as a matter of habit and without determining their necessity. If we hope to build meaningful meetings involving librarians and instructional designers, it is important that they serve a purpose that can't be replaced by something simpler, such as an e-mail or a phone call. Again, this may seem obvious, but we have all seen unnecessary meetings do more to derail than encourage commitment. Her second principle is "plan meetings with purpose."[2] Somewhat redundant with the point made in her first principle, the focus here is on spending the time to craft specific elements of the meeting, such as agenda, location, and so on. Again, this is nothing especially groundbreaking, but most of us have attended meetings that lack an agenda or perhaps fall short in planning in some other way. Other principles and strategies include running on time, balancing participation, making sure critical people but only those necessary are in attendance, recording discussions and agreements, and making clear what follow-up elements may be needed.[3] According to Patrick Lencioni, when he was writing the book *Death by Meeting*, many people "assumed I was going to make a case for having fewer meetings."[4] The issue according to Lencioni, however, is not that we need fewer meetings per se, but that the meetings need to be more integrated and meaningful. He points to the irony of people within organizations spinning their wheels or spending undue one-to-one time communicating on issues that could be resolved through good meetings.

He also conveys that holding meaningful meetings can have a significant positive impact on organizational culture and health.

So, what kinds of meetings make sense for librarians and instructional designers? Certainly anything that is connected to teaching and learning and/or the LMS is relevant to the instructional designer. While some circumspect areas such as grading may, in some instances, be an unnecessary concern for the librarian, most topics along these lines will be relevant to librarians as well. This includes a broad array of meetings about curriculum, planning, changes to the LMS, faculty development initiatives, and so forth. It behooves both groups to be involved and contribute to these types of discussions. Beyond these more obvious points, we segue to other areas that can benefit specifically by bringing the instructional designers and librarians together for discussion. These include a wide variety of topics, but most specifically any that involve connecting electronic resources and the LMS. This is perhaps the greatest point of shared opportunity for librarians and instructional designers to coordinate efforts for the benefit of the institution (aside from, perhaps, some of the possible leadership opportunities suggested in chapter 1). As addressed further later in this chapter and as a focus of chapter 8, meetings that involve the development of shared or cooperative training that will be provided to staff, faculty, or students represent another opportunity. Both librarians and instructional designers bring critical elements to such discussions.

One area that may not be so obvious but is an underlying element of having productive meetings involving instructional designers and librarians is mutual understanding. In chapter 2, it was mentioned that many instructional designers have a library background. In this case, the instructional designer may have a deeper understanding of the foundational values and principles of librarianship, and this could be a great boon to the development of relationships. However, it is not safe to assume that a library background indicates familiarity with library resources and outlook within the *specific* organization. The instructional designer can still benefit from being provided with information specific to the library, and the librarians can benefit from learning more about the specific duties of the instructional designer as defined or developed within a given specific institutional context.

Combined Messages to Faculty

One significant area of opportunity lies in messaging. Faculty at most institutions are bombarded by messages, some of which are more critical than others. While messages can be conveyed any number of ways, the most common way to inform or engage with faculty is through e-mail. Unfortunately, according to Rob Jenkins, associate professor of English at Georgia Perimeter College, "Too many campus administrators still need lessons, or a refresher course, on e-mail etiquette."[5] This probably holds true as a concern for librarians and instructional designers as well. Jenkins offers great advice: keep the message short (but not so short as to be curt); don't use slang in attempt to sound friendlier (can come across as unprofessional), be cordial (in other words not too stiff or even dictatorial), and be very, very careful about including any humor.[6]

In addition to basic advice on communicating, much research has explored the important role that communication can play in positively affecting organizational culture. According to one such study, the importance of effective collaboration may be highlighted as well in this regard: "Each department needs to use information from other departments, but they also need to provide information to these same departments in order to accomplish the tasks necessary to meet the organization's goal. This illustrates the extent to which departments in an organization may depend on one another to reduce their ambiguity."[7]According to their study, which included comprehensive interviews followed up by surveys of HR (human resources) representatives from a variety of businesses, A. Gönül Demirel and Lebriz Tosuner-Fikes indicate that productive use of e-mail for messages can have a significant impact on job satisfaction and thus, presumably, effectiveness and productivity. Their study determined that "[f]ree flow of information is a reflection of open communication climate in the organization."[8] In academia, we tend to hold up such as an ideal. What we need to do is make sure this is happening *in practice*. Within our specific context here, we must ensure that faculty are aware of issues affecting the LMS or electronic resources, for instance. They need to be kept informed, and combined messages can be an effective and efficient way to do so. One recent study explored what faculty themselves felt was most important in communicating with them. While the study looked specifically at how deans and department chairs communicated, the information is also relevant to librarians and instructional designers who are looking to combine messages. According to the study, the following are "important" or "extremely important": "Demonstrating respect for them as colleagues, showing appreciation for their professional abilities, considering them an asset to the department, respecting their opinion, responding to phone calls and e-mails in a timely manner, and understanding their scholarly interests."[9] Librarians and instructional designers alike can sometimes get so caught up in their own expertise that they fail to remember that they fundamentally share a service role in supporting faculty or teaching and learning. The findings of this study seem to show very clearly that any messaging should be especially thoughtful in this regard. For example, a combined message might look something like this:

> Welcome back, faculty! We have been working diligently this summer to incorporate the assets and capabilities you have been collectively requesting to enhance your classes. Taking into consideration a variety of elements such as typically assigned projects and resources and your scholarly interests, the library and instructional design departments

have been adding new electronic databases where appropriate and adding/exploring new functionality within the LMS. We look forward to sitting down with you and updating you on elements that could be especially useful to you in your roles as scholars and instructors. Please feel free to join us on one of the following dates for a brief overview of changes and enhancements: . . . If you are unable to make any of these dates we look forward to meeting with you personally at a time convenient to you. Our hope is to serve as a support team to meet your needs as we head into this new academic year!

Sincerely,
Susie Smith, Instructional Designer
John Smithers, Instruction Librarian

Creating and Implementing Shared Workshops

Workshops can be an excellent way to connect with and support faculty. While some workshops might be more obviously geared toward the library or educational design, many areas, especially those where information, technology, and teaching and learning intersect, present great opportunities for librarian–instructional designer partnerships. Not only is the burden of creating and implementing the workshops shared, but both benefit from the combined and complementary experiences each brings to the table.

The following examples come from the Denver campus of Johnson & Wales University and were developed by Lori Micho, Amanda Samland, and Melissa Izzo.[10] This librarian/instructional designer team put together several successful workshops for faculty at Johnson & Wales University's Denver campus for the 2014–2015 academic year. According to Micho, Director of Library Services, "By far the most popular of the workshops was Making Assignments Visual. We ended up having at least a [half] dozen or more classes take an old assignment and turn it into an 'infographic' assignment."[11]

Making Assignments Visual: Co-facilitated by Academic Technology Services and the Library, this session will expose you to ideas and tools you can use to create visual assignments. In addition to reviewing data that supports creativity in education, we will explore free tools such as Piktochart (for creating infographics), Pinterest (for creating pinboard compilations), Glogster (for creating interactive posters), and PicMonkey (for creating digital art). The session will also include examples of visual assignments from Denver campus faculty, plus some best-of-the-best ideas from the around the Web.

■ ■ ■

Making Group Work Engaging: Co-facilitated by Academic Technology Services and the Library, this session will expose you to techniques and

> best practices for designing group work that will engage students. In addition to exploring the proven benefits of group work, we will discuss how to tackle some of the common problems and view examples of unique and successful group assignments. Please come prepared with an assignment of yours (group or individual) for a session activity.
>
> ■ ■ ■
>
> **Making Finals Fun:** Co-facilitated by Academic Technology Services and the Library, Making Finals Fun will expose you to test prep games and tools for students, as well as some alternatives to the traditional final exam or final paper. We will also review the latest trends in higher ed testing and discuss some best practices for making your final assessments meaningful.

While these workshops highlighted specific topics, it should be noted that the individuals behind them have collaborated to create workshops targeting specific faculty groups or departments and continue to explore other ways of reaching faculty as well.

OPPORTUNITIES

As we explore opportunities, we will consider best practices a bit more from a sort of "cutting edge" angle. These ideas show great promise and yet may not be fully formed. They represent bold attempts by professionals in both areas to work together toward enhancing collaboration for the benefit of students and faculty. Once again, we share these ideas hoping that they encourage you to consider unique solutions and ideas of your own!

Syllabi Sandbox or "Spa" Day

The Charlotte campus of Johnson & Wales University recently organized a special day for the faculty to work on syllabi and assignments as they prepared for the 2015–2016 academic year. Spearheaded initially by the library staff and the instructional designer, the campus had set aside a day associated with faculty orientation during which faculty could gain instant access to a cross-functional support team. As stated, while initially involving the librarians and the instructional designer, this also eventually included other relevant support staff, such as those from the Writing Center and the Center for Academic Support. The concept was loosely based on an idea shared by Karla Fribley, who with her colleagues at Emerson College created a Course Design Spa. According to Fribley, "The idea for the spa grew out of conversations between librarians, instructional technologists, and campus teaching center staff in summer 2013. We were looking for an event that would allow us to join forces to support our campus faculty. Knowing many faculty feel very busy, we wanted an event that would catch their eye."[12] Their modest budget of under $1,000 allowed them to hire two massage therapists and provide coffee for the day as well. They had faculty sign up in advance, not just for the massages but also for specific assistance in developing assignments, syllabi, and learning new technologies.[13]

In implementing the idea of a Syllabi Spa Day at Johnson & Wales University in Charlotte, the decision was made not just to solicit a list of attendees in advance but to have discussions with each academic department chair as well. These meetings between library staff and department chairs sought to determine the needs as seen through the perspective of these chairs. Another idea, as espoused by the vice president and dean of academic affairs, was also to encourage chairs to help pass on the word informally to their groups, perhaps highlighting to specific faculty an area in which they could seek to improve their class. For example, if faculty members in their year-end reviews had expressed the need or interest to incorporate more flipped classroom activities through the LMS, the chair might suggest they come by to talk to the librarians and instructional designer about selecting and embedding appropriate streaming videos in their courses for the fall. It was thought that this would allow faculty to get the most synergistic or combined "bang" for their time. One side benefit, of course, relative to this text, was yet another opportunity for the librarians to learn from the instructional designer and vice versa.

In the end, a dozen faculty (of approximately 100 total) took advantage of what was billed as the Syllabi Spa Day. The library hosted representatives from experiential education and career development, health services, the center for academic support, faculty development, the Campus Read program, and, of course, instructional design. A survey was sent out to the faculty who attended and five responded. Three indicated that the day was very helpful, one that it was helpful, and one chose not to respond to this question. While none of the faculty members indicated that they had spoken to anyone from faculty development or the Campus Read program (these were late additions that didn't make it into our promotional flier), they did interact with every other area represented. About half met with a librarian, and most notably, 80 percent of the faculty who attended met with the instructional technologist! One final observation was that while the majority of faculty did not attend Syllabi Spa Day, the faculty who came took significant advantage of the opportunity. One faculty member came with a list of relevant questions and needs associated with each area and proceeded to meet with a representative from each. She indicated that this setup saved invaluable time and made her aware of services for her students about which she would not otherwise have known.

Intellectual Property and Copyright

Any discussion of best practices or opportunities for partnerships needs to include intellectual property and copyright. Librarians have played a significant historical role in assisting faculty regarding the protection of intellectual property and the application of copyright laws both as creators of knowledge and as educators who regularly employ the doctrine of fair use to disseminate, share, and discuss ideas with their students. Oftentimes at larger institutions legal assistance is provided as well through a campus attorney. As LMSs have become ubiquitous and instructional designers have been brought on board, they, too, have found themselves often on the front lines in assisting faculty with these issues.

According to John Palfrey, author of the book *Intellectual Property Strategy*, "Intellectual property is a way of describing what the people in your organization know and are capable of doing. It's the collected knowledge, work product, and skill set of all those people that make up your team."[14] In academia, of course, this often translates into support for the kind of scholarship and research found at most universities and colleges. More on this appears in the following section in terms of direct support of faculty research and teaching. In the meantime, as pointed out by Palfrey, "[A]s the global knowledge economy grows each year, the importance of intellectual property strategy also grows for nonprofit organizations such as *universities*, *libraries*, museums, public media producers, and a broad range of cultural heritage institutions" (emphasis added).[15] As duly noted, while some institutions do work directly with patents and the creation of, say, new technologies, the more common or ubiquitous application of intellectual property at institutions of higher education is through the various applications of copyright law.

From the intellectual property perspective, the focus might be a bit more on the creation of ideas, concepts, or designs and their protection. In relation to copyright, this often boils down to the written word. It can, of course, encompass quite a bit more as well, everything from videos to drawings and other creative pursuits. For our purposes here, however, librarians and instructional designers are most likely to encounter issues with copyright as they pertain to the application of the fair use doctrine and other aspects of copyright related to teaching and learning. The doctrine of fair use is the component of copyright law that encourages the limited use of intellectual property for educational purposes. Its four main tenets are "(1) the purpose and character of the use, including whether such use is of a commercial nature or is for nonprofit educational purposes; (2) the nature of the copyrighted work; (3) the amount and substantiality of the portion used in relation to the copyrighted work as a whole; and (4) the effect of the use upon the potential market for or value of the copyrighted work."[16] *Copyright for Academic Librarians and Professionals*, published by ALA in 2014, is just one example of numerous books, workshops, websites, and videos that have been created to help guide professionals such as librarians and instructional designers as they seek in turn to guide faculty. Our purpose here is not to serve as a primer on the topic but rather to recognize with some awe how daunting this issue can be for faculty. Librarians and instructional designers are both uniquely positioned with their skill sets and support roles to provide assistance and understanding in this regard. Librarians and instructional designers could work closely together to help define the application of fair use policies at their institutions through the use of library reserves and the LMS, for example. This is one case where a lack of cooperation or coordinated planning could lead to confusion. It is critical that librarians understand what the instructional designer's role is and what they will counsel faculty is or is not acceptable in the LMS under fair use. Likewise, the instructional designer, in knowing what the library is able to provide through reserves and/or database access, can provide a faculty member who is seeking guidance with a much wider array of options beyond simply uploading content into the LMS. One thing that seems to always be beneficial in working with faculty is being able to provide them with choices and alternatives so that they can best meet what they deem to be the needs of their classes and their students.

Supporting Faculty Research and Teaching

While librarians have always supported faculty research through reference and liaison services in particular, they have also played a greater role in assisting faculty with teaching and learning as well. They have typically done so more as an aside by facilitating access to information and resources. The instructional designer, of course, does this a bit more directly, often by assisting faculty in setting up online courses or online course components that often include original ideas and material created by a given faculty member. The possibility of librarians and instructional designers working more closely together to provide support to faculty in order to make them more effective researchers and instructors is an intriguing opportunity moving forward. While some issues remain more obviously mutually exclusive, the potential here for combined efforts begs for more creativity.

What if instead of thinking of faculty teaching and research in isolation, instructional designers and librarians were to work together in this area? What might that look like? We hope that simply asking this question will spur you as a reader to consider the possibilities, but some implications seem obvious. There would presumably be a much more seamless transition between a faculty member's ability to mine information, add to or enhance this information, and then convey a deeper understanding or facilitate better and more meaningful learning opportunities for their students.

Digital Scholarship

Digital scholarship is one of the fastest growing areas of our time relative to information. It is discussed throughout this text, perhaps most significantly in chapter 6 where we not only explore the state of digital scholarship in general but also provide case studies demonstrating what can be accomplished. Digital scholarship could also easily be seen to fall within the broader context of support for faculty research and teaching and thus viewed as presenting a uniquely opportune area for collaboration. Many institutions, if not most, now participate in or maintain some sort of institutional repository. Institutional repositories have the great potential of representing the collective wisdom, contributions, and knowledge as supported or sponsored by particular institutions. While a spirit of open access and open sharing of knowledge and ideas permeates these initiatives, most colleges and universities are often eager to "brand" these contributions made for the collective good. This leads to greater institutional recognition; better student, staff, and faculty recruitment and retention; and support for development initiatives of various kinds.

According to Eileen Scanlon, Associate Director of Research and Scholarship at the Institute of Educational Technology, "The potential of new forms of public engagement enabled by new technology where academic staff can make use of networked communities offers those scholars new ways to participate in wider global debates, with diverse audiences."[17]Again, our intent in this text is not to cover all that is happening within the context of digital scholarship (as if that were even possible!). There has been much written and disseminated on this topic. As indicated by Scanlon, however, it is important to note that digital scholarship has already radically changed how scholarship in general occurs in many fields. Based on an extensive series of interviews involving educational technologists and related professionals, Scanlon's article presents a variety of ways that this is occurring, inclusive of everything from blogs to institutional open-access archives. She notes that "in 2012 the UK government announced £10 million in funding for UK academics to publish their research in journals that allow free public access to the material online with a subscription. Embracing digital scholarship fits well with these new requirements."[18] She further notes that this environment is a complicated one, and one in which faculty will require guidance and support.

Clearly, the area of digital scholarship involves key elements that hit at the core of what librarians and instructional designers support. It involves supporting and educating faculty (the instructional designer's arena) and the dissemination, collection, organization, and retrieval of information (the librarian's area of expertise). A partnership on campus could result in a greater level of support and awareness among faculty about the changes taking place. As noted in the previous quote, the trend toward digital scholarship is indeed an international phenomenon that extends far beyond just the United States. While not applicable to all institutions, the case study involving Davidson

College in chapter 6 provides a detailed and successful example illustrating the great potential for collaborative projects in this area.

Embedding into the LMS for Library-Related Instruction

Embedded librarians have been around for quite some time now. The use of this approach seems to be growing by leaps and bounds, however. As with the previous topics, our intent here is not to cover this topic in-depth but rather to explore it as an avenue for partnerships and collaborations. For a comprehensive exploration of embedded librarianship, there are many great sources but perhaps none better than David Shumaker's *Embedded Librarian: Innovative Strategies for Taking Knowledge Where It's Needed.* According to Shumaker, "Embedded librarianship is a distinctive innovation that moves the librarians out of libraries and creates a new model of library and information work. It emphasizes the importance of forming a strong working relationship between the librarian and a group or team of people who need the librarian's information expertise."[19] While some institutions have actually hired librarians to fill this role explicitly, others have relied on a variety of alternative avenues to incorporate librarians into online or hybrid courses. In many cases, instruction and liaison librarians have been given access directly to classes. In other examples, some libraries have expanded their reach by recruiting MLIS students into embedded internships in the hope of reaching even more students and faculty than they could through their own onboard staff. One groundbreaking example is a very well-defined program of this sort developed by the University of North Carolina at Greensboro through partnering with a variety of other institutions in their geographic area.[20]

Getting back to our topic at hand, one of the most critical elements of embedded librarianship is that it typically involves incorporating the librarian or library intern into an LMS. This, of course, is the recognized domain of the instructional designer. While an instructional designer may be utilized to facilitate incorporation into a class, this partnership has the potential for extending further. For example, the instructional designer may be able to suggest to faculty that librarians could be embedded to provide research support in their courses. By having knowledge of just what kind of support may be provided, the instructional designer can be armed with the ability to facilitate these discussions beyond the superficial provision of specific examples of projects, assignments, or discussions that have been enhanced as a result of these efforts. Furthermore, the embedded model has yet to really reach its full potential within higher education.

With the embedded librarian as a model, the instructional designer could lead the way in incorporating other support areas, as appropriate, into online and hybrid courses. As just one example, a tool such as Starfish can be incorporated into an LMS with the instructional designer taking a lead role in its implementation: "The Starfish platform helps you eliminate the silos that make it difficult to share the information that could impact a student's ability to be successful. Our platform provides an easy way to collect data from the people and systems that are working on your campus, then provide that information to advisors and other staff at the right time to initiate and document a plan of action."[21] Starfish and similar tools have found their greatest impetus from efforts tied to student retention and success. But it is these very efforts that have become the focus of all support areas on campus of late, and rightfully so. While institutional self-interest may be involved, there is much to be said about these efforts to connect students and faculty to specific resources (e.g., librarians and other support staff) at the point of greatest need. Helping students successfully complete courses and programs is at the heart of the core values of both the instructional designers' and librarians' respective missions. Because of the importance of the modern LMS and the great potential it has for bringing librarians and instructional designers together, the entirety of chapter 8 is dedicated toward exploring this area.

Teaching Information and Digital Literacy

An additional area worth mentioning again where collaboration and partnership can have a significant impact is the teaching of information literacy skills. While this may be seen as more clearly the domain of the librarian, the instructional designer can greatly impact student learning by serving as a partner in these efforts. Some of the ways in which this may occur have been mentioned before, but many more remain. For example, the instructional designer could provide educational assistance to the library staff by offering training and assistance in the creation of meaningful online tutorials or even by helping library staff create useful assessments that test student knowledge both before and after learning occurs. Furthermore, with their in-depth knowledge of the LMS, these could be directly and seamlessly incorporated into a student's online experience within a given course. Another way in which this may occur is by providing assistance or learning opportunities with the implementation of online modules.

In 2015, the Johnson & Wales University Charlotte campus implemented the widespread use of Credo's Information Literacy Courseware, branded as "uresearch" (see the flier in figure 3.1 that was created to share this new resource with the faculty). Several companies have produced similar products. Interestingly, Credo's was created and is supported by a team of librarians and instructional designers. Together, they worked to create meaningful learning opportunities connected to information literacy and other related skill sets through online modules. These are packaged in the form of short tutorials and assessments that can be easily embedded into online courses. According to Credo's website, the product may be used for the following purposes:

- Demonstrate your institution's measurable impact on information literacy and critical thinking
- Empower your graduates with the skills demanded by employers
- Enhance cross-campus collaboration between faculty, staff, and the library
- Extend instruction and flip the classroom with engaging multi-media
- Support students in-person and online
- Free up staff time to focus on instruction rather than creating materials
- Meet accreditation requirements around information literacy and critical thinking skill standards[22]

One concern originally voiced was that this service would somehow outsource the role of the instruction librarian. In contrast, however, it became clear that the product could actually greatly enhance the opportunities for more meaningful instruction. Early on, many faculty expressed the desire to incorporate various modules into their courses. One of the points mentioned by Credo is the ability to use their product to "flip the classroom." According to Jonathan Bergmann and Aaron Sams, authors of *Flip Your Classroom: Reach Every Student in Every Class Every Day* (a great primer on the topic of flipping a classroom), "The one unifying characteristic of all flipped classrooms is the desire to redirect the attention in a classroom away from the teacher and onto

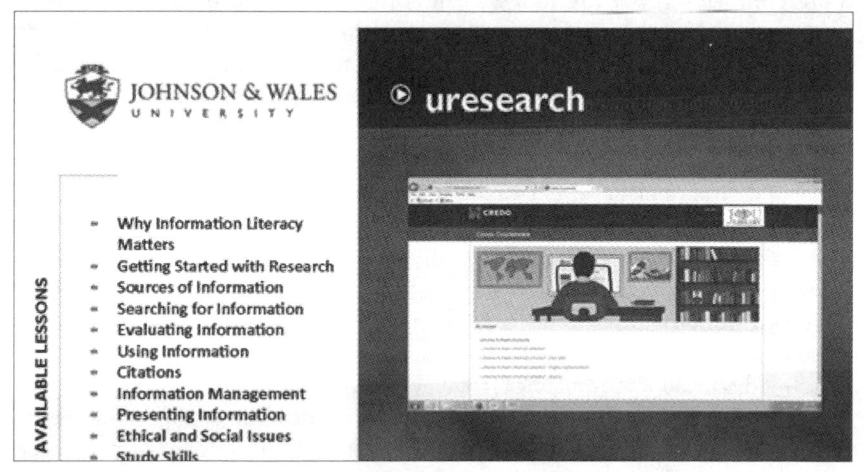

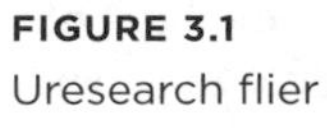

FIGURE 3.1
Uresearch flier

the learners and the learning."[23] This is one of the greatest benefits of utilizing these or similar modules. Many libraries do not have a large enough staff to create the kinds of comprehensive and sophisticated collections of online resources that this type of product provides. This type of resource allows basic content knowledge to be conveyed to and learned by students at their own pace and on their own time. This, in turn, frees the instruction librarian to focus on challenges, questions, and support for specific projects attached to a given class. According to Valerie Freeman, instruction librarian at Johnson & Wales University's Charlotte campus and contributor to *The Personal Librarian: Enhancing the Student Experience*, "Online education today is simply the latest manifestation in . . . an onslaught of technological advances in recent decades. In this rapidly changing world, it is increasingly critical for institutions to be adaptable."[24] While referring more specifically to embedded librarianship, Freeman's point is equally relevant to the use of the flipped classroom. The instructional designer can play a key role in helping librarians and faculty with the process of integrating this resource. While this perhaps more greatly benefits the domain of the librarian, the instructional designer also then has the opportunity to utilize this model to inculcate faculty about the possibilities and potentialities of flipping the classroom.

While some opportunities related to best practice points have been illustrated here, chapters 5 and 8 go even further in describing potentials and possibilities in this regard.

Digital Media

One last best practice area that needs mention here is digital media. This is a pretty broad topic as discussed within our context. It can include anything from the use of various software applications, streaming videos, or really any available digital product. Chapter 7 discusses many formats and avenues for digital media that could serve as a praxis for collaboration between librarians and instructional designers. This discussion overlaps to an extent with the discussion of the LMS, but libraries provide access to an almost mind-boggling array of digital books and videos, to name just a couple of the more obvious digital resources. Likewise, instructional designers often provide leadership and training in the creation of digital products. Less obvious areas of conjoined possibilities could be the way that librarians and instructional designers might work together to funnel students and faculty toward websites, MP3 files, and so forth.

The discussion of multimedia collaboration and best practices is indeed multifaceted in that librarians and instructional designers could team up to assist faculty in the inclusion of such resources and how to use them but also may serve as support for faculty and students to *create* digital media. This, in turn, opens up areas such as copyright, the use of equipment, and general discussions on what is meant by digital literacy. Again, this is addressed in much greater detail further on in this book. Suffice it to say that the area of digital media lies within the expertise and boundaries of each profession.

BUILDING BRIDGES AND A NEW CULTURE

Once again, building a culture of collaboration requires that we exit our comfort zone at times and build new bridges and understanding between our two professions. While not intended to be comprehensive, this chapter has hopefully provided you, the reader, with a further taste of what this book is about as well as the exciting opportunities available to us if we reach out and explore new approaches and best practices. As we move into the future, we hope that others will utilize and develop the ideas herein for the ongoing development of our partnerships and the continued support for our students and faculty! With this in mind, the next chapter takes a side step of sorts as we consider in more depth and detail the nature of collaboration within the academic enterprise.

NOTES

1. Sharon M. Lippincott, *Meetings: Do's, and Don'ts and Donuts; The Complete Handbook for Successful Meetings* (Pittsburgh, PA: Lighthouse Point Press, 1999), 19.
2. Ibid., 31.
3. Ibid.
4. Patrick Lencioni, *Death by Meeting: A Leadership Fable . . . about Solving the Most Painful Problem in Business* (San Francisco, CA: Jossey-Bass, 2004), 250.
5. Rob Jenkins, "What Did I Do Now?," *The Chronicle of Higher Education* 57, no. 33 (2011): A30.
6. Ibid.
7. A. Gönül Demirel and Lebriz Tosuner-Fikes, "The E-mail Use in Open Communication Climates: A Path-Analysis Model," *Global Media Journal: Turkish Edition* 4, no. 8 (Spring 2014): 84.
8. Ibid., 92.
9. Audrey Williams June, "Communicating with Faculty Members," *The Chronicle of Higher Education* 57, no. 40 (July 2011): A28.
10. Johnson & Wales University, Denver Campus Library, "Faculty Workshops 2014–2015: Inspiration for the Classroom," accessed April 5, 2016, http://den.library.jwu.edu/2014Workshops.
11. Lori Micho, e-mail message to author, July 15, 2015.
12. Karla Fribley, "Massages in the Library: Running a Course Design Spa for Faculty," *College and Research Libraries News* 76, no. 6 (2015): 324.
13. Ibid.

14. John Palfrey, *Intellectual Property Strategy* (Boston: MIT Press, 2011), 3, 5–6.
15. Ibid., 10.
16. Laurence and Timberg as cited in Rebecca Butler, *Copyright for Academic Librarians and Professionals* (Chicago: ALA Editions, 2014), 14–15.
17. Eileen Scanlon, "Scholarship in the Digital Age: Open Educational Resources, Publication and Public Engagement," *British Journal of Educational Technology* 45, no. 1 (January 2014): 14.
18. Ibid., 21.
19. David Shumaker, *Embedded Librarian: Innovative Strategies for Taking Knowledge Where It's Needed* (Medford, NJ: Information Today, 2012), 4.
20. University of North Carolina at Greensboro, "School of Library and Information Studies Practicum," accessed October 6, 2015, http://lis.uncg.edu/current-students/practicum (no longer available).
21. Starfish by Hobsons, "Institutional Leadership," accessed April 6, 2016, www.starfishsolutions.com/home/starfish-by-user-role/higher-education-leadership.
22. Credo, "Credo Information Literacy Courseware," accessed October 6, 2015, http://corp.credoreference.com/product-services/information-literacy-course-module.html.
23. Jonathan Bergmann and Aaron Sams, *Flip Your Classroom: Reach Every Student in Every Class Every Day* (Arlington, VA: International Society for Technology in Education, 2012), 96.
24. Valerie Freeman, "Embedded Librarianship and the Personal Librarian," in *The Personal Librarian: Enhancing the Student Experience*, eds. Richard Moniz and Jean Moats (Chicago: ALA Editions, 2014), 51.

BIBLIOGRAPHY

Bergmann, Jonathan, and Aaron Sams. *Flip Your Classroom: Reach Every Student in Every Class Every Day*. Arlington, VA: International Society for Technology in Education, 2012.

Butler, Rebecca. *Copyright for Academic Librarians and Professionals*. Chicago: ALA Editions, 2014.

Credo. "Credo Information Literacy Courseware." Accessed October 6, 2015. http://corp.credoreference.com/product-services/information-literacy-course-module.html.

Demirel, A. Gönül, and Lebriz Tosuner-Fikes. "The E-mail Use in Open Communication Climates: A Path-Analysis Model." *Global Media Journal: Turkish Edition* 4, no. 8 (Spring 2014): 82–95.

Fribley, Karla. "Massages in the Library: Running a Course Design Spa for Faculty." *College and Research Libraries News* 76, no. 6 (2015): 324–27.

Jenkins, Rob. "What Did I Do Now?" *The Chronicle of Higher Education* 57, no. 33 (2011): A30.

Johnson & Wales University, Denver Campus Library. "Faculty Workshops 2014–2015: Inspiration for the Classroom." Accessed April 5, 2016. http://den.library.jwu.edu/2014Workshops.

June, Audrey Williams. "Communicating with Faculty Members." *The Chronicle of Higher Education* 57, no. 40 (July 2011): A28.

Lencioni, Patrick. *Death by Meeting: A Leadership Fable . . . about Solving the Most Painful Problem in Business*. San Francisco, CA: Jossey-Bass, 2004.

Lippincott, Sharon M. *Meetings: Do's, and Don'ts and Donuts.* Pittsburgh, PA: Lighthouse Point Press, 1999.

Moniz, Richard, and Jean Moats (eds.). *The Personal Librarian: Enhancing the Student Experience*. Chicago: ALA Editions, 2014.

Palfrey, John. *Intellectual Property Strategy*. Boston: MIT Press, 2011.

Scanlon, Eileen. "Scholarship in the Digital Age: Open Educational Resources, Publication and Public Engagement." *British Journal of Educational Technology* 45, no. 1 (January 2014): 12–23.

Shumaker, David. *Embedded Librarian: Innovative Strategies for Taking Knowledge Where It's Needed*. Medford, NJ: Information Today, 2012.

Starfish by Hobsons. "Institutional Leadership." Accessed April 6, 2016. www.starfishsolutions.com/home/starfish-by-user-role/higher-education-leadership.

University of North Carolina at Greensboro. "School of Library and Information Studies Practicum." Accessed October 6, 2015. http://lis.uncg.edu/current-students/practicum (no longer available).

JOE ESHLEMAN

4
Collaborating to Accomplish Big Goals

This chapter is concerned with ways to collaborate and differs from chapter 3 by being more focused on the conceptual nature of collaboration. In conjunction with the preceding chapter, it provides some groundwork for developing a disposition for collaboration. For example, it attempts to answer why it would be advantageous to work together and presents environments that spur collaboration. Additionally, as opposed to offering best practices and areas for collaborative work between librarians and instructional designers, it looks instead at developing a type of collaborative mindset. The real-world practice of collaboration can often occur serendipitously. Yet, as a way to make collaboration more concrete, it is more effective to strategize and plan for it. In fact, instructional designers would consider the design of a plan for collaborating to be most useful. They would welcome the opportunity to construct a well-designed strategy for working with others. There is also the need to consider what defines the different types of collective work—whether the work should be considered cooperation or collaboration. Also, the chapter examines the different types of collaboration.

As presented earlier in the book, academic librarians have a history of collaboration, most notably with faculty and students, yet often with others on campus. While there is not a lack of desire to work together for both librarians and instructional designers, there appears to be very little structure in place for them to do so. As remarked upon in chapter 2, it is helpful to remember that librarians generally have a designated working role (liaison[1]) that is primarily concerned with forming working relationships on campus (mainly directed toward faculty). Despite this designation, they still seem to struggle with achieving a firm and consistent foothold in this position, specifically from the perspective of strong influence on the direction of the institution. In many cases, information literacy has gained ground in higher education, especially as related to learning outcomes and within mission statements. Yet in many other situations, it is confined to the library.

Although the importance of collaboration is considered a given in many places on campus, it is rare for there to be a consistent plan for two or more departments working together. Oftentimes, events or projects will bring together groups, but a concerted effort to build concrete links between departments seems to be lacking. This is understandable when contemplating organizational structures at most institutions and perhaps even advantageous in some cases. Certainly, there are instances where departments want to retain their own separate identities. It could also be confusing to students, staff, and faculty if there were fewer purposeful demarcations for support. With these hurdles recognized, there are cases where departments pool their resources, and these often benefit the collaborators as well as the institution.

One idea that has been offered for impact is for librarians to "[p]artner on campus with faculty, deans, provosts, and other administrators."[2] While it may be beneficial to do this, there must be a consideration of the size of the library and its staff. The current perception of librarian work at specific institutions also may not allow for these partnerships. As discussed in the section on human-centered design in chapter 6, this often limited or false perception of librarians can lead to situations in which they are not thought of as first-choice partners for collaboration. The lack of deep knowledge regarding librarian roles and librarian potential can be a large hurdle to surmount when seeking cooperative opportunities. Again, a great deal of the responsibility for this rests on librarians' shoulders, and changing such perceptions needs to be a greater priority moving forward.

In "Librarians as Academic Leaders: Uniquely Qualified for the Job," Maureen Diana Sasso and David A. Nolfi exhort librarians to lead and list numerous reasons librarians are well qualified for this role: "Academic librarians are innovative problem solvers, expert at working within financial, space, and time constraints, and skilled at collaborating in cross-disciplinary teams and working with diverse populations."[3] They are quick to caution that "[a]cademic librarians who are too closely identified with support services rather than academic affairs risk being seen as tangential rather than central to the educational mission of the institution."[4] This is a situation with an effect that cannot be underestimated. While librarians are well aware that they contribute to the idea that they are generally considered to be in support roles rather than ones of leadership, there is a catch-22 here.

Although frequently invoked, the full meaning of catch-22 is often only vaguely understood. Aspects of it include a "situation in which a desired outcome or solution is impossible to attain because of a set of inherently contradictory rules or conditions" and one that "often result[s] from rules, regulations, or procedures that an individual is subject to but has no control over because to fight the rule is to accept it."[5] Both of these concepts imply a form of helplessness and an inability to move forward or make changes. How is this conundrum overcome? One idea to start with is the development of a collaborative mindset. Rather than feeling that a specific outcome or project needs to take place to "fix" the situation, another tactic may be more helpful. Stepping back and thinking about ways in which to collaborate and designing a plan can help here. As part of a tiered approach, cultivating an open mental state that understands the importance of focusing on process over finished product is one way forward.

Steven Bell often offers well-thought-out solutions about how librarians can respond to the challenges faced by higher education. By mapping specific strategies to the different types of transformations occurring within higher education, he analyzes the situations and proposes focused plans. In *Five Ways Academic Libraries Support Higher Education's Reboot*, Bell positions libraries as support systems reacting to five educational transformations and says that libraries can respond by concentrating on openness, online learning, higher productivity, alt-higher ed, and user-design-driven higher education.[6] He reinforces the importance of conversations around these topics and the significance of collaboration. He concludes with this advice for other campus associates:

> Take time to visit your campus library, talk to your academic librarian colleagues and discover what the library can offer to higher education in transformation. Working collaboratively, we can begin the reboot and make sure the college or university we create is the one shaped by our vision of academic success for our students and faculty.[7]

Bell's comments here imply that there needs to be a two-way-street mentality in place, and that those in campus leadership roles need to recognize librarians' value and work.

In their book *Organizing Higher Education for Collaboration: A Guide for Campus Leaders*, authors Adrianna J. Kezar and Jaime Lester are careful to detail how ingrained ideas such as individualism and organizational design create a culture against collaboration.[8] This needs to be met with a focused mindset and a mission that embraces collective work and is initiated by leadership. In a review of the book, Connie D. Foster points out, "Creating a collaborative campus is an intentional and deliberate process. It does not happen by accident and, according to Kezar and Lester, it will not occur until major organizational systems are intentionally redesigned."[9] This intentionality stems from self-reflective analysis, discussions, planning and designing, and then action.

Sasso and Nolfi highlight a central tenet of librarian leadership that is at the core of this book, that is, how librarians can act as agents with interdisciplinary roles that allow them to collaborate more freely:

> As campus leaders we can better position the library within the larger campus agenda and further the reputation of librarians as collaborators and valued contributors to the achievement of the institutional mission and goals. Additionally, we can more clearly assess faculty and student needs in order to improve planning for the services and collections that will most benefit our campuses.[10]

An important distinction here is the use of the phrase "further the reputation of librarians as collaborators and valued contributors," which is another in a long line of initiatives that librarians know they need to accomplish. Yet it appears as if a heightened reputation for librarians on the college campus has yet to reach critical mass. As pointed out previously, it does not appear as if librarians can achieve this alone and collaboration may shine a brighter light on librarians' value.

One of the roadblocks that can occur with collaboration is the concern of "stepping on toes," that is, moving out of one's silo and into another's sphere of influence. Although it may sound obvious, this type of barrier can not only do harm by inhibiting collaboration and innovation but also cause futile competition for resources. A good collaborative model will use resources well (not duplicate them) and ideally find innovative ways to use added resources more efficiently. Organizational silos are certainly not a new idea; one definition puts it this way: "The term 'silos' is quite commonly used in literature on organisational performance to describe inwardly focused organisational units where external relationships are given insufficient attention."[11] As a librarian, it can be a thought-provoking exercise to consider where you expend your time and energy: Is it inwardly focused or outwardly focused as it relates to the library itself? As part of their landmark document *New Roles for New Times: Transforming Liaison Roles in Research Libraries*, Janice M. Jaguszewski and Karen Williams begin with this:

> Engagement requires an outward focus. By understanding the changing needs and practices of scholars and students, librarians can help shape future directions for the library and advance the library's mission within the larger institution. Building strong relationships with faculty and other campus professionals, and establishing collaborative

> partnerships within and across institutions, are necessary building blocks to librarians' success.[12]

Connect, Collaborate, and Communicate is the leading title of *A Report from the Value of Academic Libraries Summits*, prepared by Karen Brown and Kara J. Malenfant. In it, they conclude:

> Academic librarians can serve as connectors and integrators, promoting a unified approach to assessment. As a neutral and well-regarded place on campus, the academic library can help break down traditional institutional silos and foster increased communication across the institutional community. Librarians can bring together people from a wide variety of constituencies for focused conversations and spark communities of action that advance institutional mission.[13]

Moving away from silos and into places of conversation also helps to create higher visibility. In "Collaboration or Cooperation? Analyzing Small Group Interactions in Educational Environments," Trena M. Paulus states, "Dialogue, then, is critical to collaboration, because it creates awareness of one's own thinking processes as multiple perspectives are shared through discussion."[14] Before dealing with dialogue, it is important to spend some time with one's own thinking process and examine how the development of a specific mindset can set the tone for good collaboration.

DEVELOPING A COLLABORATIVE MINDSET

Stepping back a bit before delving into how to develop a mindset, we need first to define what a mindset is. Mindset as something that is "fixed" or "given" differs from other ways to conceptualize an approach, such as an attitude or a disposition. It is interesting to consider for a moment how important dispositions are to the ACRL's *Framework for Information Literacy for Higher Education* (ACRL *Framework*).[15] Dispositions are a core element of this recent guiding document for instruction librarians. They are connected to each of the six "frames" developed within the ACRL *Framework*. These frames in turn are influenced by threshold concepts. Such concepts give "a name to points in new learning that mark a departure from old ways of viewing the world and entrance into new ways that may be counterintuitive and thus upsetting (troublesome), and yet they are ways that must be grasped in order to go forward in learning."[16] Threshold concepts can be defined for different disciplines. They allow for a type of demarcation in knowledge growth, and though they are difficult to assess, there is an attraction to them for instruction librarians hoping to converse with specific faculty. More information about threshold concepts and the ACRL *Framework* appears in chapter 5 of this book.

Points in new learning and the effect of dispositions can also be closely aligned to mindset. Perhaps the most influential current mindset strategy is the one developed by Carol Dweck, growth mindset. On her website, Dweck states, "Mindsets are beliefs—beliefs about yourself and your most basic qualities. Think about your intelligence, your talents, your personality. Are these qualities simply fixed traits, carved in stone and that's that? Or are they things you can cultivate throughout your life?"[17] The idea that there is a choice in how personal capabilities are perceived is highly influential for teaching and learning. What makes for additional impact here is the work toward the nurturing of certain mindsets.

At the core of Dweck's ideology is the notion that challenges are what help to change mindsets and that students can learn more effectively when they let go of the idea that their capabilities are fixed. In the same way, it is beneficial to understand that the ability to collaborate is ever present and that one's capability to work together is not a static set point. One's capacity to collaborate can always change and grow. The viewpoint that equates to a fixed notion about how collaboration cannot be achieved needs to be challenged and overcome. Certainly there is the reality that collaboration takes more than one person, but opening up to opportunity breaks down preconceived notions and then silos. All of the documented cases in this book prove that librarians have collaborated and will continue to do so. What we need are even more such endeavors.

When attempting to develop a collaborative mindset as a librarian, one instinctive approach is an understanding of shared responsibility to students. This outlook can help to minimize barriers when working with others. Although it is obvious that student growth and achievement is a shared concern, it can still be helpful to constantly remain conscious of this and often vocalize its significance. As Susan E. Shepley puts it, "Librarians must determine how plans to collaborate would benefit everyone involved, from graphic artists to instructional designers in online courses to faculty and, most importantly, to students."[18] Shared goals are often a way to remove barriers to collaboration, so instructional designers and librarians should contemplate the similar outcomes they desire.

Although Amber Chandler's blog post "What Growth, Innovation and Collaborative Mindsets Look Like for Students and Teachers" does not focus on librarianship, it has numerous relevant points here, especially the connection to growth and collaborative mindsets. She notes, "Truth be told, standing up there and 'teaching' is outmoded and ineffective. As a 21st century teacher, your job is to rally the disjointed group to prepare them for a future that doesn't exist yet. With this in mind, teachers must tap into important mindsets to be successful in creating powerful, personalized learning experiences."[19] In a similar way, most of the focus of a librarian's job has changed and continues to change. Realizing the importance of shaping the future for students is an important outcome for instruction librarians. Bringing a growth mindset to this academic challenge means coming to a realization that this situation has the potential to be changed.

One important approach that can help when developing a collaborative mindset is increasing mindful habits. Mindfulness can lead to a focus on process rather than on an end result, and when done properly, it can alleviate anxiety and judgment. The latter two attributes are enemies of collaboration. Additionally, it can be helpful to remember that small collaborative efforts have numerous advantages over larger ones. For example, collaborating with one or two people allows for a deeper understanding of those with whom you work. Small cooperative ventures are sometimes easier to manage and control and can of course lead to larger efforts, if desired. In fact, in our cases, the collaborative efforts began as individual connections and grew from there. This scaffolding concept also allows for a mindful or paced propulsion toward action in small ways rather than overly self-conscious inertia. Once this small but crucial step of developing the proper mental state is achieved, it is time to move on to discussion. Along with more conversation, informal learning can impact collaborative ventures.

THE POWER OF CONVERSATION AND INFORMAL LEARNING

Often overlooked as a step for fostering collaboration is the power of conversation. Daily discussions in the library about the state of higher education and issues that affect librarianship can contain seeds for future endeavors. These day-to-day talks can act in the same manner as brainstorming sessions during meetings and retreats. As one of the frames in ACRL's *Framework* points out so well, scholarship is conversation: "Communities of scholars, researchers, or professionals engage in sustained discourse with new insights and discoveries occurring over time as a result of varied perspectives and interpretations."[20] Building from this helpful metaphor leads naturally to the idea of collaboration as conversation. Dovetailing with this slogan, the exchange of ideas that can occur between librarians and instructional technologists are manifold. What needs to occur is a breakdown in the divisions that are denying them the ability to have consistent and collaborative conversations.

Upon closer examination, what are these divisions? Usually they are a combination of organizational demarcations combined with daily work habits that do not allow for creative collaborations. This is why there needs to be a great deal of thought put into planning to work together. Without directives or task-oriented projects, there are few opportunities for librarians and instructional designers to get together. The previous chapter offered some creative ideas, such as workshops and events, but are there other prospects?

Librarians are generally skilled in understanding information networks and finding ways to retrieve information. Instructional designers understand how learning occurs and have an awareness of how learning development tools and software function. In both cases, experienced people in these fields should have some knowledge of emerging technologies and can communicate well with one another about their passions. It would seem to be the case that some of these overlapping interests would lead to many more collaborations than we see. Proposing that these two departments on campus get together more frequently to discuss these overlapping interests would be a good start to collaborative ventures. Of course, some libraries have already accomplished this, for example, Kenyon College's Library and Information Service (https://lbis.kenyon.edu/about-lbis), Hamilton College's Library and Information Technology Service (www.hamilton.edu/lits/news) and Libtech at the University of Central Florida (https://library.ucf.edu/services/computers-technology/libtech).

The Hamilton College merger is a good one in which to take a deeper dive. One of the ways in which the administration settled on combining the library and IT departments was to talk about it: "'With the impact of new technologies on the production and retrieval of knowledge, such a merger seems to me the way of the future,' Stewart [president of the college] said in a statement. 'At Hamilton it was the result of extensive conversation and careful planning.'"[21] The two entities involved had the added advantage of sharing space prior to the merger. This situation is obviously conducive to collaboration: "'We lived together for 40 years before we got married,' Smallen [vice president for libraries and information technology] said. 'There's no substitute for people interacting with each other over the coffeepot. That was a real benefit.'"[22] Despite this case being one that has gone rather smoothly, there must be consideration given for each institution making its own decision. A cursory look at the comments for the article on the merger attests that some librarians do not support this type of decision. One of the reasons is that the identity of the library (and the librarians) can be subsumed. The final summation: "'If you merge the organizations, you should do it for strategic purposes, not to save money or just for efficiency,' Smallen said. Hamilton wasn't trying to fix an 'organizational problem' with the merger, he said, but to find the best way to support the college's academic programs 'in a world in which information and technology are changing in many different ways.'"[23]

Conversations are great starting points and can keep collaborative opportunities alive. Although the perspective in the blog post "Librarians as Instructional Designers: Strategies for Engaging Conversations for Learning" is that of a school librarian, Buffy J. Hamilton speaks of her efforts working with faculty, and her approach can also apply in the academic library: "I take whatever material and ideas the teachers [have] sent to me and use that as a starting point for an ongoing conversation."[24] After working with faculty on an instructional design project, Hamilton concludes:

> My hope is that this initial kind of instructional collaboration will lead to future work and design thinking that will help us, in the words of Kristin Fontichiaro, "nudge toward inquiry" and spark additional conversations about teaching and learning that will ultimately impact students in meaningful and positive ways. By meeting learners—both teachers and students—at the point of need, we can nurture trust and build a climate that invites partnerships to help us identify challenges, wonder and ideate a range of solutions, implement those strategies, and learn from our experiences together. Even when circumstances are not ideal, I do believe it is possible to open up entry points that can lead to more nuanced ideation, implementation, and assessment if we contextualize collaborative partnerships as a continuum of trust and relationship building, the anchors of libraries that embody participatory culture and learning.[25]

As Amanda Hovius states, in her blog *Designer Librarian*, "While there is a tendency for librarians to focus heavily on information technology fluency skills in beginning IL instruction (which is important) *another approach would be for librarians to partner with technology instructors* to ensure that the skills are fully addressed in the types of required technology-focused courses that can be found in both K–12 and in higher education" (emphasis added).[26]

Developing a collaborative mindset that initiates conversations that lead to consistent working relationships sounds like a nice packaged plan. But, once more, a consideration of the real-world situations on your campus may not allow for these types of platitudes. Taking a look at the reasons that librarians may not connect with instructional designers can be a helpful exercise. What are the places on the Venn diagram where we do not meet? Designers usually understand the technical underpinnings of the networks; they often can code and create digital technologies; they comprehend usability and experience design and, often, information design. Librarians may not have these skills. Conversely, what are instructional designers "missing" when they consider the opportunity to work with librarians? Librarians may have more comprehensive knowledge of how information is created, processed, and organized. It could be said that as part of an instructional technologists' education and need for lifelong learning, they have a better understanding of their field in relation to higher education. As a newer profession compared to librarianship, instructional design has an advantage in that it is more precisely defined. Perhaps the more singular focus on the role of the instructional designer allows for more intentional professional development. Thinking about these different roles may allow us to step back and take stock of ways in which we may be able to work cooperatively.

One reason that librarians can be thought of as "natural collaborators" is that they are required to develop proficiencies in (or, at minimum, have knowledge of) a wide variety of responsibilities and disciplines. For example, they may not be experts in copyright or intellectual property law necessarily (i.e., they generally cannot or should not give legal advice when it comes to these issues), but they do have enough information expertise to collaborate with a lawyer, if needed. In the same way, some teaching librarians (who are given faculty status or tenure in some cases) are often willing to collaborate with others, for example, graduate students,[27] instructional technologists,[28] and writing programs.[29] The overlap of technology skills and the allure of design thinking are paving the way for librarian–instructional designer projects. We can see that although librarians and instructional designers may not individually possess all of the aforementioned attributes, *combined* they bring to the table a fair amount of skill and knowledge that can help move higher education forward. Collectively, it would seem as though the combined knowledge and skill sets of the two would be something any institution would desire and use to their advantage.

How then do instructional designers and librarians begin the process of joining forces? There are many ways, some of them detailed through the examples in this book. One more recent opportunity is through the online tool called Slack (https://slack.com). Advertised as a messaging app for teams, it allows sharing of collaborative objects (files, images, workspaces) and, most distinctively, retains conversations and group efforts in one collaborative space. Other options here are software such as Trello (https://trello.com) and Asana (https://asana.com). There are also, of course, the tried-and-true academic avenues, such as creating more cohesive ties together through committees, affinity groups, and task forces.

Perhaps there is a difference in professional outlook between these two roles that creates less collaboration. Librarians, for all their wonderful traits, can sometimes be lulled into a type of stasis. One place where instructional technologists/designers and librarians may part or even be at odds is when looking at some of the underlying approaches to their own fields. Technologists and designers are in a constant state of rethinking and evaluating. Due to their close connection to the changes in technology, they are daily engaged in assessing learning technologies, platforms, and tools and very often are in "critique mode." It could be energizing and insightful for more academic librarians to tap into this state of mind. That is to say, librarians could unbind themselves from focusing so intently on their role on campus and how they are perceived.

Librarians, often with a heavy history and more stringent academic requirements placed upon them, can on occasion become more deeply invested (especially emotionally) in how they are viewed. An interesting take on this concept is the post "Librarianship Doesn't Need Professionals" by Madison Sullivan in *ACRLog*. As a new librarian trying to navigate the position and attempting to figure out "[h]ow to be taken seriously as a 'new professional,' and how to 'be yourself' at the same time,"[30] she is a bit overwhelmed by this enigma. Wrestling with the idea of professionalism, Sullivan states, "Professionalism is a word people use to maintain and enforce the status quo. Professionalism doesn't take risks; it encourages conformity. Can you simultaneously call yourself a professional and advocate for radical change? Professionalism is safe and it is boring."[31] She concludes, "Librarianship doesn't need more professionals. Librarianship needs people who can look critically at our field and feel compelled to bring about change. We need leadership that actively encourages this. How can we create work cultures conducive to this?"[32] While it is certainly easy to take context out of any writing, what is interesting here is that new academic librarians often feel this way when confronted with perceived notions of the behavior expected of them. To continue on with the earlier distinction between librarians and instructional designers, it would be difficult to imagine an instructional technologist or designer having a similar set of concerns about being a "professional," at least from the point of view of outside pressure. An instructional technologist is not beholden to a learning management system (as opposed to how a librarian may feel about a collection), and an instructional designer is more interested in evaluation and function than angst associated with finding the "best" resource. Keeping in mind that these are perceptions and not value judgments, analyzing how these two positions approach their work can lead to more empathy and connections for each.

And it is also here where an exaggerated focus on perception (inner and outer) puts librarians at a distinct disadvantage. An often-heard lament from academic librarians is the weariness that accompanies having to explain what they do. As stated earlier, this concept ties in with how each institution perceives and values its librarians. This facet is one factor that leads to librarian burnout. Maria Accardi (https://mariataccardi.com) is a librarian who has experienced this situation and speaks about it with great insight. Other components of librarian burnout include feeling as though you must do everything and please everyone, the taxing effect of emotional labor, and feelings of isolation. Obviously, good collaborative efforts can alleviate some of these effects. Attempting to fully decide why burnout occurs can be an exercise in futility. Part of the reason is the usual cadre of numerous culprits; the wide range of reasons includes poor messaging and communication on the part of librarians, stereotyping of positions and roles, and constantly shifting job titles and goals due to the influence of technology. Yet this quandary is surely not limited to librarians because every instructional designer has certainly grappled many times with the question, "What do you do in that job?" It is almost as if academic librarians and instructional designers must be resigned to the fact that their jobs will be either trite caricatures or puzzles to many forever. This is why it may be the case that elevated positions on campus may lessen some of these problems.

All of this heavy introspection is merely raised to quantify the point that librarians are hitting a peak in relation to how they are being defined. Perhaps this anxiety is tapped into when collaboration or merging of roles is mentioned. They are questioning themselves in the same way that their jobs are continually being questioned. Librarians do seem to have a tendency to look inward,[33] and they are very loyal to their values, such as equal access to information, protection for patrons, and Ranganathan's Laws of Library Science.[34] A great deal of controversy and animosity occurs when the idea of merging departments is brought up, especially from the perspective of librarians who feel they are being subsumed by information technology. Again, the development of a collaborative mindset may alleviate these fears.

The differing nature of cooperation in relation to collaboration warrants some discussion. Collaboration needs to be demarcated from ideas such as working together or even an ephemeral team event. Collaboration is a consistent partnering that takes on well-defined and focused projects. Additionally, collaboration needs to be seen as achievement based in some manner; that is, there needs to be an accomplishment that can be measured. Ideally, a venture that is collaborative between instructional designers and librarians would be planned, documented, and assessed in some way. Other chapters in this book detail numerous combinations of librarians working with others, primarily instructional technologists and designers. In many cases, there are specific projects that detail ways in which the separate positions or departments work together. In the document *Think Global, Act Local—Library, Archive and Museum Collaboration*, Günter Waibel and Ricky Erway from OCLC (Online Computer Library Center) Research say that for cooperation to move to collaboration, five aspects must be present: vision, mandate, incentives, change agents, and mooring.[35] In using the term *mooring*, they mean this:

> Collaborations thrive and survive when they have an administrative mooring or a home base from which they can conduct operations, communicate with others, and incorporate their efforts into the broader mission of their institution. Collaborations that operate on the periphery of their institution's administrative structure have a difficult time situating themselves among existing committees or programs, and find it hard to get their voice heard among a cacophony of competing interests.[36]

Surely many academic libraries are well immersed in existing committees and programs, but there do not appear to be numerous unified and vocal librarian–instructional designer/technologist teams consistently representing an integrated mission to their institutions. When looking at deep and radical collaborations in the next section of this chapter, we can see that there are a few and the potential for more, so that is inspiring. Still, as many of the examples detailed in this book prove, there is work to be done to move from simple cooperation to consistent collaboration.

Informal learning is the name given to what can transpire outside a formal learning space. One of the intriguing aspects of informal learning is how it brings into question what spaces are considered to be those that are for "formal" learning. One that most frequently comes to mind is the classroom. Yet for some students, the academic library is thought of as a type of classroom, or a formal learning area. What makes informal learning interesting in an academic environment is that it could be considered to be somewhat antithetical to part of the mission of higher education, in particular the idea that informal learning diverges from learning acquired from a teacher. Informal learning is also difficult to quantify and not easily assessed. With all of this said, how can informal learning between librarians and instructional designers be of benefit?

Knowledge creation is at the core of R. David Lankes's influential book *The Atlas of New Librarianship*. As a way to lift librarians away from and above their continued association with the physical library itself, he states, "The mission of *librarians* is to improve society through facilitating knowledge *creation* in their communities" (emphasis in original).[37] As opposed to knowledge acquisition, knowledge creation is sometimes associated with informal learning and is considered to be more self-determined. Still, there are often social and support elements to this, therefore a need for communities and librarians to support them. As a way to amplify Lankes's idea with numerous added components, Roy Tennant relayed his version in "The Mission of Librarians Is to Empower."[38] One of the ways in which librarians empower is to stay current, Tennant says: "Society evolves, and librarians evolve with it. . . . So I have great confidence in the ability of librarians to adapt and to continue to offer services that our users find compelling."[39]

The informal learning in libraries now is connected to such exciting initiatives as gamification, makerspaces and 3-D printing, virtual reality, digital media creation, and active learning spaces. The collaborative aspect of all of these informal learning ideas intersects with technology and often elevates the library from preconceived ideas about its function. Those who see the library strictly as an academic support system may feel as though that mission is being compromised. Being reminded of the library as a growing organism may make them reconsider. Or as Lankes has done, perhaps it should first be considered whether or not the librarians are growing (as opposed to diminishing).

As mentioned in previous chapters, although formal institutional roles (and job titles) are significant, there can be more essential attributes to look for when attempting to do work together. Moving away from a preoccupation on established roles can be beneficial to the creation of cooperative projects. One of the interesting aspects of living and working in a world heavily dominated by online communication and presence is how academic identities are now being influenced. Bonnie Stewart explores "social media identity and its implications for higher education" and "the intersections of knowledge and technologies, and currently researches the implications of networks for scholarship, attention, care and vulnerability."[40] She is interested in how the changing of academic reputation and influence is affected by social media and online interaction. As part of the changes that the intersection of the public and workplace personas brings to academic work, she urges us to begin talking to and educating students (and one another) about this. Once more, conversation (in the form of both academic and technological focus) is a way forward and librarians and instructional designers need to start talking.

What is applicable here is the idea that roles in academia are changing often and changing quickly. And that is certainly the case when it comes to librarians. Yet more than the fact that job titles, responsibilities, and areas of focus are in a swift state of change, all of higher education must be braced for an acceptance of the need to develop a rapid response. Seemingly caught in an unprepared state of inertia, higher education in some cases is not able to act fast. There are numerous valid reasons for this, but still, it is the rare institution that looks to its instructional designers or its librarians as resources to help with this condition. The point here is that librarians have once again been at the forefront of this issue. They have needed to adapt and change perhaps more than anyone else on campus. The insight that they can bring to adaptability and flexibility in relation to job roles would seem to be something campus administrators should be interested in.

The development of a collaborative mindset can lead to the strategy that prompts conversations that in turn create opportunities for informal learning—all of which can lead to collaboration. Conversations are a way to break through the "culture of silence" that Paulo Freire says helps to reinforce a diminished self-image.[41] These breakthroughs bolster confidence and lead to connections and collaborations. And although collaboration is the objective, there can be even greater goals to pursue.

DEEP AND RADICAL COLLABORATION

Begun in 2009, "2CUL is a transformative partnership between two major academic research libraries, the Columbia University Libraries and the Cornell University Library, based on a broad integration of resources, collections, services, and expertise."[42] The idea of libraries joining together, especially from the perspective of sharing their collections in some manner, is a time-honored practice. Libraries have been borrowing from and lending to one another since the 1890s.[43] But the 2CUL partnership reaches much further than previous library consortia and shared storage endeavors between libraries. One of the interesting deviations in this partnership is the sharing of staff. The "About" page on the 2CUL website summarizes the chronology and main highlights of the project, one of which is this:

> Phase 2 of 2CUL (2013–2015) is designed to consolidate the partnership, create the requisite infrastructure to build deeper collections through integration, and develop new capabilities for meeting 21st century research, teaching, and learning needs. Both partners believe that addressing such challenges successfully will require new organizational models that embrace deep collaboration.[44]

Anne R. Kenney, in the presentation "2CUL: Emerging Model of Deep Collaboration?" presents these points as "Some 'Ah Ha' Moments":

- Bringing two organizations together to perpetuate traditional library models is not a goal but a dead end
- It's got to be seen as being about more not less
- Enabling prerequisites for radical collaboration are key[45]

Kenney, who is the Carl A. Kroch University Librarian at Cornell, is also the author of *Leveraging the Liaison Model: From Defining 21st Century Research Libraries to Implementing 21st Century Research Universities*. In it, she states, "As demands and expectations rise, it is clear that no one liaison can do it all and research libraries have begun to pair disciplinary experts with functional specialists (such as those familiar with intellectual property issues) and are teaming up with others on campus, including information technologists and instructional designers."[46] Deep and radical collaborations are happening and they are fascinating to watch, especially from the perspective of the history of libraries. As in the adage "Everything old is new again," the case can certainly be made that these efforts have echoes of library consortial arrangements, interlibrary loan services, and other local, regional, national, and international library ventures. Yet technological pervasiveness seems to be a factor this time, and it is a driver that cannot be ignored. Once again, working with instructional designers as a way to move toward the personal development of an improved technological skill set with the added advantage of design thinking seems to be an excellent choice for librarians.

Another recent example of libraries combining resources is the announcement that Georgia Tech Library and Emory University Libraries are working together on a joint Library Service Center, which "is a collaborative project that will house a shared collection of materials, provide delivery services and free up space on the main campuses at both universities."[47] While this effort fits more closely under the category of a shared collection—of which there are several cases, such as the Preservation and Access Service Center for Colorado Academic Libraries and the joint library depository of the University of Texas system and Texas A&M University—it does add an element that sets it apart from a storage facility by allowing patrons to visit, and there are plans for the combined sharing of digital resources.

Emblematic of the ways in which far-reaching ideas are expanding is the example provided in the article "Building a New Research-University System" by Jonathan R. Cole. Here the radical collaborative idea put forth is modeled on another system: "In the next 25 or 30 years, we ought to shift our glance away from intercollegiate athletics associations to academic associations. These would not be formal mergers, but 'academic leagues' that would enhance the capabilities of great universities and, at least potentially, lower the cost of education."[48] Interestingly, the author is "a university professor at Columbia University, where he was provost and dean of faculties from 1989 to 2003."[49] He notes, "The library is the one feature of academic research organization that has flourished through partnerships," alluding to the earlier partnership with Cornell.[50] An interesting rejoinder to this comes from the comments on the article, where the idea of library consortia is raised and then this point is made: "But then, the mindset of people who choose to work in libraries is fundamentally one of wanting to share, rather than compete; after all, sharing is what libraries do. So maybe if you want to transform American higher ed into a more sharing/collaborative framework, you should start by recruiting leaders from the ranks of library directors."[51]

Valerie Horton defines deep collaboration as "two or more people or organizations contributing substantial levels of personal or organizational commitment, including shared authority, joint responsibility, and robust resources allocation, to achieve a common or mutually-beneficial goal."[52] Although deep collaboration is generally referred to in reference to libraries and organizations working more closely together, in some cases, it is used in conjunction with librarians' work. One of the prime movers for collaboration is the continued growth of the use of digital resources. Horton concludes, "It is apparent to me that libraries are at the beginning of a new transformation movement with deep collaboration as one of the critical tools."[53] And John Helmer, the Executive Director of the Orbis Cascade Alliance, has this to say:

> I think that deep collaboration based on shared human resources is a very exciting area. People are so important, so expensive, and many are trying to do too many things and not feeling good enough at any of them. The strong network tools we have now make a truly effective distributed workforce not only possible but, in some cases, the best way to go. Creating a shared labor force has the promise of making jobs better and improving services but it requires careful thought and trust that encourages a willingness to depend on others. Library A has to be willing to say "I depend on Library B to accomplish my mission." I see it as a long-term commitment, not a convenient arrangement you can easily get out of. Marriage, not just a hookup.[54]

The group behind the *Journal of Radical Librarianship* is the Radical Librarians Collective in the United Kingdom. The group is looking to uphold library values against the tide of "the marketisation of libraries and commodification of information."[55] In the journal article "Radical Librarian-Technologists," John Schriner notes:

> The role of the academic librarian continues to change. It seems that there has been no better convergence of academic departments around technology than at this moment: the librarian speaks with journalism students about secure communications and privacy tools; to computer science faculty and students about setting up anonymity network relays to give censored users a voice; to student groups to help rein in unconstitutional surveillance.[56]

As the collaborative mindset continues to grow and as librarians think of ways to begin the conversations that lead to collaboration, they will act upon this foundation. What once was an idea that seemed beneficial is now an imperative as the roles on campus expand and librarians and instructional designers find themselves getting out and working together more frequently. Writing about collaboration during hard times in *Library Journal*, Irene Gashurov and Curtis L. Kendrick sum up the drive behind the need to collaborate:

> If we don't join in creating the future, we may find that the future does not include us. We can make ourselves an integral part of the future by working together. Collaboration, as much as competition, is here to stay. By scrutinizing each project's potential to add to the bottom line and paying attention to human factors like trust, commitment, and a culture of collaboration, we can increase our chances of leading our partnerships to innovation, forging new value rather than just perpetuating the status quo.[57]

NOTES

1. For more information about the current state of library liaisons, see Janice M. Jaguszewski and Karen Williams, *New Roles for New Times: Transforming Liaison Roles in Research Libraries* (Washington, DC: Association of Research Libraries, 2013), www.arl.org/storage/documents/publications/nrnt-liaison-roles-revised.pdf; Anne R. Kenney, *Leveraging the Liaison Model: From Defining 21st Century Research Libraries to Implementing 21st Century Research Universities* (report published by Ithaka S+R, March 25, 2014), www.sr.ithaka.org/wp-content/mig/files/SR_BriefingPaper_Kenney_20140322.pdf; and Barbara Rockenbach, Judy Ruttenberg, Kornelia Tancheva, and Rita Vine, *Association of Research Libraries/Columbia University/Cornell University/University of Toronto Pilot Library Liaison Institute Final Report* (Washington,

DC: Association of Research Libraries, 2015), www.arl.org/storage/documents/publications/library-liaison-institute-final-report-dec2015.pdf.
2. Rockenbach et al., *Pilot Library Liaison Institute Final Report*, 8.
3. Maureen Diana Sasso and David A. Nolfi, "Librarians as Academic Leaders: Uniquely Qualified for the Job" (paper presented at the ACRL Thirteenth National Conference, Baltimore, MD, April 1, 2007), 325, www.ala.org/acrl/sites/ala.org.acrl/files/content/conferences/confsandpreconfs/national/baltimore/papers/325.pdf.
4. Ibid., 326.
5. *The Free Dictionary*, "Catch-22," accessed January 28, 2016, www.thefreedictionary.com/Catch-22; *Wikipedia*, "Catch-22," accessed January 28, 2016, https://en.wikipedia.org/wiki/Catch-22_%2810gic%29.
6. Steven Bell, "Five Ways Academic Libraries Support Higher Education's Reboot," *The EvoLLLution* (online newspaper), February 18, 2013, http://evolllution.com/opinionsfive-ways-academic-libraries-support-higher-educations-reboot.
7. Ibid.
8. Adrianna J. Kezar and Jaime Lester, *Organizing Higher Education for Collaboration: A Guide for Campus Leaders* (San Francisco: Jossey-Bass, 2009).
9. Connie D. Foster, "Review of *Organizing Higher Education for Collaboration: A Guide for Campus Leaders*, by Adrianna J. Kezar and Jaime Lester," *Planning for Higher Education* 38, no. 3 (2010): 66.
10. Sasso and Nolfi, "Librarians as Academic Leaders," 326.
11. Tony Fenwick, Erica Seville, and Dave Brunsdon, *Reducing the Impact of Organizational Silos on Resilience*, Resilient Organisations Research Report—2009/01 (New Zealand: Resilient Organisations Research Programme, March 2009), www.resorgs.org.nz/images/stories/pdfs/silos.pdf.
12. Jaguszewski and Williams, *New Roles for New Times*, 4.
13. Karen Brown and Kara J. Malenfant, *Connect, Collaborate, and Communicate: A Report from the Value of Academic Libraries Summits* (Chicago: Association of College and Research Libraries, 2012), www.ala.org/acrl/sites/ala.org.acrl/files/content/issues/value/val_summit.pdf.
14. With reference to Arvaja, Hakkinen, Etelapelta, and Rasku-Puttonen (in press), Trena M. Paulus, "Collaboration or Cooperation? Analyzing Small Group Interactions in Educational Environments," in *Computer-Supported Collaborative Learning in Higher Education*, ed. Tim S. Roberts (Hershey, PA: Idea Group, 2005), 113.
15. Association of College and Research Libraries, *Framework for Information Literacy for Higher Education* (Chicago: American Library Association, 2016), www.ala.org/acrl/sites/ala.org.acrl/files/content/issues/infolit/Framework-ILHE.pdf.

16. Jan H. F. Meyer and Ray Land (eds.), *Overcoming Barriers to Student Understanding: Threshold Concepts and Troublesome Knowledge* (New York: Routledge, 2006), 1.
17. Carol Dweck, "The Mindsets," MindsetOnline.com, accessed January 28, 2016, http://mindsetonline.com/whatisit/themindsets/index.html.
18. Susan E. Shepley, "Building a Virtual Campus: Librarians as Collaborators in Online Course Development and Learning," *Journal of Library Administration* 49, no. 1/2 (2009): 280.
19. Amber Chandler, "What Growth, Innovation and Collaborative Mindsets Look Like for Students and Teachers," *Getting Smart* (blog), September 17, 2015, http://gettingsmart.com/2015/09/what-growth-innovation-and-collaborative-mindsets-look-like-for-students-and-teachers.
20. Association of College and Research Libraries, *Framework for Information Literacy*.
21. Carl Straumsheim, "How and Why Hamilton College Merged Library, IT." *Inside Higher Ed*, December 4, 2015, www.insidehighered.com/news/2015/12/04/how-and-why-hamilton-college-merged-library-it.
22. Ibid.
23. Ibid.
24. Buffy J. Hamilton, "Librarians as Instructional Designers: Strategies for Engaging Conversations for Learning," *The Unquiet Librarian* (blog), December 6, 2013, https://theunquietlibrarian.wordpress.com/2013/12/06/librarians-as-instructional-designers-strategies-for-engaging-conversations-for-learning.
25. Ibid.
26. Amanda Hovius, "The 4 Facets of Information Literacy," *Designer Librarian* (blog), November 2, 2015, https://designerlibrarian.wordpress.com/2015/11/02/the-4-facets-of-information-literacy.
27. Alexander Watkins and Katherine Morris, "Can Only Librarians Do Library Instruction? Collaborating with Graduate Students to Teach Discipline-Specific Information Literacy," *The Journal of Creative Library Practice*, February 27, 2015, http://creativelibrarypractice.org/2015/02/27/can-only-librarians-do-library-instruction.
28. Bonnie W. Oldham and Diane Skorina, "Librarians and Instructional Technologists Collaborate," *College and Research Libraries News* 70, no. 11 (2009): 634–37, http://crln.acrl.org/content/70/11/634.full.
29. Lily Griner, Yelina Luckert, Judy Markowitz, and Nevenka Zdravkovska, "Supporting the Professional Writing Program with Online Modules—Collaboration and Engagement, Theory and Reality." *The Journal of Creative Library Practice*, November 4, 2015, http://creativelibrarypractice.org/2015/11/04/supporting-the-professional-writing-program-with-online-modules.

30. Madison Sullivan, "Librarianship Doesn't Need Professionals," *ACRLog*, January 19, 2016, http://acrlog.org/2016/01/19/professionalism.
31. Ibid.
32. Ibid.
33. Nicole Pagowsky and Miriam Rigby (eds.), *The Librarian Stereotype: Deconstructing Perceptions and Presentations of Information Work* (Chicago: Association of College and Research Libraries, 2014); Ashanti White, *Not Your Ordinary Librarian: Debunking the Popular Perceptions of Libraries* (Oxford, UK: Chandos, 2012).
34. S. R. Ranganathan, *The Five Laws of Library Science* (London: Edward Goldston, 1931).
35. Günter Waibel and Ricky Erway, "Think Global, Act Local—Library, Archive and Museum Collaboration," *Museum Management and Curatorship* 24, no. 4: preprint, www.oclc.org/research/publications/library/2009/waibel-erway-mmc.pdf.
36. Ibid., 13.
37. R. David Lankes, *The Atlas of New Librarianship* (Cambridge, MA: MIT Press, 2011).
38. Roy Tennant, "The Mission of Libraries Is to Empower," *The Digital Shift*, January 15, 2014, www.thedigitalshift.com/2014/01/roy-tennant-digital-libraries/mission-librarians-empowerment.
39. Ibid.
40. Bonnie Stewart, "Contributions and Connections," *Higher Ed Beta* (blog), accessed January 28, 2016, www.insidehighered.com/blogs/bonnie-stewart.
41. Paulo Freire, *Pedagogy of the Oppressed* (New York: Continuum, 2000).
42. 2CUL, "FAQ," accessed January 28, 2016, www.2cul.org/node/1.
43. James Buckley, "Behind the Scenes of College's Interlibrary Loan Staff, Process," *The Highland Echo*, April 17, 2013, http://highlandecho.com/behind-the-scenes-of-colleges-interlibrary-loan-staff-process.
44. 2CUL, "About 2CUL," accessed January 28, 2016, www.2cul.org/node/17.
45. Anne R. Kenney, "2CUL: Emerging Model of Deep Collaboration?" (presentation at the ASERL Fall 2010 Membership Meeting, What Is 2CUL?), slide 18, accessed April 8, 2016, www.aserl.org/meetings/archive-meetings/2010_11_mtg_materials.
46. Kenney, *Leveraging the Liaison Model*, 8.
47. Emory News Center, "Emory, Georgia Tech to Open Joint Library Service Center," November 19, 2014, http://news.emory.edu/stories/2014/11/upress_library_service_center/index.html.
48. Jonathan R. Cole, "Building a New Research-University System," *The Chronicle of Higher Education*, January 17, 2016, http://chronicle.com/article/Building-a-New/234906.
49. Ibid.
50. Ibid.

51. Ibid., comment by mbelvadi.
52. Valerie Horton, "Going 'All In' for Deep Collaboration," *Collaborative Librarianship* 5, no. 2 (2013): 65–69.
53. Ibid.
54. John F. Helmer and Valerie Horton, "Finding Joy in Our Profession: John F. Helmer on Library Consortia," *Collaborative Librarianship* 7, no. 3 (2015): 139–44.
55. Radical Librarians Collective, "Radical Libraries," accessed January 28, 2016, https://rlc.radicallibrarianship.org/radical-libraries.
56. John Schriner, "Radical Librarian-Technologists," *Journal of Radical Librarianship* 1 (2015), https://journal.radicallibrarianship.org/index.php/journal/article/view/6/1.
57. Irene Gashurov and Curtis L. Kendrick, "Collaboration for Hard Times," *Library Journal*, October 2, 2013, http://lj.libraryjournal.com/2013/10/managing-libraries/collaboration-for-hard-times/#_.

BIBLIOGRAPHY

Association of College and Research Libraries. *Framework for Information Literacy for Higher Education*. Chicago: American Library Association, 2016. www.ala.org/acrl/sites/ala.org.acrl/files/content/issues/infolit/Framework-ILHE.pdf.

Bell, Steven. "Five Ways Academic Libraries Support Higher Education's Reboot." *The EvoLLLution* (online newspaper), February 18, 2013. http://evolllution.com/opinions/five-ways-academic-libraries-support-higher-educations-reboot.

Brown, Karen, and Kara J. Malenfant. *Connect, Collaborate, and Communicate: A Report from the Value of Academic Libraries Summits*. Chicago: Association of College and Research Libraries, 2012. www.ala.org/acrl/sites/ala.org.acrl/files/content/issues/value/val_summit.pdf.

Buckley, James. "Behind the Scenes of College's Interlibrary Loan Staff, Process." *The Highland Echo*, April 17, 2013. http://highlandecho.com/behind-the-scenes-of-colleges-interlibrary-loan-staff-process.

Chandler, Amber. "What Growth, Innovation and Collaborative Mindsets Look Like for Students and Teachers." *Getting Smart* (blog), September 17, 2015. http://gettingsmart.com/2015/09/what-growth-innovation-and-collaborative-mindsets-look-like-for-students-and-teachers.

Foster, Connie D. "Review of *Organizing Higher Education for Collaboration: A Guide for Campus Leaders*, by Adrianna J. Kezar and Jaime Lester." *Planning for Higher Education* 38, no. 3 (2010): 66–68.

Freire, Paulo. *Pedagogy of the Oppressed*. New York: Continuum, 2000.

Gashurov, Irene, and Curtis L. Kendrick. "Collaboration for Hard Times." *Library Journal*, October 2, 2013. http://lj.libraryjournal.com/2013/10/managing-libraries/collaboration-for-hard-times/#_.

Griner, Lily, Yelina Luckert, Judy Markowitz, and Nevenka Zdravkovska. "Supporting the Professional Writing Program with Online Modules—Collaboration and Engagement, Theory and Reality." *The Journal of Creative Library Practice*, November 4, 2015. http://creativelibrarypractice.org/2015/11/04/supporting-the-professional-writing-program-with-online-modules.

Hamilton, Buffy J. "Librarians as Instructional Designers: Strategies for Engaging Conversations for Learning." *The Unquiet Librarian* (blog), December 6, 2013. https://theunquietlibrarian.wordpress.com/2013/12/06/librarians-as-instructional-designers-strategies-for-engaging-conversations-for-learning.

Helmer, John F., and Valerie Horton. "Finding Joy in Our Profession: John F. Helmer on Library Consortia." *Collaborative Librarianship* 7, no. 3 (2015): 139–44.

Horton, Valerie. "Going 'All In' for Deep Collaboration." *Collaborative Librarianship* 5, no. 2 (2013): 65–69.

Hovius, Amanda. "The 4 Facets of Information Literacy." *Designer Librarian* (blog), November 02, 2015. https://designerlibrarian.wordpress.com/2015/11/02/the-4-facets-of-information-literacy.

Jaguszewski, Janice M., and Karen Williams. *New Roles for New Times: Transforming Liaison Roles in Research Libraries*. Washington, DC: Association of Research Libraries, 2013. www.arl.org/storage/documents/publications/nrnt-liaison-roles-revised.pdf.

Kenney, Anne R. *Leveraging the Liaison Model: From Defining 21st Century Research Libraries to Implementing 21st Century Research Universities*. Report published by Ithaka S+R, March 25, 2014. www.sr.ithaka.org/wp-content/mig/files/SR_BriefingPaper_Kenney_20140322.pdf.

———. "2CUL: Emerging Model of Deep Collaboration?" Presentation, ASERL Fall 2010 Membership Meeting, What Is 2CUL? Accessed April 8, 2016. www.aserl.org/meetings/archive-meetings/2010_11_mtg_materials.

Kezar, Adrianna J, and Jaime Lester. *Organizing Higher Education for Collaboration: A Guide for Campus Leaders*. San Francisco: Jossey-Bass, 2009.

Lankes, R. David. *The Atlas of New Librarianship*. Cambridge, MA: MIT Press, 2011.

Meyer, Jan H. F., and Ray Land (eds.). *Overcoming Barriers to Student Understanding: Threshold Concepts and Troublesome Knowledge*. New York: Routledge, 2006.

Oldham, Bonnie W., and Diane Skorina. "Librarians and Instructional Technologists Collaborate." *College and Research Libraries News* 70, no. 11 (2009): 634–37. http://crln.acrl.org/content/70/11/634.full.

Pagowsky, Nicole, and Miriam Rigby (eds.). *The Librarian Stereotype: Deconstructing Perceptions and Presentations of Information Work*. Chicago: Association of College and Research Libraries, 2014.

Paulus, Trena M. "Collaboration or Cooperation? Analyzing Small Group Interactions in Educational Environments." In *Computer-Supported Collaborative Learning in*

Higher Education, edited by Tim S. Roberts, 100–24. Hershey, PA: Idea Group, 2005.

Ranganathan, S. R. *The Five Laws of Library Science*. London: Edward Goldston, 1931.

Rockenbach, Barbara, Judy Ruttenberg, Kornelia Tancheva, and Rita Vine. *Association of Research Libraries/Columbia University/Cornell University/University of Toronto Pilot Library Liaison Institute Final Report*. Washington, DC: Association of Research Libraries, 2015. www.arl.org/storage/documents/publications/library-liaison-institute-final-report-dec2015.pdf.

Sasso, Maureen Diana, and David A. Nolfi. "Librarians as Academic Leaders: Uniquely Qualified for the Job." Paper presented at the ACRL Thirteenth National Conference, Baltimore, MD, April 1, 2007. www.ala.org/acrl/sites/ala.org.acrl/files/content/conferences/confsandpreconfs/national/baltimore/papers/325.pdf.

Schriner, John. "Radical Librarian-Technologists." *Journal of Radical Librarianship* 1 (2015). https://journal.radicallibrarianship.org/index.php/journal/article/view/6/1.

Shepley, Susan E. "Building a Virtual Campus: Librarians as Collaborators in Online Course Development and Learning." *Journal of Library Administration* 49, no. 1/2 (2009): 89–95.

Straumsheim, Carl. "How and Why Hamilton College Merged Library, IT." *Inside Higher Ed*, December 4, 2015. www.insidehighered.com/news/2015/12/04/how-and-why-hamilton-college-merged-library-it.

Sullivan, Madison. "Librarianship Doesn't Need Professionals." *ACRLog*, January 19, 2016. http://acrlog.org/2016/01/19/professionalism.

Waibel, Günter, and Ricky Erway. "Think Global, Act Local—Library, Archive and Museum Collaboration." *Museum Management and Curatorship* 24, no. 4 (2009). Preprint, www.oclc.org/research/publications/library/2009/waibel-erway-mmc.pdf.

Watkins, Alexander, and Katherine Morris. "Can Only Librarians Do Library Instruction? Collaborating with Graduate Students to Teach Discipline-Specific Information Literacy." *The Journal of Creative Library Practice*, February 27, 2015. http://creativelibrarypractice.org/2015/02/27/can-only-librarians-do-library-instruction.

White, Ashanti. *Not Your Ordinary Librarian: Debunking the Popular Perceptions of Librarians*. Oxford, UK: Chandos, 2012.

JOE ESHLEMAN

5
Where Librarians and Instructional Designers Meet

Because there is an overlap in the focus of the institutional roles for both librarians and instructional designers, that is, teaching, library instruction could be considered to be the most natural collaborative connection between them. The most obvious intersection between the librarian and the instructional designer comes when the specific case of the instruction librarian's role is added to the discussion. The question of where librarians and instructional designers meet can be addressed in several ways. These two positions can encounter each other online or face-to-face during meetings, and they can connect in the classroom or work together on projects away from it. Certainly there have been numerous cases where librarians have asked for pedagogical help from instructional designers, whether formally or informally.

Due to many factors, instruction librarians are always looking for new ways to teach. The constraints of compressing a number of objectives into a small amount of time influence the desire to always be at the top of your pedagogical game when teaching students about information literacy. Meeting once with a class of students during a term or semester creates a scenario in which every decision takes on heightened importance. When you only get "one shot" (i.e., a fifty-minute session with students), you have to make it count. The ability to plan and design that one-shot session so that it carries impact and the information can be retained lies at the core of instructional design. And despite a history that has separated silos in its past, keeping these two roles away from each other, a closer look shows numerous similarities in these two fields of endeavor. As a way to help our institutions recognize our current worth and our potential to help higher education during this crucial time of change, we need to be proactive and express the value of these collaborations to our institutions. And as time goes on, there continue to be more aspects in which these roles have commonalities. In fact, the idea that instruction librarians (and even other librarians) are becoming instructional design librarians continues to gain momentum.

THE ROLE OF THE INSTRUCTION LIBRARIAN AND THE DEVELOPMENT OF THE BLENDED LIBRARIAN

A basic yet satisfactory definition of an instruction librarian is this perfunctory explanation: "the term *instruction librarian* refers to any librarian with instruction responsibilities."[1] There are those who feel as though "[e]very librarian in an academic environment is a teacher."[2] In many academic libraries, some librarians are designated specifically as teaching librarians. Yet as time goes on and "[a]ll roles in an academic library are impacted and altered by the changing nature of scholarly communication and the evolution of the dissemination of knowledge,"[3] there continues to be a widening of the type of instruction that all librarians do. In the same way that job definitions and responsibilities are expanding and morphing, a classroom with a teaching librarian and students doesn't define the whole of an instruction librarian's role. There are opportunities for teaching in a surprisingly wide variety of librarian positions. Teaching librarians obviously have some parallels to faculty and can therefore use the help of instructional designers. Yet there are numerous pedagogical and design elements that can work to benefit all librarians, even those who may not be considered instruction librarians by title.

As librarians are being asked to support (often with instructional technologists and designers) LMSs, archives, digital humanities, MOOCs, and other related technologies, such as open-access initiatives and data curation, they are required to develop new skill sets. This can be difficult for those who attempt to go it alone, and one added advantage of teaming up with other campus colleagues is an expanded and collective set of skills. Technological changes occur so quickly that they do not allow for anticipation or preparation, yet these same upheavals can allow for opportunities. This state is nicely summarized by Steven Bell and John D. Shank: "The why is more significant than [the] how of what librarians do, since the latter is going to be subject to constant, perhaps increasingly faster change."[4]

All of these changes portend more to come. But looking back, again from the librarian position, it can be difficult to pinpoint if librarians were slow or quick to adhere to the ideas of instructional design. Bibliographic instruction, which mainly helps students become acclimated to library information sources, has been around for quite some time. It began to be taught by librarians in a more formal sense in the beginning of the 1960s. This design was replaced later with information literacy initiatives that focused on a much broader spectrum of information sources and more concepts related to information use. Interestingly, librarians have had a history of reacting to the effects of technology on information use as a driver for the need for library instruction and then the desire to adapt it. For example, the revision from the *Information Literacy Competency Standards for Higher Education* from the year 2000 to the *Framework for Information Literacy for Higher Education* in 2016 (both documents created by ACRL) was affected in part by technological changes to the information landscape.[5] The ACRL *Framework* is discussed in more detail later in this chapter.

As in most backward-looking searches with regard to technology, the definitions of terms used do not stay consistent through time. That is to say, it is difficult to look back at previous technologies through the subjective lens of today; for example, "cutting edge" CD-ROMs now seem quaint by comparison. Despite these ever-changing effects, an interesting proposition that ties librarians with instructional technology and design is the development of the idea of the blended librarian. Responding to "profound societal confusion over the future relevance of the academic library and the uncertain role of future college and university librarians,"[6] Steven Bell and John D. Shank focus on the growing strength of instruction in the academic library and shed light on the fact that many librarians are combining elements of instructional technology and instructional design in their daily work. But these librarians do not fully recognize it or outwardly define this role. In *Academic Librarianship by Design: A Blended Librarian's Guide to the Tools and Techniques*, Bell and Shank summarize this situation:

> Have you ever helped a faculty member learn how to use a library database? How about integrating links to library resources into a course management system (courseware) site? Have you ever done a survey to determine how to best meet the information needs of a set of students and then developed a tutorial to resolve that information need? At one time or another, most academic librarians have likely accomplished a number of tasks that could fit into instructional design or instructional technology without even knowing it. In fact, of the many kinds of designers in different professions, academic librarians may identify most closely with instructional designers or instructional technologists.[7]

Blended librarianship, first proposed in 2004, gained momentum and with the help of the Learning Times Network, an online learning workspace and community, gained some adoption. In essence, a goal for this book, and in particular this chapter, aligns with one of the vision statements of the blended librarian community: blended librarianship "[b]rings together librarians, faculty, and other academic support professionals to find ways to effectively collaborate for the benefit of our students. Members are committed to helping students achieve designated institutional learning outcomes."[8] This idea in turn becomes even more focused, with this specific principle proposed as one of six for the blended librarian: "Collaborating and engaging in dialogue with instructional technologists and designers, which is vital to the development of programs, services, and resources needed to facilitate the instructional mission of academic libraries."[9]

It is a bit difficult to determine if blended librarianship has "caught on" and has had the desired effect. Revisiting the impact of the blended librarian concept in 2011, both Bell and Shank contributed their thoughts in the article "Blended Librarianship: [Re]Envisioning the Role of Librarian as Educator in the Digital Information Age." They conclude:

> Perhaps the principal impact blended librarianship has had is as a metaphor that clarifies the educational role of today's librarian. It depicts the librarian as an essential partner and leader in the educational process, working with and among many different campus departments, to enhance the teaching, learning, and research environment. Standing at the intersection of the learning and knowledge hub online or on campus, the blended librarian is the leader, who acts as the mediator and guide, to accessing and making sense of the ever expanding universe of information in all the forms that it takes.[10]

The primary need here is for librarians to work with instructional designers and instructional technologists, an idea that Bell and Shank often address; they also give some tips on how to collaborate and present to the reader some valuable case studies. They point out that it should be a primary goal of higher education to supply some more specific institutional paths for collaboration. How can ingrained academic divisions be reimagined to create more spaces and opportunities for collective work? Perhaps there would be more collaborative efforts pairing librarians and instructional designers in academic settings in the future if more librarians move from the role of partner to that of leader.

LIBRARIAN APPROACHES TO DESIGNING LIBRARY INSTRUCTION

Blended librarianship did initiate more librarian focus on instructional design. There were more singular instructional design approaches put forward by and for teaching librarians. Perhaps one of the more noteworthy and influential attempts to bring a sense of instructional design to librarians is Char Booth's 2011 book *Reflective Teaching, Effective Learning: Instructional Literacy for Library Educators*.[11] In it, Booth advances the focus on instructional design. She puts forward the design acronym USER, the components of which are understand, structure, engage, and reflect. She posits that by developing our own instructional literacy, that is, having a greater awareness of how to design the way in which we teach students about information use, we can create more impact as teaching librarians.

Two books that came out in 2014 took similar approaches by proposing design as a way to teach information literacy. *Designing Information Literacy Instruction: The Teaching Tripod Approach* by Joan R. Kaplowitz uses three design elements to prepare and define library instruction: expected learning outcomes, developing learning activities, and assessment.[12] Yvonne Mery and Jill Newby's *Online by Design: The Essentials of Creating Information Literacy Courses* focuses on online information literacy course planning, with the course design broken up into two sections in the book: "Developing the Course" and "Developing the Units."[13] Di Su takes an interesting path in his *Library Instruction Design: Learning from Google and Apple*; seeing Google as reflecting a "bottom-up" aesthetic and Apple conversely taking a "top-down" approach, Su applies these to library instruction design.[14]

Connecting with others on campus both personally and professionally is a time-honored theme for the librarian. In many cases for the instruction librarian, a first thought when discussing collaboration would be faculty as partners. Yet there have been some other interesting and creative partnerships that have led to a number of unique and uncommon instruction opportunities. Illuminating some of the more impactful collaborations that have involved instruction librarians and instructional designers is a good place to begin to see where these two roles meet. Perhaps what is most interesting regarding these types of collaborations is who initiated them.

The article "Talking toward Techno-Pedagogy: IT and Librarian Collaboration—Rethinking Our Roles" details an event that took place in 2000 at Bryn Mawr College in Pennsylvania where teams of librarians and instructional technologists (and others) worked together in a retreat environment for a week. They then shared information about their roles. The authors conclude: "The overall spirit gained from the week at Bryn Mawr was a reminder of the vast resources available from different constituencies on campus—constituents can continue to learn from one another and navigate this sea of constant change together. Specifically, librarians, instructional technologists, faculty, and students should not plod onward in isolation."[15]

Another team effort of note took place in 2007 at the University of Massachusetts–Dartmouth: "A multidisciplinary team of faculty and librarians, along with the UMass Dartmouth Instructional Development (ID) team, came together to develop new delivery mechanisms for information literacy instruction and a model for their implementation. A central component of this effort was the collaborative design, development, and implementation of reusable learning objects (RLOs) focused on information literacy skills in the online classroom."[16]

The article "Moving beyond the Org Chart: Library and IT Collaboration for Course Design and Support" begins in its overview with this: "College courses are complicated productions. Creation and management of a course can benefit from a range of educational professionals working in partnership with faculty."[17] They go on to describe and detail a pilot project that helps faculty with course design and delivery. Their four takeaways and advice for others, based on five staff members from "Dartmouth's Computing Services, library and Dean of Faculty divisions"[18] working as a team, are these: "See the Problem through Faculty Eyes," "Emphasize Building on Existing Strengths (Rather Than Filling Deficits)," "Have a Core Team, but Strive to Be Inclusive," and, most importantly from the perspective of a learning goal for this chapter, "Lead from the Middle (and the Institution Should Encourage This)."[19] This important takeaway is further encouraged: "Librarians and learning technologists should not wait to be directed to initiate these collaborations, and the leadership of the library and of computing has the opportunity to catalyze these collaborations by actively promoting (and recognizing) any efforts towards these ends."[20]

THE ACRL *FRAMEWORK* AND OPPORTUNITIES FOR COLLABORATION

In 2007, the ACRL approved the *Standards for Proficiencies for Instruction Librarians and Coordinators*, within which the proficiencies are divided into twelve categories. Category six, which is instructional design skills, lists numerous abilities that "the effective instruction librarian" uses: collaborates with classroom faculty, sequences information, creates learner-centered course content and incorporates activities, assists learners to assess their own information needs, scales presentation content appropriately, designs instruction to meet learning characteristics of students, and integrates technology appropriately.[21] Another proficiency category, planning skills, lists this as a proficiency: "Seeks potential partners to create new instruction opportunities."[22] This document is currently being updated to respond to and reflect many of the changes that have occurred in the intervening years. Scheduled for completion in January 2016, the rationale for revision includes such factors as the evolving higher education environment, the changing role of the instruction librarian, the new vision of information literacy, and the practical nature of the ACRL five-year review cycle for standards and guidelines. As part of the change, a move from proficiencies to roles is being considered. According to an *ACRLog* update post, the roles, which will be expanded upon, will be advocate, coordinator, learner, teaching partner, instructional designer, leader, and teacher.[23] Note that instructional designer is included here.

The changing role of the instruction librarian (and, by proxy, information literacy) is of particular interest here. Another set of ACRL standards from 2000, the ACRL *Information Literacy Competency Standards for Higher Education*, was revised to (although not fully replaced by) the ACRL *Framework for Information Literacy for Higher Education* in 2016.[24] The ACRL *Framework* is a more open and conceptually leaning document than the earlier ACRL *Standards*. In an interesting parallel to the aforementioned definition of a blended librarian, the ACRL *Framework* focuses on addressing the "why" behind the research process and information use rather than the "how." How to find information is more closely aligned to the ACRL *Standards*. This conceptual nature of the ACRL *Framework* is most evident in its significant use of threshold concepts, which are core concepts within a discipline that are central to mastery of a subject. A threshold concept "gives a name to points in new learning that mark a departure from old ways of viewing the world and entrance into new ways that may be counterintuitive and thus upsetting ('troublesome'), and yet they are ways that must be grasped in order to go forward in learning."[25] The creation of and the theories behind threshold concepts were developed by Ray Land and Jan Meyer. Threshold concepts commonly have five characteristics:

> **Transformative:** Once understood, a threshold concept changes the way in which the student views the discipline.
>
> **Troublesome:** Threshold concepts are likely to be troublesome for the student. Perkins . . . has suggested that knowledge can be troublesome, e.g., when it is counter-intuitive, alien or seemingly incoherent.
>
> **Irreversible:** Given their transformative potential, threshold concepts are also likely to be irreversible; i.e., they are difficult to unlearn.
>
> **Integrative:** Threshold concepts, once learned, are likely to bring together different aspects of the subject that previously did not appear, to the student, to be related.
>
> **Bounded:** A threshold concept will probably delineate a particular conceptual space, serving a specific and limited purpose.[26]

Additionally, some other features of threshold concepts not remarked upon in detail in the ACRL *Framework*—in particular, the idea of liminality—are pertinent to our discussion of how librarians and instructional designers can work together to support higher education in the future. These other attributes of threshold concepts follow:

> **Discursive:** Meyer and Land . . . suggest that the crossing of a threshold will incorporate an enhanced and extended use of language.

> **Reconstitutive:** "Understanding a threshold concept may entail a shift in learner subjectivity, which is implied through the transformative and discursive aspects already noted. Such reconstitution is, perhaps, more likely to be recognised initially by others, and also to take place over time . . ."[27]

And, as such, place the learner in a state of liminality:

> **Liminality:** Meyer and Land . . . have likened the crossing of the pedagogic threshold to a "rite of passage" (drawing on the ethnographical studies of Gennep and Turner in which a transitional or liminal space has to be traversed; "in short, there is no simple passage in learning from 'easy' to 'difficult'; mastery of a threshold concept often involves messy journeys back, forth and across conceptual terrain. . . ."[28]

Before moving on to how the ACRL *Framework* uses threshold concepts practically to push forward a greater understanding of information literacy, it can be illuminating to discuss threshold concepts and how instruction librarians have reacted to the ACRL *Framework*. At this point in time, there is an interesting either-or acceptance. Librarians embrace the ACRL *Framework* and the threshold concepts or they have found them to be unwieldy to use in the classroom and difficult to assess (among some other grievances). Despite this, those who find excitement and freedom when discussing and presenting threshold concepts to faculty and students still remark on the difficulties when attempting to teach them. In fact, threshold concepts cannot be taught; they must be presented and experienced. Instructional design strategies are one solution here. An interesting blog post from the *ACRLog* zeroes in on this very subject, as Eveline Houtman, Coordinator of Undergraduate Library Instruction at the Robarts Library, University of Toronto, uncovers an overlooked reference in the ACRL *Framework* to the work of Grant Wiggins and Jay McTighe, whose book, *Understanding by Design*, "focuses on the importance of drawing on core concepts or 'big ideas' in order to teach for understanding."[29] Houtman also notes that "their design approach is likely to be very helpful in redesigning our instruction, learning outcomes and assessment around our big ideas."[30] In tandem with these big ideas, Wiggins and McTighe also suggest the importance of asking "big questions," which some librarians are connecting to the ACRL *Framework*, particularly Nicole Pagowsky.[31] Houtman uncovers some overlooked information, connects some interesting dots, and lays out ideas in a series of four takeaways that point out how librarians can use big ideas and instructional design to present threshold concepts.[32]

Jonathan McMichael and Liz McGlynn's presentation "Information Literacy by Design: Unlocking the Potential of the ACRL Framework" relays how the University of North Carolina's librarians use an Information Literacy by Design (ILbD) template composed of preplanning and Understanding by

Design's three stages: desired results, evidence, and learning plan.[33] Each of these stages has additional steps. Contending that "ILbD unlocks the Framework"—"it enhances that which is revolutionary and provides solutions to that which is problematic about the Framework"—and that "ILbD is changing the way we teach"—"it prioritizes student learning by enhancing the visibility of their learning"—the presenters align Wiggins and McTighe's big ideas with authentic tasks.[34] These tasks help to propel threshold concepts and use backward design (beginning the lesson with outcomes) to help "unlock" the framework using Understanding by Design, which is focused on continuous improvement and student understanding. This well-thought-out use of several of the key elements that are currently impacting information literacy and library instruction comes together quite nicely.

A forward-looking example of good collaborative work between librarians and instructional designers is summarized in the presentation "Shifting Our Focus, Evolving Our Practice: A Collaborative Conversation about the ACRL Framework for Information Literacy for Higher Education."[35] This cross-institutional demonstration from Donna Witek (Public Services Librarian, University of Scranton), Danielle Theiss (Director, De Paul Library, University of Saint Mary), and Joelle Pitts (Instructional Design Librarian, Kansas State University) was presented at the ACRL conference in 2015. In it, the presenters point to instructional design elements in the ACRL *Framework* and relay tips for collaboration, one of which is this: "Identify potential collaborators whose work demonstrates obvious overlap with the Framework and reach out to start a conversation."[36] Of course, one such potential collaborator would be an instructional designer.

Amanda Nichols Hess's presentation from the LOEX (Library Orientation Program) Fall Focus 2015 conference mixes some of the ideas relayed here; "Becoming USERs of the *Framework*: Building New Information Literacy Instructional Practices in a Library Faculty Learning Community" applies Char Booth's USER Model to the ACRL *Framework* to help librarians themselves understand it, structure it, engage with it, and reflect on it.[37] Another redesign that helps librarians once again transition to the ACRL *Framework* comes from Robert E. LeBlanc and Barbara Quintiliano, who take the research evaluation mnemonic CRAP (currency, reliability, authority, and purpose/point of view—and its many iterations) and repurpose it for the ACRL *Framework* thusly: conversation, revision, authority, and property.[38] This low-level design change enhances student understanding and can also spark conversations that help change library instruction strategies.

As pointed out earlier, the ACRL *Framework* was designed to use information literacy threshold concepts, which in the document are designated as "frames." Bolstering each of the initial six frames are a set of knowledge practices, and a set of dispositions. The frames continue to gain adherents because they specifically address how to enter into conversations with faculty, students, and other campus colleagues. The frames are somewhat complex, but we provide here a brief rundown of them and use one as an example of how librarians and instructional designers can work together. The six frames are as follows:

- Authority Is Constructed and Contextual
- Information Creation as a Process
- Information Has Value
- Research as Inquiry
- Scholarship as Conversation
- Searching as Strategic Exploration[39]

The ACRL *Framework* itself does excellent work expanding upon the meaning of these frames. We examine the first frame in more detail and also include the ACRL *Framework* description here:

> **Authority Is Constructed and Contextual**
>
> Information resources reflect their creators' expertise and credibility, and are evaluated based on the information need and the context in which the information will be used. Authority is constructed in that various communities may recognize different types of authority. It is contextual in that the information need may help to determine the level of authority required. . . .
>
> ■ ■ ■
>
> **Dispositions**
>
> Learners who are developing their information literate abilities
>
> - develop and maintain an open mind when encountering varied and sometimes conflicting perspectives; . . .
> - develop awareness of the importance of assessing content with a skeptical stance and with a self-awareness of their own biases and worldview; . . .[40]

A type of assignment that may be considered to be structured with instructional design in mind for this frame would be one that allows students to reflect and ask questions about their own creative work. To minimize the "in between" feeling referenced earlier with the liminal state, there would need to be some type of connection to familiar ideas. In conjunction with this is a need to move toward a threshold conversation about the concepts. Designing an assignment like this takes into some consideration the student's position and puts emphasis on reflection and self-awareness. The assignment presented in the sidebar was designed by this author with the editing help of Committee Chair Karen Tercho for the ALA's Learning Instruction Round Table, Teaching, Learning, and Technology Committee.

As part of this topic, the role of the teaching librarian (and, therefore, any teacher) comes with a sense of authority, yet as can be seen when discussing the ACRL *Framework* and critical pedagogy (which is dealt with in more detail later in this chapter), relinquishing authority may be a much more valuable option. Beth McDonough, in her comprehensive dissertation on the subject,

SAMPLE ASSIGNMENT

Authority Is Constructed and Contextual

> Information resources reflect their creators' expertise and credibility, and are evaluated based on the information need and the context in which the information will be used. Authority is constructed in that various communities may recognize different types of authority. It is contextual in that the information need may help to determine the level of authority required. (ACRL, *Framework for Information Literacy for Higher Education*)

For a teaching librarian hoping to help students with this threshold concept, the instruction session could be spent exploring what it means when someone says he or she is an authority or an expert. What does it mean when we say that authority is contextual? One response to this question is that *authority* is not a concrete term that can be applied uniformly to any resource. How *authority* is interpreted by someone using information can change based on the context of the information itself. It's important to help students understand that what is meant by authority here is not the common use of authority as power, but authority as a basis for trust and credibility. Emphasizing the appearance of the word *author* in *authority* should help drive this point home.

A potential assignment based on this frame using social media could begin with this question posed to students: Are you an expert and/or an authority? On what? And why? Students will choose their preferred social media platform (e.g., Pinterest, Twitter, or Facebook) and then "inventory" and reflect on various social media content that they have produced. Follow-up questions to students include the following: Is there content that you have produced or skills or experience that you have that make it feasible that you could be considered to be an expert or an authority on a certain topic? For example, are you an expert on basketball or on how to throw a party?

In small groups, students will comment on one another's expertise, and a wrap-up discussion could center around the use of social media as a reliable source for academic work. For students not active in social media, workarounds include asking students to look at various Twitter feeds of those considered experts in certain fields. Alternatively, discussion could center around what constitutes a "scholarly" source and analyzing the various credentials that authors present to the world.

"Critical Information Literacy in Practice: An Interpretive Synthesis," examines how "[c]ritical information literacy librarians embrace new roles for themselves and students" with a focus on the concept of the ability to move away from being an authority to being a "dynamic co-creator, facilitator, enabler, and guide."[41] One interesting question here is whether or not instructional technologists and designers have this capability (over instruction librarians). And if they do, perhaps librarians could learn this from them.

As headlined in a *Blended Librarian* blog post, "Are We Becoming Information Literacy Designers?," continuing discussions point to the need for the proficient instruction librarian to be well-versed in instructional design.[42] It is interesting (and perhaps a bit sobering when thinking about predictions) to read this prognostication, made by Cherrie Noble in 1998: "Will our current library instruction screens and tutorials evolve into a more complex system of instructional design? Will we become instructional designers as well, or at least become part of an instructional design team, perhaps composed of both librarians and non-librarians?"[43]

Another blog post points to a more comprehensive look: "From Teaching to Consulting: Librarians as Information Literacy Designers; an Interview with Carrie Donovan," from the *Ubiquitous Librarian* blog of Brian Mathews.[44] In the interview, Mathews asks Donovan about a direction library instruction seems to be taking toward a more consultant-driven model; in response, she states:

> At my institution, the reasons for librarians to adopt more consultative approaches to designing information literacy education, rather than focusing entirely on the delivery of library instruction sessions, have really been practical: dropping numbers of requests for one-shot library instruction sessions for core first-year courses (our students are coming in having already taken these courses or they are fulfilling these credits elsewhere) with the resulting opportunity to focus more on integration of research methods and info lit concepts into upper division courses (through our assignment design consultation, incentives for faculty and librarians to partner through library-led grant initiatives, and support for subject liaisons in developing course assignments and assessments around info lit).[45]

She later surmises, "I don't exactly know what will be next in the evolution of librarians' teaching, but I do think it will become more and more about collaborative, campus-level initiatives that situate information literacy firmly and securely in the student experience—both in and beyond the classroom."[46] If this is the direction that teaching librarians take, then surely working with those on campus who create and support instructional design efforts would be beneficial.

An interesting tangent that the Donovan interview takes is her reference to an article that stresses a deeply reflective look at information literacy and proposes the idea that libraries should consider "letting go" of information literacy. The article, "Information Literacy: The Battle We Won That We Lost?" by Susanna M. Cowan, raises a thought-provoking point about differing institutions and how information literacy (as a term) cannot possibly cover all of what is occurring in them, and, therefore, why feel committed to that term?[47] Cowan concludes, "Information literacy is alive and well. And should be. But perhaps not by that name, and perhaps not in the hands—at least not mostly in the hands—of librarians."[48]

One aspect of the ACRL *Framework* that can be overlooked is the undercurrent within it that attempts to create a common conversation about information literacy and gain a much wider understanding of it across campus. This idea corresponds to the effort to move information literacy from the purview of librarians and have it more evenly understood and taught on the college campus. Often, the first conversations are thought to be those designated as discussions with faculty, yet this book posits that perhaps others are just as, if not more, important to have these conversations with. In our case, we suggest beginning a conversation with your instructional technology and design department and staff.

How does this current assessment of the library instruction landscape and the important influence of the ACRL *Framework* inform how and why librarians (particularly teaching librarians) and instructional designers should work together? It is important to note here that whatever direction information literacy and library instruction take, the need for an awareness of instructional design skills by librarians will still have value because, as mentioned previously, librarians are at core teachers (even if they are not teaching information literacy in a one-shot session). Developing a design focused mindset and planning instruction can be considered to be the expertise that instructional designers have. But in an exchange of ideas and mixing of skills, librarians can work with design colleagues on campus to move forward information literacy and instructional designers can collaborate with librarians to advance instructional design.

CRITICAL INFORMATION LITERACY, AGENCY, COLLABORATION, AND DESIGN

Returning to the Donovan and Mathews interview, and positioning another direction for library instruction, there is a current focus on critical information literacy, as Carrie Donovan states in the interview:

> I started wondering if critical theory wasn't the underlying thing, the hook, the foundation, that information literacy and (maybe) librarianship had needed from the start . . . it seemed to be a way better match for librarians (especially for those of us with teaching in our hearts, anyway) than neutrality and it already made so much sense because of the

> radicalism, the social justice aspects, and the desire to empower people that is inherent to our practice.[49]

In much the same way that this chapter does not desire to comprehensively present the ACRL *Framework*, it is not a goal to introduce all aspects of critical pedagogy, the underlying concept from which critical information literacy branches. Before describing this theory (and practice), it is worth noting there is also a critical librarianship movement. Paulo Freire put forth ideas that made educators realize that getting students to become more active social agents and teaching them to recognize how their own knowledge advances them and others in society are more important goals than good grades and sending people through a system.[50] Rather than thinking of themselves as docile and empty "buckets" to be filled by a teacher's wisdom, students in a class based on critical pedagogy learn to bring a more authentic mindset to learning and can begin to understand how ownership of a self-directed education connects to personal agency and an independent life. In reference to library instruction and information literacy, as more instruction librarians examine the content of their library instruction, they are forced to recognize that there are numerous changes occurring that affect what they are teaching. Foremost among these are the ideas that students should be learning more about how information is constructed and presented so that the students may become more aware of their role in the information landscape. That is to say that having an awareness of how information is constructed gives students more personal agency and allows them to explore and understand their own role as a creator rather than as a consumer (or bystander).

Understanding the importance of the ability to gain agency for one's own actions can be considered to be one of greatest of all threshold concepts. As more librarians take heed of the importance of teaching with an eye on critical pedagogy, more campus colleagues will see the value, and, ideally, so will students. In the particular situation here (librarians and instructional designers working together), it appears as if there is an opportunity to teach each other core concepts such as design practice, threshold concepts, and critical pedagogy.

A LOOK AHEAD AND THE IMPORTANCE OF THINKING COLLABORATIVELY

Perhaps the most difficult initial step is how to get started once an institution realizes the benefits of collaboration between departments and, more specifically for our purposes, the value of librarians and instructional designers (and, on occasion, faculty) working together. Many of the schools that have collaborative initiatives under their belts point to a type of disruptive mentality that needs to be developed. The merger article "Making a Difference: Moving Your Organization from Transactional to Transformational" details Bucknell

University's efforts to create a unified organization between its library and information technology department. Two of the takeaways from the article offer advice on how to combine forces:

- Involving the campus community early in these conversations makes them part of the process when you need to make choices and focus and what to stop doing.
- When considering reallocation of resources in libraries and information technology divisions, universities should take a holistic look at services across the organization.[51]

Consistently, the main discussion point when addressing the need for collaboration between librarians and other instructional partners is how to convince the institutions of the value. The only big question that is left unanswered is, "When are you ready to begin collaborating to get that goal accomplished?" Let's meet.

NOTES

1. Association of College and Research Libraries, *Standards for Proficiencies for Instruction Librarians and Coordinators: A Practical Guide* (Chicago: American Library Association, 2008), 4, www.ala.org/acrl/sites/ala.org.acrl/files/content/standards/profstandards.pdf.
2. Association of College and Research Libraries, Working Group on Intersections of Scholarly Communication and Information Literacy, *Intersections of Scholarly Communication and Information Literacy: Creating Strategic Collaborations for a Changing Academic Environment* (Chicago: Association of College and Research Libraries, 2013), 4, www.ala.org/acrl/sites/ala.org.acrl/files/content/publications/whitepapers/Intersections.pdf.
3. Ibid.
4. Steven Bell and John D. Shank, "Blended Librarianship: [Re]Envisioning the Role of Librarian as Educator in the Digital Information Age," *Reference and User Services Quarterly* 51, no. 2 (2011): 106, https://journals.ala.org/rusq/article/download/4025/4567.
5. Association of College and Research Libraries, *Information Literacy Competency Standards for Higher Education* (Chicago: American Library Association, 2000), www.ala.org/acrl/sites/ala.org.acrl/files/content/standards/standards.pdf; Association of College and Research Libraries, *Framework for Information Literacy for Higher Education* (Chicago: American Library Association, 2016), www.ala.org/acrl/sites/ala.org.acrl/files/content/issues/infolit/Framework-ILHE.pdf.
6. Bell and Shank, "Blended Librarianship," 106.
7. Steven Bell and John D. Shank, *Academic Librarianship by Design: A Blended Librarian's Guide to the Tools and Techniques* (Chicago: American Library Association, 2007), 3.

8. Steven Bell and John D. Shank, "About BL: Vision Statement," Blended Librarian, accessed May 2, 2016, http://blendedlibrarian.learningtimes.net/about-bl/#.VydNFfnK6rA.
9. Bell and Shank, *Academic Librarianship by Design*, 8.
10. Bell and Shank, "Blended Librarianship," 109.
11. Char Booth, *Reflective Teaching, Effective Learning: Instructional Literacy for Library Educators* (Chicago: ALA Editions, 2011).
12. Joan R. Kaplowitz, *Designing Information Literacy Instruction: The Teaching Tripod Approach* (Lanham, MD: Rowman and Littlefield, 2014).
13. Yvonne Mery and Jill Newby, *Online by Design: The Essentials of Creating Information Literacy Courses* (Lanham, MD: Rowman and Littlefield, 2014).
14. Di Su, *Library Instruction Design: Learning from Google and Apple* (Oxford, UK: Chandos, 2014).
15. Juliet Habjan Boisselle, Susan Fliss, Lori S. Mestre, and Fred Zinn, "Talking toward Techno-Pedagogy: IT and Librarian Collaboration—Rethinking Our Roles," *Resource Sharing and Information Networks* 17, no. 1/2 (2004): 125.
16. Matthew C. Sylvain, Kari Mofford, Elizabeth Lehr, and Jeannette E. Riley, "Reusable Learning Objects: Developing Online Information Literacy Instruction through Collaborative Design," in *Teaching Information Literacy Online*, eds. Thomas P. Mackey and Trudi E. Jacobson (New York: Neal-Schuman, 2011), 25.
17. Joshua Kim, Ridie Wilson Ghezzi, Anthony Helm, Laura Barrett, and Michael Beahan, "Moving beyond the Org Chart: Library and IT Collaboration for Course Design and Support," *ECAR Research Bulletin* 14 (2010), 2, www.dartmouth.edu/~library/col/1011/docs/ERB1014.pdf?mswitch-redir=classic.
18. Ibid., 2.
19. Ibid., 8–9.
20. Ibid., 9.
21. Association of College and Research Libraries, *Standards for Proficiencies*, 8.
22. Ibid., 9.
23. Sara Harrington, "Update on the Standards for Proficiencies for Instruction Librarians and Coordinators," *ACRLog*, November 24, 2015, http://acrlog.org/2015/11/24/update-on-the-standards-for-proficiencies-for-instruction-librarians-and-coordinators.
24. Association of College and Research Libraries, *Standards for Proficiencies and Framework for Information Literacy*.
25. Jan H. F. Meyer and Ray Land (eds.), *Overcoming Barriers to Student Understanding: Threshold Concepts and Troublesome Knowledge* (New York: Routledge, 2006), 1.
26. Mick Flanagan, "Threshold Concepts: Undergraduate Teaching, Postgraduate Training, Professional Development, and Secondary School Education; a Short Introduction and Bibliography," last updated April 12, 2016, www.ee.ucl.ac.uk/~mflanaga/thresholds.html.

27. Ibid.
28. Ibid.
29. Eveline Houtman, "Teaching with Big Ideas: How a Late Addition to the ACRL Framework Might Make Us Rethink Threshold Concepts," *ACRLog*, March 16, 2015, http://acrlog.org/2015/03/16/teaching-with-big-ideas-how-a-late-addition-to-the-acrl-framework-might-make-us-rethink-threshold-concepts.
30. Ibid.
31. Nicole Pagowsky, "#acrlilrevisions Next Steps," *Pumped Librarian* (blog), December 9, 2014, http://pumpedlibrarian.blogspot.com/2014/12/acrlilrevisions-next-steps.html.
32. Houtman, "Teaching with Big Ideas."
33. Jonathan McMichael and Liz McGlynn, "Information Literacy by Design: Unlocking the Potential of the ACRL Framework" (slide presentation), accessed April 14, 2016, https://docs.google.com/presentation/d/1P0PAuI-zkDmcM2tkc4XFruItFAdK2tjyZ4iXmUarZ1M/present?ueb=true#slide=id.gd80476bcf_2_48.
34. Ibid., slides 9–10.
35. Donna Witek, Danielle Theiss, and Joelle Pitts, "Shifting Our Focus, Evolving Our Practice: A Collaborative Conversation about the ACRL Framework for Information Literacy for Higher Education" (presentation at the ACRL 2015 conference, March 25–28, 2015, Portland, OR).
36. Ibid.
37. Amanda Nichols Hess, "Becoming USERs of the *Framework*: Building New Information Literacy Instructional Practices in a Library Faculty Learning Community" (presentation at LOEX Fall Focus 2015: Becoming USERs of the Framework), accessed April 14, 2016, https://sites.google.com/a/oakland.edu/loex-fall-focus-2015-becoming-users-of-the-framework/home.
38. Robert E. LeBlanc and Barbara Quintiliano, "Recycling C.R.A.P.: Reframing a Popular Research Mnemonic for Library Instruction," *Pennsylvania Libraries: Research and Practice* 3, no. 2 (2015), http://palrap.org/ojs/index.php/palrap/article/view/105/482.
39. Association of College and Research Libraries, *Framework for Information Literacy*.
40. Ibid.
41. Beth Allsopp McDonough, "Critical Information Literacy in Practice: An Interpretive Synthesis" (Dissertation, Graduate School, Western Carolina University, March 2014), 61, 62, http://libres.uncg.edu/ir/wcu/f/McDonough2014.pdf.
42. John Shank, "Are We Becoming Information Literacy Designers?," *Blended Librarian* (blog), June 10, 2015, http://blendedlibrarian.learningtimes.net/218647/#.Vw-rM3o6GSo.
43. Cherrie Noble, "Reflecting on Our Future: What Will the Role of the Virtual Librarian Be?" *Computers in Libraries* 18, no. 2 (1998): 50.

44. Brian Mathews, "From Teaching to Consulting: Librarians as Information Literacy Designers; an Interview with Carrie Donovan," *The Ubiquitous Librarian* (blog), June 8, 2015, http://chronicle.com/blognetwork/theubiquitouslibrarian/2015/06/08/from-teaching-to-consulting-librarians-as-information-literacy-designers-an-interview-with-carrie-donovan/?cid=pm&utm_source=pm&utm_medium=en.
45. Ibid.
46. Ibid.
47. Susanna M. Cowan, "Information Literacy: The Battle We Won That We Lost?," *portal: Libraries and the Academy* 14, no. 1 (2014): 23–32, www.press.jhu.edu/journals/portal_libraries_and_the_academy/portal_pre_print/current/articles/14.1cowan.pdf.
48. Ibid.
49. Mathews, "From Teaching to Consulting."
50. Paulo Freire, *Pedagogy of the Oppressed* (New York: Continuum, 2000).
51. Param Bedi and Jason Snyder, "Making a Difference: Moving Your Organization from Transactional to Transformational," *EDUCAUSE Review*, March 16, 2015, http://er.educause.edu/articles/2015/3/making-a-difference-moving-your-organization-from-transactional-to-transformational.

BIBLIOGRAPHY

Association of College and Research Libraries. *Framework for Information Literacy for Higher Education*. Chicago: American Library Association, 2016. www.ala.org/acrl/sites/ala.org.acrl/files/content/issues/infolit/Framework-ILHE.pdf.

———. *Standards for Proficiencies for Instruction Librarians and Coordinators: A Practical Guide*. Chicago: American Library Association, 2008. www.ala.org/acrl/sites/ala.org.acrl/files/content/standards/profstandards.pdf.

———. Working Group on Intersections of Scholarly Communication and Information Literacy. *Intersections of Scholarly Communication and Information Literacy: Creating Strategic Collaborations for a Changing Academic Environment*. Chicago: Association of College and Research Libraries, 2013. www.ala.org/acrl/sites/ala.org.acrl/files/content/publications/whitepapers/Intersections.pdf.

Bedi, Param, and Jason Snyder. "Making a Difference: Moving Your Organization from Transactional to Transformational." *EDUCAUSE Review*, March 16, 2015. http://er.educause.edu/articles/2015/3/making-a-difference-moving-your-organization-from-transactional-to-transformational.

Bell, Steven, and John D. Shank. *Academic Librarianship by Design: A Blended Librarian's Guide to the Tools and Techniques*. Chicago: American Library Association, 2007.

———. "Blended Librarianship: [Re]Envisioning the Role of Librarian as Educator in the Digital Information Age." *Reference and User Services Quarterly* 51, no. 2 (2011): 105–10. https://journals.ala.org/rusq/article/download/4025/4567.

Flanagan, Mick. "Threshold Concepts: Undergraduate Teaching, Postgraduate Training, Professional Development, and Secondary School Education; a Short Introduction and Bibliography." Last updated April 12, 2016. www.ee.ucl.ac.uk/~mflanaga/thresholds.html.

Freire, Paulo. *Pedagogy of the Oppressed*. New York: Continuum, 2000.

Kim, Joshua, Ridie Wilson Ghezzi, Anthony Helm, Laura Barrett, and Michael Beahan. "Moving beyond the Org Chart: Library and IT Collaboration for Course Design and Support." *ECAR Research Bulletin* 14 (2010). www.dartmouth.edu/~library/col/1011/docs/ERB1014.pdf?mswitch-redir=classic.

Mathews, Brian. "From Teaching to Consulting: Librarians as Information Literacy Designers; an Interview with Carrie Donovan." *The Ubiquitous Librarian* (blog), June 8, 2015. http://chronicle.com/blognetwork/theubiquitouslibrarian/2015/06/08/from-teaching-to-consulting-librarians-as-information-literacy-designers-an-interview-with-carrie-donovan/?cid=pm&utm_source=pm&utm_medium=en.

McDonough, Beth Allsopp. "Critical Information Literacy in Practice: An Interpretive Synthesis." Dissertation, Graduate School, Western Carolina University, March 2014. http://libres.uncg.edu/ir/wcu/f/McDonough2014.pdf.

Meyer, Jan H. F., Ray Land, and Caroline Baillie. *Threshold Concepts and Transformational Learning.* Rotterdam: Sense, 2010.

Noble, Cherrie. "Reflecting on Our Future: What Will the Role of the Virtual Librarian Be?" *Computers in Libraries* 18, no. 2 (1998): 50–54.

Sylvain, Matthew C., Kari Mofford, Elizabeth Lehr, and Jeannette E. Riley. "Reusable Learning Objects: Developing Online Information Literacy Instruction through Collaborative Design." In *Teaching Information Literacy Online*, edited by Thomas P. Mackey and Trudi E. Jacobson, 25–45. New York: Neal-Schuman. 2011.

Talking toward Techno-Pedagogy: A Collaboration across Colleges and Constituencies. Last updated May 13, 2002. http://serendip.brynmawr.edu/talking.

Witek, Donna, Danielle Theiss, and Joelle Pitts. "Shifting Our Focus, Evolving Our Practice: A Collaborative Conversation about the ACRL Framework for Information Literacy for Higher Education." Presentation at the ACRL 2015 conference, March 25–28, 2015, Portland, OR.

Woodworth, Andy. "The Master's Degree Misperception." *Agnostic Maybe* (blog), September 2, 2010. https://agnosticmaybe.wordpress.com/2010/09/02/the-masters-degree-misperception.

JOE ESHLEMAN AND
KRISTEN ESHLEMAN

6
Innovation and Cooperative Ventures

Although this chapter includes cursory attempts to define and introduce relevant topics, there is much more emphasis placed here on spurring thoughts and conversations. Rather than exhaustively exploring each opportunity, we present ideas as ways to excite the inquisitive. Ideally, those thus inspired would then pursue some of these ideas on their own and begin enthusiastic discussions on campus. Those discussions (leading to collaborative work) would focus on ways to implement projects and initiatives that map to similar work or connect to the ideas presented in this chapter's case studies.

THE DIGITAL HUMANITIES

In 2011, at the Modern Language Association (MLA) conference, Stephen Ramsey blithely tossed out this idea: "Personally, I think Digital Humanities is about building things. . . . [I]f you are not making anything, you are not . . . a digital humanist."[1] And though there was backlash and some controversy about this summation, he stood by it. Librarians have struggled with the concept of what it means for them to "make" something as it is sometimes thought that their role is one of support to the makers. One of the more famous recent guideposts for librarians comes from R. David Lankes in *Atlas of New Librarianship*: "The mission of librarians is to improve society through facilitating knowledge *creation* in their communities" (emphasis added).[2] One could interpret this as meaning that librarians do not necessarily create but instead help those who create, which is an interesting variation on the old adage "Those who can't do, teach" ("Those who can't create, facilitate"). Yet even if it is the case that librarians are primarily facilitators, higher education administrators need to have a better understanding of that campus role, especially how it relates to digital technologies. Librarians are needed to work on digital humanities (DH) projects because they bookend the process, starting with discovery and ending with preservation. They can advocate for fair use in DH projects, and they can help move higher education to open-access publishing. Here, as in other cases throughout this book, the preconceived, misunderstood, or static role of librarians sometimes plays a part in how they are engaged as agents on campus.

It can be quite a chore to pinpoint a definition of digital humanities, but it is necessary for us to try. The website What Is Digital Humanities?, built and designed by Jason Heppler, currently offers numerous quotes that attempt to answer that question from different perspectives. These answers are "pulled from participants from the Day of DH between 2009–2014," and "[a]s of January 2015, the database contains 817 rows and randomly selects a quote each time the page is loaded."[3] The Day in the Life of the Digital Humanities (or Day of DH) "is an open community publication project that will bring together scholars interested in the digital humanities from around the world to document what they do on one day. . . . The goal of the project is to create a web site that weaves together a picture of the participant's activities on the day which answers the question, 'Just what do digital humanists really do?'"[4]

Digital humanities can be thought of as a process or a product, but for some, it is an even larger entity. According to Matthew G. Kirschenbaum, "At its core, then, digital humanities is more akin to a common methodological outlook than an investment in any one specific set of texts or even technologies."[5] The digital humanities are another place where the roles of instructional designers and librarians (as well as other scholars and students) intersect. Because an emphasis on humanities research has been part of some of the definitions, that aspect has appealed to librarians interested in the subject. Additionally, there are the historical roles of archivist and collector to fuel librarians' interest. And because the focus on newer tools and digital environments separates digital humanities from earlier types of research, this area has attracted a set of librarians with a special affinity toward the use of these new tools. Therefore, there are numerous entry points and appealing aspects for librarians. But it is the sharing aspect of the digital humanities landscape that has the greatest impact for this discussion. Jonathan Senchyne's webinar,

"An Introduction to the Digital Humanities for Librarians," offers this as one definition: "think of DH as the space (real or imagined) of collaborative contact between people with various skills and interests coming together to pursue questions of culture and technology or culture through technology."[6]

More than anything, the collaborative nature of the digital humanities is what takes precedence: "Because they cross over boundaries between disciplines; between theoretical and applied knowledge; and among the humanities, library science, information technology, and design, Digital Humanities projects typically require support structures that cut across conventional department and school organizational lines."[7] Not only are congenital lines dismantled, digital humanities create environments that allow for more use of open educational resources (similar to MOOCs). A trend that appears to be in its initial phase is libraries from different institutions "joining forces" to leverage space, resources (including human resources and talent), and budgets for gain. For example, as mentioned in chapter 4, Georgia Tech and Emory as well as 2CUL with Columbia and Cornell have developed meaningful alliances that appear primed for growth. By pooling resources, these united libraries have more collections and resources from which they can create DH projects.

As a way to briefly introduce the topic to those who are new to it, it can be helpful to point librarians in directions in which they can learn more about digital humanities. A very good introduction for librarians new to the concept of the digital humanities can be found by viewing the presentation "Introducing Digital Humanities" by Korey Jackson and Aaron McCollough.[8] This excellent tutorial can also be found at the University of Delaware's "Digital Humanities: Home" LibGuide.[9] This guide points to other useful primers and sources as well. The ACRL website and community dh+lib ("where the digital humanities and librarianship meet") is also an excellent foundational space for librarians.[10] One final excellent entry point is the CUNY Academic Commons wiki, particularly the Hot Topics area that provides links to the history of the digital humanities and relevant discussion around the topic.[11]

Often, the way in which DH projects get started is with already initiated relationships between faculty and staff. For librarians, this can be a situation where the liaison role helps to get things started. As the article "Librarians and Scholars: Partners in Digital Humanities" notes:

> Over the past few years, many of our faculty began their digital humanities projects by first consulting with their liaison librarian. Some of these scholars have project ideas, but lack the technological expertise to get started. Librarians can make connections with experts across campus, provide a guided path at the journey's start, and then identify resources (physical, technological, human) to help them at each stage of their project.[12]

Work in the digital humanities between librarians and faculty is usually where this type of collective work begins, but it also exemplifies cases of instructional designers and librarians working together. In the document *New Roles for New Times: Transforming Liaison Roles in Research Libraries*, Janice M. Jaguszewski and Karen Williams point out how "[l]ibrarians work directly with faculty, students, and other campus stakeholders to create services and training that support the digital humanities. Data and digital resources produced by these campus initiatives present librarians with a unique opportunity to learn about and advise faculty how to provide persistent, secure, and copyright-compliant access to the digital research underlying their scholarship."[13]

In his blog *Scholarship, Libraries, Technology*, Stewart Varner, Digital Scholarship Librarian at the University of North Carolina, characterizes how he feels the library should be viewed in relation to digital humanities:

> I like to think of the library as the research co-op of the university. It is a place to centralize some things that lots of people can use but not everyone needs to buy. Maybe that's a subscription to a journal, maybe that's a 3D printer, maybe that is a special piece of software for digital publishing. The library also wants to talk to you about your digital work because we might eventually be where your digital work goes for preservation. That is seriously hard work but it gets slightly easier if you think about it before you start working rather than after-the-fact.[14]

This idea of a library as a centralized place for sharing on campus is, of course, not a new idea, but the "things" being shared are now often not "in" the library. Speaking to the collaborative prompts that digital humanities makes for the library, Trevor Muñoz, Assistant Dean for Digital Humanities Research at the University of Maryland Libraries and Associate Director of the Maryland Institute for Technology in the Humanities (MITH), says, "Librarianship is intellectual work. Doing digital humanities in the library should be (re)centered on the research questions and intellectual agendas of librarians. I believe that the good work that comes from this re-centering will attract partners—whether they be faculty, other librarians, students, or the public."[15] Although all of these statements portray the librarian as a willing collaborator, there are also cases where there may be a desire for less librarian interaction. Mark Sample's tweet from the MLA's annual convention in 2016 notes, "Some DH projects benefit from not being affiliated with libraries or DH centers, where they have to compete with new projects."[16] This underscores that there are good matches for librarian collaboration but not all DH projects need it.

As an example of how collaborative ventures can take many twists and turns, a recent edition of *Digital Humanities Quarterly* relays some challenges:

> We've held a reading seminar and it's been held at the humanities institute on campus. Most of the research reading seminars tend to attract almost exclusively professors and graduate students. However, the DH reading seminar has attracted many, many librarians and technologists, sometimes more so than professors and grad students. That's been great, but I think it's raised some unwritten hierarchies at the university. My impression is the more librarians and technologists come, the fewer faculty and graduate students come. They arrive . . . and see there aren't people from their immediate circle of colleagues. The librarians . . . ask some different questions. There's been a real challenge in working across the boundaries of training and perspective in one group.[17]

Later in this same article, which discusses collaborative research relationships in digital humanities, is this quote, which underscores the notion that skills will continue to be more important than roles in digital areas: "As one faculty participant noted, there seems to be a natural affinity between the digital humanities and librarians: 'There's often a sense where librarians aren't appreciated for their expertise as real scholars, and I think that's often true of the digital humanities. There tends not to be as much focus on rank and where you're at [in digital humanities], it's more the expertise you bring to the table.'"[18] Jennifer Schaffner and Ricky Erway ask a question in the title of their report: *Does Every Research Library Need a Digital Humanities Center?*[19] Attempting to answer this question, they come up with some perceptive thoughts for library directors and librarians in general. Beginning with the idea that many libraries currently have services that act as support for digital humanities, they say, "Perhaps the simplest way to improve support for the digital humanities is to package these existing library services so that it becomes obvious that they are there to be used by DH scholars. Give your 'virtual DH center' a name and publicize it to DH researchers."[20] They give inspiration to all academic librarians when they conclude, "No matter which approaches to supporting the digital humanities you opt to take, keep in mind that what we call 'The Digital Humanities' today will soon be considered 'The Humanities.' Supporting DH scholarship is not much different than supporting digital scholarship in any discipline. Increasingly, digital scholarship is simply scholarship."[21]

Before reviewing a case study that employs faculty, a librarian, and an instructional designer, the following quote helps clarify why librarians are good DH associates: "Libraries embody commitment to discovery through research activities, teaching practices, and aspirations for student learning; it is not surprising that they serve as connectors, collaborators, partners, and initiators in digital humanities work."[22]

Case Study

DIGITAL HUMANITIES

Since 1999, several generations of Davidson College students have built an online, open-access bibliographic database, *Index of Modernist Magazines*[a] (http://sites.davidson.edu/littlemagazines; see figure 6.1), as part of a collaborative research seminar. The *Index* serves as model for how faculty, librarians, and instructional technologists can collaborate to create, support, and sustain undergraduate digital research projects that promote undergraduate learning while furthering scholarship in new areas of study. It also attests to the value and importance of bibliographic research in an era of proliferating digital information and archives. This case study discusses the pedagogical practices that make the *Index of Modernist Magazines* a model of sustainability (the project is ongoing and ever-expanding), scope (it is manageable for students while also requiring significant research), and impact (it allows students to contribute to a vibrant, expanding field of scholarly inquiry).

With their emphasis on small classes, student-faculty relationships, interdisciplinary study, and undergraduate research, liberal arts colleges seem like ideal environments for the digital humanities. Yet as Bryan Alexander and Rebecca Frost Davis point out, liberal arts campuses often lack the resources, infrastructure, and emphasis on research needed to generate and sustain digital humanities projects; they recommend that liberal arts colleges should forge a "separate path" in digital humanities, "one based on emphasizing a distributed, socially engaged *process* over a focus on publicly shared *products*" (emphasis in original).[b] Working at Davidson College, a small, private, liberal

FIGURE 6.1

The *Index of Modernist Magazines* (2012–present)

arts college in North Carolina, we appreciate their recognition of the specific challenges we face in the field of digital humanities. Like the small colleges they discuss, we do not have a "center" or department of digital humanities and have only recently hired our first tenured faculty member specializing in the field. Our primary focus is on teaching, and the liberal arts commitment to a broad-based education means that our students are more likely to diversify their interests than to specialize; their commitment to a given topic or project may last only a semester, until the next set of courses demands their time and attention. Yet even without the benefits of a digital humanities center, department, or graduate student body, we have forged a path that combines a collaborative learning process with a publicly shared digital product. Our experience suggests that digital products need not be sacrificed in service of the learning process but can be tailored to complement and enrich undergraduate education. Moreover, given their potential broader impact, digital projects should be afforded the same dedication to rigor that we apply to the marriage of process and product in writing instruction. The key to the successful union of process and product in digital humanities is collaboration.

The *Index of Modernist Magazines* is maintained as part of a collaborative research seminar on modernism in magazines. Working closely with a professor, a librarian, and an instructional technologist, students in the seminar identify little magazines to research and add to the database. Suzanne Churchill and Adam McKible define little magazines as "non-commercial enterprises founded by individuals or small groups intent upon publishing the experimental works or radical opinions of untried, unpopular, or underrepresented writers. Defying mainstream tastes and conventions, some little magazines aim to uphold higher artistic and intellectual standards than their commercial counterparts, while others seek to challenge conventional political wisdom and practice."[c] The student-authored *Index* now includes sixty magazines and has become a research tool used by professors, graduate students, and undergraduates in the United States, Canada, and Great Britain. As Jerome McGann avers, in the digital age, "textual and editorial work are once again being seen for what they are and always have been: the fundamental ground for any kind of historically-oriented intellectual work."[d] This textual and editorial work—which McGann calls philology and which includes bibliographic research—is intellectual effort eminently suited to undergraduates and readily fitted to digital products.

Partners

The success of our project is due to the innovative design of the seminar and the ways in which a librarian (Susanna Boylston), an instructional technologist (Kristen Eshleman), and a professor (Suzanne Churchill) partner to support it. We each draw upon our respective areas of expertise to help students learn how to conduct primary research, organize bibliographic data, and use new digital media to share their findings. But the success of this project may be less instructive than the obstacles encountered along the way. Research in positive psychology shows that if you see only a successful outcome, you are likely to conclude that the venture is unattainable for you. But according to psychologist Ellen Langer, "By investigating how someone got somewhere, we are more likely to see the achievement as hard-won and our own chances as more plausible."[e] The following recounts the story behind the *Index,* including mistakes made and lessons learned along the way. By demonstrating that our achievement has been hard-won, we hope you will see your own chances of success as more plausible.

Design

In his manifesto "Post-Artifact Books and Publishing," Craig Mod observes, "Everyone asks, 'How do we change books to read them digitally?' But the more interesting question is, 'How does digital change books?'"[f] The *Index of Modernist Magazines* was born out of Churchill's desire to see how digital could change one particular book—Frederick J. Hoffman, Charles Allen, and Carolyn F. Ulrich's *The Little Magazine: A History and a Bibliography.* Cary Nelson asserts that this 1946 volume "remains the single most useful source for the study of modern literary magazines," and Mark Morrisson hails it as "an indispensable resource for anyone delving into the sometimes arcane world of modernist magazine publication."[g] Conscious of the book's strengths (so much information in one compact, searchable volume) as well as its weaknesses (the neglect or exclusion of women, African Americans, and political radicals), Churchill envisioned an online, expandable, hypertext version that would not only fill these gaps but also supply color illustrations of the rich visual culture contained in these magazines and include hyperlinks between magazines, digitally mapping the intricate web of modernism. Like the celebrated Homer Multitext,[h] this digital project originated in a revered work of print scholarship, seeking to use digital tools to overcome the limitations of a print reference and teach undergraduates that they can make genuine contributions to scholarship.

Implementation

PHASE 1

On Lines: The Web of Modernism (1999)

Churchill did not have much technological expertise at this point, and she knew she could not realize her vision on her own. She sought out Susanna Boylston for help locating and getting access to little magazines, and Kristen Eshleman for advice and assistance with the website construction. To recruit a team of student workers, she designed a new seminar called On Lines: The Web of Modernism, with a focus on poetry and the goal of using little magazines to recover links between Anglo-American modernism, the Harlem Renaissance, and leftist political poetry of the same period (see figure 6.2). The course was a fairly traditional seminar, with a strong literary focus and a large packet of readings. Although the seminar thematically linked the construction of the website to the goal of tracing lines of connection between disparate modernist movements, structurally, the digital database was an add-on to a traditional course design.

In this first attempt, Churchill did not have a clear vision of what the website would look like. She conceived of it as a repository of factual information but thought the students should have freedom to express the styles and personalities of the individual magazines in the designs of their respective webpages. At the outset, she required each

Modernist Little Magazines HomePage

Broom
Camera Work
Contempo
Close-Up
The Crisis
The Glebe
The Egoist
The Liberator
The Little Review
The Masses
Opportunity
Others
Poetry
Seven Arts
Transatlantic Review
Transition

This website will provide information about modernist little magazines, linking three contemporaneous traditions that are usually studied as separate and distinct: Anglo-American modernism, the Harlem Renaissance, and political poetry from the 1920s and '30s. The website will address key figures from each movement--modernists such as T.S. Eliot, James Joyce, Mina Loy, Ezra Pound, and Gertrude Stein; Harlem Renaissance writers such as Sterling Brown, Countee Cullen, Langston Hughes, and Jean Toomer; and political activists such as Edna St. Vincent Millay, Carl Sandburg, and Genevieve Taggard. It will also include information about such transitional and unclassifiable figures as Kay Boyle, Bob Brown, Nancy Cunard, Lola Ridge, Carl Van Vechten, and the notorious Baroness Elsa von Freytag-Loringhoven, whose Dada performance art defied not only the boundaries between artistic traditions, but also the very division between modern art and life. By returning to the little magazines that provided the publishing base for these revolutionary writers, we will recover "links" between diverse modernist movements. Using technology to support our theoretical aims, our website will demonstrate how common influences, aesthetic affinities, political sympathies, and unorthodox attitudes and behaviors entangle disparate writers, artists, and activists in the complex "web" of modernism.

This website will be written and designed by students participating in the seminar, "On Lines: The Web of Modernism" (ENG 487, Fall 99) in consultation with Suzanne W. Churchill, Assistant Professor of English, Davidson College.

View syllabus for "On Lines: The Web of Modernism" (ENG 487, Fall 99) | Return to S.W. Churchill's home page

FIGURE 6.2
The *Index of Modernist Magazines* (1999–2004)

class member to be responsible for composing two informational webpages: one about a little magazine and one about a related writer. Once they created these pages, they would collaborate to establish "links" between them. To provide students with the necessary technical training, she set aside one three-hour seminar meeting for an "Introduction to Web-Authoring" workshop.

PHASE 1: Lessons Learned

1. Collaborate with librarians to gather relevant resources. Boylston was able to acquire microfilm collections of little magazines that expanded our library's holdings exponentially, allowing students to select from a broad range of magazines. Today, searchable digital archives such as the Modernist Journals Project, the Modernist Magazines Project, and the Blue Mountain Project provide access to more and better quality reproductions of little magazines, but librarians are still valuable partners for researching new digital resources. In fact, the sheer proliferation of digital information available today makes partnering with librarians more essential than ever.
2. Budget more time for repeated sessions dedicated to technical training and support. Although students are catching on faster every year and some now come with experience in web-authoring, their skill levels are inconsistent. They may also have technological fluency, yet lack crucial digital literacy skills in evaluating and designing online resources.

3. Scale back on literary content to allow time to discuss and theorize web content; teaching three branches of literary modernism, poetry reading skills, methods of periodical studies, and digital writing was simply too much to cover in a single seminar. The problem of syllabus overload is articulated by Alexander and Davis when they ask, "How can digital humanists assemble the combination of skills and technology infrastructure needed to conduct digital humanities work such as coding, media production and aggregation, and the creation and development of information architecture, not to mention conducting the essential work within a humanities subject?"[i] Their answer involves scaling back in order to "limit the scope and scaffold the learning process."[j] For Alexander and Davis, that means establishing a "process-over-product focus,"[k] but we were able to balance process and product by limiting the humanities content and scaffolding the technology learning curve. Having well-designed information architecture in place allows students to contribute to a DH product, as they gradually acquire understanding of its infrastructure.
4. Establish a clear rubric and set manageable technological goals. To be useful and legible, an online, multiauthored database requires consistent formatting, style, and content. When students tried to reflect the individual aesthetics and ethos of their respective magazines in their webpages, the result was visual chaos in the collective website. Churchill also had to drop the idea of author pages because getting the magazine pages created, written concisely, and formatted consistently was sufficiently challenging. Making and maintaining links between pages proved too complicated and served a function more easily fulfilled by a search engine.
5. Rather than trying to anticipate and prevent such "mistakes," expect them and welcome them as part of the discovery process.

PHASE 2

The Web of Modernism (2004)

In the second version of the seminar, Churchill moved little magazines front and center, reducing the emphasis on poetry. In an attempt to re-create the tangible pleasures of reading and handling little magazines, she made spiral-bound photocopies of single issues of selected little magazines. For example, students read Mina Loy in *The Little Review,* Claude McKay in the *Liberator,* and Langston Hughes in the *Crisis.* In this second attempt, Churchill had a clearer vision of the website as a bibliographic database, called "Housing Modernism: A Bibliography of Selected Little Magazines" (see figure 6.3).

The college hired local freelance web designers to redesign the site on a Dreamweaver platform, and they came up with what at the time was a sophisticated, professional-looking layout. To develop students' digital literacy skills, Churchill and Eshleman scheduled a design workshop, a training workshop, a computer lab session and conference, as well as several optional lab sessions. Hoping to link the work on the website more closely to their students' research papers, they also added a journal of undergraduate research to the website, where students would publish their final research papers.

FIGURE 6.3
The *Index of Modernist Magazines* (2004–2007)

PHASE 2: Lessons Learned

1. A professor teaching full time should not try to run a small press. The spiral-bound, photocopied magazines failed to capture the thrill of reading little magazines. The print quality was poor, aesthetically unappealing, and difficult to read. The increasing availability of full-color digital facsimiles only heightens the inadequacy of bound photocopies for capturing the aesthetics of little magazines.
2. A professor teaching full time should not try to edit a journal of undergraduate research single-handedly. *ELM (Essays on Little Magazines)* was attractive and functional but lacked necessary peer review mechanisms. Churchill did not have the time to edit and fact-check the students' research papers. When a respected colleague complained that a student had misrepresented his work, she decided to take the journal down and focus the site exclusively on bibliographic data about the magazines. Although misrepresentation of scholarship may be endemic to the humanities profession, the potential for gross misinterpretations is greater among amateurs. Christopher Blackwell and Thomas R. Martin recommend that instead of asking our students to produce "a diluted version of professional scholarship," we are better off having them "undertake the too often ignored task of ascertaining and explaining primary evidence" or, in our case, the tasks of locating, researching, interpreting, describing, and presenting print artifacts.[1] Instead of trying to turn undergraduates, most of whom will not go on for PhDs, into miniature professional

scholars, we can set them to work on information gathering, analysis, and synthesis—tasks well within their ken, yet still intellectually challenging.

3. Bibliographic research is just as valuable as critical essays. To embrace the value of bibliographic research, we must, as D. F. McKenzie argues, broaden our definition: "bibliography is the discipline that studies texts as recorded forms, and the processes of their transmission, including their production and reception."[m] Bibliography thus involves the study of not only print objects but also their history and the cultures that produce and consume them. Bibliography is increasingly important in the digital age, when the sheer volume of data available at our fingertips makes the task of curating and organizing information more crucial than ever. Undergraduates have the ability to gather, organize, and present such data, and in the process, they acquire skills in digital literacy, including an understanding of the importance of metadata. By undertaking bibliographic research, students can contribute to scholarship while learning practical, portable skills that can be applied outside academia.
4. Collaboration with instructional technologists is essential. The extra technical support paid off doubly because Kristen Eshleman taught both the students and the professor to use Dreamweaver, to understand metadata, and to write appropriately for web publication.
5. A well-designed, well-researched, and well-organized database is a valuable resource, and investment yields surprising dividends. The professional-looking website attracted notice across the country. Out of the blue, Churchill received an e-mail message, flagged "important," from a man who had original copies of *Close Up* and *The Mask* from 1927–1930. The magazines had belonged to his deceased father, and he was looking for a library to donate them to. He was even willing to pay shipping expenses. Alexander and Davis assert that "undergraduates can play an important role translating our digital humanities work to the general public";[n] in this case, their digital project also allowed the public to give resources back to humanities research.
6. Communication and collaboration with librarians are essential. As much as these magazines seemed like manna from heaven, libraries cannot accept unsolicited donations without considering the costs, maintenance, and storage needs to house the acquisitions. Fortunately, our library was willing and enthusiastic. This unexpected donation sparked the beginning of a growing collection of original issues of little magazines, an effort driven by Boylston (see the following section), which proved to be a far better way to ignite student interest in the materiality of little magazines.

PHASE 3

Modernism in Black and White (2007)

In the third iteration, Churchill redesigned the course completely, based on a model developed by John Wertheimer, a history professor at Davidson College. Wertheimer taught a collaborative research seminar on legal history and had published a collection of essays based on his collaborative research with undergraduates. He generously supplied his syllabus and accrued wisdom, which Churchill adapted to the topic of modernist little magazines. Perhaps it was the excitement of thinking that her own research interests might dovetail with her students' investigations, but she forgot the lesson about the need to scale back on literary content. She designed her most ambitious seminar yet: Modernism in Black and White, a course investigating both the print culture and the race issues that shaped modernism. Utilizing modernist magazines to challenge the "color line" dividing modernism and the Harlem Renaissance, the seminar had four main components:

1. critical reading and student-led discussion of modernist texts, periodicals, and criticism;
2. a collaborative research paper written jointly by members of the seminar;
3. an individual research paper; and
4. expansion of the student-authored website, "Little Magazines & Modernism: A Select Bibliography" (see figure 6.4).

The collaborative papers were to be submitted for presentation at an aptly timed scholarly symposium, Modernism beyond Little Magazines, hosted at the University of Delaware later that semester. The ultimate aim, after further collaboration with the professor, was to generate a publishable article.

FIGURE 6.4
The *Index of Modernist Magazines* (2007–2012)

The weekly, three-hour seminar meetings were divided into two parts: the first half focused on masterworks of modernism and the Harlem Renaissance, and the second half was devoted to the collaborative research project, with carefully sequenced assignments, including a topic proposal, an exploratory "think piece," primary and secondary source note cards, a scholarship review essay, section drafts, a full draft, and a final paper. Each week, students would read the assigned texts and complete the next step in the research paper. In theory, the two halves of the course would fuse into a harmonious whole, with the readings providing a foundation in modernism and the Harlem Renaissance, and the collaborative research unearthing connections between the two movements. In practice, the two parts often competed for attention. Scarcely had the class begun to scratch the surface of *Souls of Black Folks* or *Jacob's Room* when it would be time to turn their attention to periodical studies and collaborative research. The digital component also was not sufficiently integrated into the course. The students did not choose research projects related to their work on the website, so here again the two enterprises competed with each other. Although the seminar ultimately met its goal of producing a published, multiauthored article, it was splitting at the seams, straining under the weight of its own ambitions.

PHASE 3: Lessons Learned

1. Collaboration remains essential, and it works even better when students are involved and collaborating with one another. They can do so much more. The research topics this semester were original and groundbreaking: youth culture in *Crisis* and *Fire!!* and the rise and fall of Japan as an influence on American modernism. Although the study of youth culture in *Crisis* and *Fire!!* eventually got published, at the end of the semester, everyone was exhausted, and the course evaluations were cranky.
2. You cannot simply add on periodical studies to a traditional great books course on modernism. You cannot build a modernist canon and break it down with the magazines, all in one semester. Set realistic goals, especially when forging new territory.
3. IT staff and librarians are not just technical support; they are intellectual partners. Churchill would have given up on the *Index* if it were not for Kristen Eshleman, the director of instructional technology. She provided vital intellectual energy when Churchill felt most depleted. Eshleman introduced Churchill to the burgeoning field of digital studies and helped her see that the project was not marginal, isolated, or futile, but part of a growing trend in humanities. On a small campus, it is easy for professors to feel as though they are lone practitioners of digital humanities. Instructional technologists bring important professional knowledge to the table that can help link professors to a broad, interdisciplinary community of educators. And, of course, instructional technologists also provide practical expertise and knowledge of new platforms and tools in a rapidly changing digital environment. Eshleman suggested simplifying the website design and title and migrating it to a blog platform, which made the work of expanding and maintaining the site much more manageable. It also enabled us to scaffold the technology side of the learning

process; with a WordPress platform, students can learn to post without needing to know how to code. Finally, Eshleman also supported Churchill's effort to get funding for a summer research assistant to fact-check and edit the site for accuracy and stylistic consistency.

Susanna Boylston was also a crucial ally, trolling eBay and "winning" originals of the *Liberator,* and forming contacts with rare booksellers who notified her when they came across magazines that might be of interest to us. The original issues she acquired, now preserved in Davidson's Special Collections, offer students the tactile pleasures of handling individual little magazines, as they turn to ever-expanding digital archives to examine the full runs. We are fortunate because the Davidson College library is not organized like many research libraries, with separate budgets or line items for acquisitions of periodicals. Instead, we have one big budget that enables us to take advantage of acquisition opportunities. The opportunity cost for acquiring original copies of little magazines is quite small. It typically costs $100 to $250 for a single issue, which is comparable to the cost of an academic book or a video with public performance rights. Acquiring original print copies requires no investment in equipment for reading them (and relieves us of the misery of poring over microfilm). The magazines can be digitized but do not have to be. As a small library, we are also not burdened by the expectation that we acquire complete runs. In fact, we are more interested in individual copies and are developing a collection with samples of a broad range of modernist magazines. We want students to get their hands on originals—to have tangible access to history. Working with originals also encourages students to think about differences between the print and digital forms when they turn to digital archives to further their research. Using digital archives thus does not have to mean losing touch with print artifacts but can actually emphasize their value.

WORKING MODEL

Modernism, Magazines, and Media (2012)

In the most recent iteration, we think that we have arrived on a model that works. Migrating the entire seminar to WordPress was an important move because it enabled us to successfully integrate the website expansion into the coursework, all of which is now conducted on a WordPress website. Churchill used to dismiss blogs as "blah, blah, blog"—vehicles for self-indulgent blather—but prodded by Eshleman, she came to recognize the intellectual potential of blogging. As Kathleen Fitzpatrick points out, "the blog is not a form but a platform. . . . [It is a] stage on which material of many different varieties—different lengths, different time signatures, different modes of mediation—might be performed."[9] The blog has become the stage not only for the retitled, redesigned *Index of Modernist Magazines* but also for the coursework leading to the collaborative research project.

The seminar, now called Modernism, Magazines, and Media, begins with a six-week minicourse on modernist periodicals and digital media, in which students post short assignments to a website (http://sites.davidson.edu/modmags) and add a new journal to the *Index of Modernist Magazines* (http://sites.davidson.edu/littlemagazines; see figure 6.5).

The first half of the course introduces students to modernism, methodologies of periodical studies, digital media, and bibliographic research. That is still a tall order, but Churchill is no longer teaching a modernist canon and then asking students to subvert it. Instead she lets them discover and define modernism on their own. Students purchase copies of the magazines currently available in reprint editions: *Blast, Fire!!,* and *Survey Graphic.* They also work with the originals in our library collection and use digital magazine archives.

The second half of the course is devoted solely to the collaborative research projects. Students propose research paper topics, vote on them, form teams, and embark on a collaborative research project on modernist magazines. With this arrangement, the bibliographic work on the *Index* lays a foundation of research, writing, and technology skills that they continue to develop through their collaborative research projects. Although students may aim to collaborate with Churchill to produce a publishable article, they can also seek out online publication venues that do not require the same level of research, revision, and professional peer review. Indeed, students may use their

FIGURE 6.5

The *Index of Modernist Magazines* (2012–present), 291 Gallery heightened digital literacy skills to discover publication opportunities and platforms of which their professors are not aware. They may also be discovered by other scholars, as when an undergraduate in the seminar received an invitation to submit an essay she had published on the course blog for inclusion in a scholarly volume.

WORKING MODEL: Lessons Learned

1. Let go of the controls. Entering the world of modernist magazines requires you to go into unchartered territory, where you are no longer the expert. One group wrote about the pulp magazine *Ranch Romances,* which was way out of Churchill's field. The burgeoning field of modern periodical studies is also new and vast enough that an undergraduate has the capacity to contribute original research. In entering this field, the students not only produced "popularizing" scholarship—what Blackwell and Martin describe as work "aimed at bringing a topic to the less-informed masses"[p]—but also investigated popular cultural forms that have historically been denigrated and neglected by scholars.
2. Allow digital tools to transform what you do. Instead of simply asking, "How do we change our scholarship to publish it digitally," we should follow Mod's lead and ask the more interesting question: "How does digital change scholarship?"[q] In this case, Churchill realized that going digital meant letting go of the "hierarchies of expertise"[r] that limited the path to publication to collaboration with her. It was Kristen Eshleman who prodded her to let go of her academic and print cultural biases, asking, "Why do students have to seek publication through collaboration with you?" In attempting to answer this question, Churchill realized that she wanted control over the students' final product in order to guarantee a certain level of expertise before their work would be made public. But once students started publishing their research findings on the course blog, Churchill was contacted by a professor who was editing a volume on pulp magazines and wanted to include a student's essay on *Ranch Romances.* By delving into the rich but understudied realm of the pulps, this student had acquired knowledge and expertise Churchill and many other academics lack—and her research was publication worthy without professional intervention.

Conclusion

Digital platforms are changing the nature and process of scholarly publication, opening up new possibilities. Reflecting the networked structure of the Internet, digital scholarship moves education toward "connectivist" learning. As George Siemens argues, "learning (defined as actionable knowledge) can reside outside of ourselves (within an organization or a database), is focused on connecting specialized information sets, and the connections that enable us to learn more are more important than our current state of knowing."[s] As digital networks alter consumption of information and creation of knowledge, the roles of educators and students change as well. Siemens describes this as "blending the concept of educator expertise with learner construction."[t] The blending of the roles of teacher and student transforms a once hierarchical relationship into a more collaborative one. Cathy Davidson and David Goldberg observe that "the relative horizontality of access to the Web has . . . flattened out contributions to knowledge making, . . . making them much less the function of a credentialed elite and increasingly collaboratively created."[u] Scholarship in a digital age is no longer a hierarchical enterprise governed by experts with PhDs and institutional titles, but a democratic, open exchange of ideas, in which all creative, intellectual minds are welcome, regardless of reputation or credentials. Come to think of it, the digital age of modernist studies is starting to resemble the print culture of modernist little magazines. Then, as now, collaboration across disciplines stimulated creative production and generated hundreds of new publication platforms of all shapes, sizes, and dispositions. These public platforms fostered artistic alliances and intellectual networks, generated new forms and genres, and transformed processes of knowledge production.

To document the full range and diversity of modernist little magazines, we look forward to collaborating with other colleges and universities, allowing their students to work with their own professors, librarians, instructional technologists, and archives—and with us—to expand the *Index.* In this way, we might extend what Davidson and Goldberg call "participatory learning"[v] beyond the borders of our small college campus. Partnering with other institutions would allow us to grow the *Index* at a faster pace than we can with a single biannual seminar that adds, on average, six magazines per year. It also opens up possibilities for undergraduate peer review and exchange across institutional borders. While Davidson and Goldberg argue that academic institutions should be rethought of as "mobilizing networks" that stress "flexibility, interactivity, and outcome,"[w] if we want our digital scholarly products to have credibility, we must balance openness and flexibility with a commitment to scholarly rigor and consistency. While it is tempting to reimagine the *Index* as a *Wikipedia*-like public collective, such a model has limitations for an undergraduate DH product. An undergraduate project has a greater chance of success if its scope is limited, but a narrow focus reduces the number of participants likely to provide quality checks and corrections. The *Index* is currently designed to give individual authors ownership of their pages, with a byline at the bottom of each page. This byline not only holds individual students accountable for upholding the scholarly standards of the *Index* but also allows them to get academic credit for their work and to showcase that work to future employers, fellowship providers, and graduate programs. In the future, we may want to let go of this system of acknowledging individual authors and instead embrace a self-regulating network of anonymous collaborators. We proceed with cautious optimism, however, because just as we seek to marry a sustainable digital product with the undergraduate learning process, so we seek to balance our desire to innovate and expand our horizons with a commitment to preserving academic rigor and integrity.[x]

---

a. *Index of Modernist Magazines,* accessed January 29, 2016, http://sites.davidson.edu/littlemagazines.

b. Bryan Alexander and Rebecca Frost Davis, "Should Liberal Arts Campuses Do Digital Humanities? Process and Products in the Small College World," in *Debates in the Digital Humanities,* ed. Matthew K. Gold and Lauren F. Klein (Minneapolis: University of Minnesota Press, 2012), 2013 digital edition, accessed January 29, 2016, http://dhdebates.gc.cuny.edu/debates/text/25.

c. Suzanne W. Churchill and Adam McKible (eds.), *Little Magazines and Modernism: New Approaches* (Burlington, VT: Ashgate, 2007), 6.
d. Jerome McGann, "Radiant Textuality," *Victorian Studies* 39, no. 3 (Spring 1996): 381.
e. Ellen J. Langer, *Mindfulness* (Reading, MA: Addison-Wesley, 1989), 76.
f. Craig Mod, "Post-Artifact Books and Publishing," *Journal* (blog), June 2011, http://craigmod.com/journal/post_artifact.
g. Cary Nelson, *Repression and Recovery: Modern American Poetry and the Politics of Cultural Memory, 1910–1945* (Madison: University of Wisconsin Press, 1989), 316; Mark Morrisson, "Preface," in *Little Magazines and Modernism: New Approaches,* ed. Suzanne W. Churchill and Adam McKible (Burlington, VT: Ashgate, 2007), xv.
h. The Homer Multitext Project, "The Homer Multitext: Home Page," accessed January 29, 2016, www.homermultitext.org.
i. Alexander and Davis, "Should Liberal Arts Campuses Do Digital Humanities?"
j. Ibid.
k. Ibid.
l. Christopher Blackwell and Thomas R. Martin, "Technology, Collaboration, and Undergraduate Research," *DHQ: Digital Humanities Quarterly* 3, no. 1 (2009): para. 5, 13, www.digitalhumanities.org/dhq/vol/3/1/000024/000024.html.
m. D. F. McKenzie, "The Book as an Expressive Form," in *The Book History Reader,* ed. David Finkelstein and Alistair McCleery (New York: Routledge, 2002), 29.
n. Alexander and Davis, "Should Liberal Arts Campuses Do Digital Humanities?"
o. Kathleen Fitzpatrick, "Networking the Field," *Planned Obsolescence* (blog), January 10, 2012, www.plannedobsolescence.net/blog/networking-the-field.
p. Blackwell and Martin, "Technology, Collaboration, and Undergraduate Research," para. 5, 13.
q. Mod, "Post-Artifact Books and Publishing."
r. Cathy N. Davidson and David Theo Goldberg, *The Future of Learning Institutions in a Digital Age,* John D. and Catherine T. MacArthur Foundation Reports on Digital Media and Learning (Cambridge, MA: MIT Press, 2009), 11.
s. George Siemens, "Connectivism: A Learning Theory for a Digital Age," *International Journal of Instructional Technology and Distance Learning* 2, no. 1 (2005), www.itdl.org/Journal/Jan_05/article01.htm.
t. George Siemens, "Learning and Knowing in Networks: Changing Roles for Educators and Designers" (paper presented to the Instructional Technology Forum, Department of Instructional Technology, University of Georgia, January 27, 2008), www.ingedewaard.net/papers/connectivism/2008_siemens_Learning_Knowing_in_Networks_changingRolesForEducatorsAndDesigners.pdf.
u. Davidson and Goldberg, *The Future of Learning Institutions in a Digital Age,* 11.
v. Ibid., 35.
w. Ibid., 12–13, 33–34.
x. This case study, in somewhat different form, was originally published online at www.academiccommons.org/2014/08/26/the-digital-database-a-model-of-student-staff-and-faculty-collaboration and is distributed under a Creative Commons Attribution-ShareAlike 3.0 Unported License.

MOOCS AND COLLABORATION

Librarians have also had a difficult time figuring out where they "fit in" when it comes to massive online open courses. In a 2013 article, Kerry Wu ponders, "If MOOCs are going to transform higher education, it will undoubtedly have a significant impact on the way libraries work and the role they play in the future of learning."[23] She notes that "library participation in MOOCs fall[s] into the following three categories: copyright clearance and locating alternatives such as Creative Commons materials and other free sources; course production; and development of policies and best practices. Other possible, but less well-defined areas include archiving class materials, curating user-generated content such as forum discussions and student projects, providing leadership (rather than just "partnership"), and teaching information literacy to MOOC students."[24]

It would initially appear to be the case that the collaborations that occur in campus efforts to support the learning management system would organically flow into MOOC initiatives. Librarians in an LMS class environment might be in a role such as an embedded librarian that can entail a wide range of commitments, whereas an instructional designer might also have "LMS to MOOC" mapped responsibilities based on his or her role. But while there are a few overlapping similarities, there are obvious and noteworthy differences. As mentioned in chapter 1, the demographics that make up modern (and online) students are different from residential students and those of the past (and this situation continues to change). In a similar fashion, the MOOC student appears to represent the modern learner in the digital age and can be different from those registered on a campus. All of this is said not only to differentiate the design of the LMS course from the MOOC but to gain an understanding of the student in each environment.

Joseph Esposito, writing for the blog *The Scholarly Kitchen* and surveying the state of the MOOC at the end of 2015, echoes the concern presented by Clay Shirky in chapter 1 (the disconnect between current students and those making higher education decisions) and states:

> The MOOC, in other words, has not disappeared. It has begun to adapt to the world it operates in, starting with a big utopian idea and gradually finding new uses and new users. This is the way it is with digital media, indeed of all media. The new medium starts out as an alleged replacement for an established medium and then gradually finds its own way as it discovers its underlying nature and marries those capabilities to genuine interest and demand in the marketplace. We will be seeing more MOOCs (no doubt expressed as a different acronym) in the future, which represents a genuine area for growth for publishers that are stymied by what appears to the unimaginative as a flat or declining marketplace.[25]

It appears as though some of the excitement, hype, and predictions surrounding MOOCs have had to come to grips with reality. Proponents of MOOCs and those who work extensively in them would be quick to protect them from criticism and point out many of their positives, one of which is their versatility. They will continue to be useful but will go through numerous phases. One consensus for a "good fit" for MOOCs moving forward is in support of professional development, which may appeal more to librarians and instructional designers as *users* rather than as part of the support teams for the construction of MOOCs.

The present and potential future conditions of MOOCs entail a running debate that currently hints toward the overall viability of the concept, but with a need to morph and adapt. Copyright and access issues concern university administrators and, therefore, librarians. One possible solution for how librarians may be part of MOOCs moving forward is offered by Curtis Kendrick and Irene Gashurov: "As librarians, we are in the best position to confront these challenges, because we work at the intersection of technology and pedagogy, and we are well equipped to understand technology's broader implications and impact on teaching, learning, and scholarship. We understand what infrastructure is essential for a flipped classroom or what licensed resources can be extended to faculty and students."[26] They conclude, referencing James Michalko, Vice President of the OCLC Research Library Partnership:

> At a minimum, the library should join the university support team to oversee MOOC development; Michalko also recommends that we bring together our copyright, open access, and permission staff members and get our experts to join or lead any cross-institutional teams—such as for instructional technology, licensing, or preservation—that might be formed to bring MOOCs to the campus.
>
> Libraries should not miss out on a chance to get involved in the future of MOOCs on campus; as Michalko noted, "At the times that libraries were slow to help, slow to reconfigure their resources, and waited to see what might develop, they lost chances to renew their importance to their home institution."
>
> The MOOC frontier offers new opportunities for librarians to provide leadership and guidance in advising administration, faculty, and students about changes in higher education. But first, we must study and analyze the MOOCs landscape so that we can shape the conversation about MOOCs and their successors in a more purposeful and organized way.[27]

Aligning MOOCs with open educational resources (OERs), Carmen Kazakoff-Lane, in "Environmental Scan and Assessment of OERs, MOOCs and Libraries: What Effectiveness and Sustainability Means for Libraries' Impact on Open Education," reviews how these two concepts overlap for librarians and higher education.[28] She points out how MOOCs offer a potential way out of the escalating cost of higher education and how OERs offer sustainability by creating commitment from their communities. Concluding that libraries and librarians need to educate themselves on these two open education possibilities and then make others aware about the effectiveness and sustainability of these initiatives, she references instructional design as an element:

> No one believes it to be easy, but libraries' battles on behalf of open access, together with their increasing encapsulation of relevant publication, multimedia, instructional design, and intellectual property services, means they have the credibility, knowledge, and relationships needed to argue for and support an open education consistent with all of their values, not just some. In so doing, libraries might ensure that higher education
>
> - is not entering into a world where it loses control of its content again,
> - is not the sole property of a few major institutions, with potentially devastating impacts on tuition and research in smaller universities,
> - is capable of both developing and taking advantage of open content in a rationalized and sustainable fashion, and
> - is providing content that aids people with diverse cultural, linguistic, and learning needs.
>
> That is a vision of open education that all libraries could get behind, champion and sustain.[29]

Like digital humanities collaboration, it is more often the case that a librarian will be asked to support faculty and may "end up" working with an instructional designer. Of course, as is the case for almost all digital learning tools and technologies, the instructional designer is needed (or certainly it is advisable that one be consulted). As is so often the case when thinking about the type of work that librarians and instructional designers can do together, there is, on one side, a conceptual viewpoint and, on the other side, a practical design to things. While ideas help to propel action, a balance needs to exist between reading, researching, discussing, and thinking about how to translate concepts into reality. A vision or intention must be backed with stepwise concrete goals or accomplishments; otherwise it dies on the vine. The key is *implementation* as a way to sustain collaborative ideas, and design is a lynchpin in that process.

Although he is focused on how MOOCs bring "more attention and investment in residential learning," Joshua Kim states, "The most important innovations catalyzed by MOOCs have very little to do with technology, or even pedagogy. Rather, they are innovations at the level of *institutional organizational and cultural change*" (emphasis in original).[30] He adds, "The same teams of faculty, instructional designers, media educators, librarians, and assessment experts who have gained trust and experience in working on MOOCs will also work on redesigning large-enrollment residential classes."[31] This section's case study is a good example of this type of synergy.

Case Study

MOOCS: A STUDY IN COLLABORATION

This residential class engages students in a transdisciplinary conversation about representations of HIV/AIDS in science writing, journalism, visual art, literature, drama, and popular culture. The hypothesis is that scientists and cultural critics can learn valuable lessons from one another, even as they create their own responses to HIV/AIDS. The pandemic remains a major health concern throughout the world. Recognizing this is a global issue, Davidson College offered its second MOOC on the topic in an effort to engage a global audience of artists, scientists, medical practitioners, and people living with HIV/AIDS in this conversation. Using technology to bring divergent voices into the classroom, the experiment aims to break down the walled gardens of higher education toward real-world problem solving.

What is a MOOC?

At face value the concept is a simple one—a massive open online course, or MOOC, is an online course designed for unlimited participation and open access. The term originated with Dave Cormier, an educational activist, researcher, and online community advocate who coined the acronym in 2008 to describe the first online course of this kind, Connectivism and Connective Knowledge.[a] George Siemens and Stephen Downes, both leading scholars in the field of networked and digital learning, taught the first MOOC.

It is easy to see how MOOCs became the poster child for disruption in higher education, but the MOOC experiment by Siemens and Downes was not designed with an eye toward providing a low-cost alternative degree. It was a scholarly effort to understand how optimal learning happens in digital spaces where the rate of information and knowledge creation has exploded. At their core, digital environments are composed of networks of connections—connections between information (data) and connections between individuals and ideas. Siemens's theory on connectivism describes digital learning as a similarly networked process. Knowledge is less about mastery of content and more about wayfinding—navigating, connecting, and synthesizing rapidly changing nodes of information. How we interact with the new information network within a learning process that is also going digital is the key here. MOOCs embody the intersections between teaching and learning, information literacy, inclusive pedagogies, open access, and digital technologies. MOOC experiments have been a key driver in the renewed interest in learning research and, as a result, have changed the conversation about the role of digital learning in higher education. In our case, they have also been a key driver in elevating the roles of technologists and librarians as intellectual partners in the important conversation about the future of higher education.

Why did Davidson College enter into the MOOC experiment?

When Davidson College joined in 2013, edX had emerged as the lone nonprofit MOOC provider dedicated to improving higher education. Participating as a charter member gave us a seat at the governing table, allowing us to exert some degree of influence over the future of the edX platform as well as a more powerful voice in the national conversation around MOOCs and their impact on higher education. In our minds, we could either help shape this direction or risk being shaped by it.

Davidson President Carol Quillen said, "This partnership exemplifies our obligation to understand how new technologies might strengthen the hallmarks of the academic experience at Davidson."[b] Davidson was primarily interested in the residential impact of MOOCs—on our college's professors, students, and the DavidsonX team. To get at those insights, the DavidsonX team took two approaches. First, the DavidsonX blogged openly, reflecting on early experiences developing our initial four MOOCs.[c] Second, in two MOOC-infused residential courses, we designed a formal qualitative study of the Davidson student and faculty experience. From these we hoped to add value to the existing body of knowledge about the potential for digital technologies in higher education.

Teaching is moving away from the lone practitioner.

At a 2014 SXSWedu panel, Making MOOC Magic: What Students Have to Say, Steven Mintz described the handwringing around MOOCs as not really about MOOCs at all, but about the future of higher education, including course delivery and faculty roles. He argued that the explosion of information resources (much of it open and digital) increasingly requires a course design process that is collaborative.[d] We experienced a similar shift—away from our traditional roles in residential teaching toward a new model of collaboration in the development of DavidsonX MOOCs. Traditional residential courses typically include academic technologists and librarians mostly on the edges, cycling in and out in support of student projects. Projects range from traditional research papers to new forms of digital scholarship. Although our contributions are valued, rarely are we consulted on the full syllabus or incorporated into the course in deeply embedded ways. By contrast, we participated fully in the creation and running of our MOOCs. DavidsonX course teams on average consisted of the faculty, two to three academic technologists, one to two librarians, three to five student TAs (teaching assistants), and a project manager. Library and academic technology participation was critical to the success of these courses. Absent an office of online learning, our academic technologists assumed all of the technical, instructional design, and, to a smaller degree, project management roles on the DavidsonX course team. At the same time, our librarians were key experts in all aspects of content procurement, intellectual property, and copyright. To a lesser degree, both roles were also involved in the running of some courses—serving as TAs in the discovery and creation of student-generated content. At the core, we guided faculty through the development of their courses within the framework and affordances of the new digital knowledge process. In developing and running our MOOCs, we realized that the combined expertise that served our faculty and students so well might also serve the institution at a higher level. This is not just an argument that there is strength in numbers. These two fields are symbiotic because of their overlap, and not in spite of it.

Information specialists take on a new role.

A notable and significant precursor to MOOCs that paved the way for deeper library and academic technology collaborations emerged in 2001, with the MIT OpenCourseWare (OCW) project. Massive, open, and enabled by technology, OCW made course content for fifty MIT courses free and accessible to anyone. By the end of 2014, OCW boasted the following statistics:

- 2,250 courses were published.
- 1 billion page views and 170 million visits occurred.
- 100 courses had complete video lectures.
- 900 older versions of courses had been updated.[e]

As the project grew, so did questions about intellectual property and copyright.[f] Who owned the content produced at MIT? The professor? The institution? Both? The same questions applied to our MOOC courses, and as our librarian Sara Swanson discovered, "It was clear from the beginning that we would need to tackle many intellectual property (IP) issues as we created our MOOCs. As I set out to explore what those issues might be, I quickly realized that I had entered a whole new world, much of which hasn't yet been thoroughly mapped."[g] Educating the faculty about fair use was the most efficient obstacle to remove in order to meet course deadlines. To accomplish this, Swanson developed a guide for faculty to review at the start of course planning and for future MOOC proposals. In the end, the guidelines streamlined her work on the team, as faculty leaned heavily on her expertise to guide them on content choices. Copyright and IP in the context of open access are important and somewhat obvious spaces for library inclusion in MOOCs. What might get overlooked are the additional ways librarians can, and in our case did, contribute more deeply to the course—research and information literacy.

It's a team sport.

Navigating the affordances of digital learning as well as providing open access to information meant all members of the DavidsonX team were equally invested in the outcomes. Ownership of the course design was shared. This was the first time faculty, staff, and students were central to the input and execution of courses, from start to finish, and participated in all aspects of the instructional design, including syllabus design, course material production, instruction, quality assurance, and research. Teaching in digital spaces, we learned, is a team sport.

We relied on innovation and creativity.

At the start, the sense of shared ownership of the course grew out of a need to overcome resource constraints. At one level, this comes naturally to smaller schools like

Davidson, where we have experience being strategic and creative in the face of limited resources. Where our larger peer institutions dedicated people to their MOOC efforts, we had to absorb the work within our existing academic technology and library departments. This meant we had to balance existing residential course needs with those of the DavidsonX MOOCs. The challenges in doing so were very real and, at peak times, quite stressful. But constraints and stressors breed creativity. We discovered that this structural shortcoming had a silver lining: "[E]mbrace the constraints you've been given. Use them as assets, as an opportunity to be the one who solved the problem."[h]

Partly out of necessity and partly by design, the DavidsonX team jumped into our MOOC course development process feet first. Limited resources were not our only constraints. Time was another. MOOCs take months to build and test. We did not have the time to develop a deep plan for execution. We found ourselves in the role of a startup, learning by doing. Recognizing this, our project manager, Allison Dulin Salisbury, astutely studied and borrowed from the principles of lean startup and applied the methodology of "build-measure-learn."[i] We created, tested, and pivoted as we designed and ran the courses. We worked in scrums. We adjusted budget priorities on the fly. We empowered everyone to contribute ideas. Because we lacked dedicated online instructional designers and producers, our academic technologists and librarians were deeply involved in the instructional design and production of DavidsonX courses. We watched one another rise to the occasion many times, and we were a stronger team as a result. The collaboration and creativity around the DavidsonX experiment deepened our pedagogical understanding, expanded our skills in digital learning, honed in on the symbiotic strengths of every member, and added value to our ongoing work with existing residential courses.

Working in this way was not without its pain points, but the exercise in collaboration and creativity epitomizes a new academic model that we (academic technologists and librarians) now strive to replicate in much of our work with faculty. It also prepared us for a bold new R&D (research and development) initiative in digital learning that is empowering us to enter a cycle of experimentation necessary to address the current uncertainty around the future of higher education.[j] In the end, this integrated MOOC experiment served as a boot camp to position academic technologists and librarians to better serve innovative, emerging digital pedagogy in collaboration, whether or not the application was residential or fully online.

We learned that research anchors good innovation.

In May 2014, Fiona Hollands and Devayani Tirthali, from the Center for Benefit-Cost Studies of Education at Teachers College, Columbia University, published a cost-benefit study of MOOC experiments.[k] Two leading goals for the twenty-nine institutions interviewed include expanding access to higher education and improving economics through lowered costs or increased revenues. The Columbia team's research suggests, however, that the likelihood that MOOCs will achieve either of these goals is unclear. In contrast, improving educational outcomes, fostering innovation, and conducting learning research are the least-cited reasons for creating MOOCs. In our experience, these lesser goals have proven to be the areas where we have seen the greatest potential benefits. The first two are anchored by the third. The research efforts have aided us in understanding how we might look at educational outcomes residentially and how to advance innovation through formal experimentation.

At Davidson, we started with the simple question, "How, if at all, is the MOOC experiment impacting residential teaching and learning?" In response, we undertook a mixed-method research study of two MOOC-infused residential courses during the fall semester of 2014. Ours was primarily a traditional case study, examining the human side of learning that cannot be measured in clickstreams. How learners experience the knowledge process in digital environments is important to understanding optimal designs for open, social learning. Quantitative data can track student pathways online, but it cannot tell us why a student chose that path, or whether that experience was seamless and intuitive or frustrating and fraught with hurdles. Where quantitative data leaves off, qualitative data picks up, giving us a clearer picture of learning.[i] We documented the experiences of our faculty and residential students in the classroom and in the MOOC, using observation, interviews, focus groups and surveys.

Conclusion

Online education is not central to the mission of Davidson College, nor is it likely to become central. From the outside, a MOOC experiment at a small liberal arts college seems out of place. The once popular notion of MOOCs as an alternative to college is waning, but higher education will continue to embrace digital environments where people connect and create knowledge.

As we discovered, digital technology reaches far beyond the traditional online course, enhancing residential teaching and learning toward new collaborative models with an emphasis on creating knowledge rather than consuming it. Where the inclusion of digital spaces makes a residential education more relevant for tomorrow's professors and students, they should be an integral part of the fabric of teaching and learning.

---

a. Stephen Downes, "Welcome to CCK11," Connectivism and Connective Knowledge 2011, accessed January 30, 2016, http://cck11.mooc.ca.

b. Davidson College, "Davidson Joins Leading Online Learning Consortium EdX," Davidson College News, May 21, 2013, www.davidson.edu/news/news-stories/130521-edx-announcement.

c. Davidson College, "DavidsonX," accessed January 30, 2016, http://blogs.davidson.edu/davidsonx.

d. SXSW PanelPicker, "Making MOOC Magic: What Students Have to Say," accessed January 30, 2016, http://panelpicker.sxsw.com/vote/26156?__hstc=264666192.fdd7a7debc8575bac5a80cf7e168316a.1448668800095.1448668800096.1448668800097.1&__hssc=264666192.1.1448668800098&__hsfp=3972014050.

e. MIT OpenCourseWare, "Our History," accessed January 30, 2016, http://ocw.mit.edu/about/our-history.

f. MIT OpenCourseWare, "FAQ: Intellectual Property," accessed May 3, 2016, http://ocw.mit.edu/help/faq-intellectual-property.

g. Sara Swanson, "Copyright Cop on the MOOC Beat," *DavidsonX* (blog), March 24, 2014, http://blogs.davidson.edu/davidsonx/2014/03/24/copyright-cop-on-the-mooc-beat.

h. Seth Godin, "Embracing Constraints," *Seth's Blog*, July 20, 2011, http://sethgodin.typepad.com/seths_blog/2011/07/embracing-constraints.html.

i. The Lean Startup, "Methodology," accessed January 30, 2016, http://theleanstartup.com/principles.
j. Davidson College, "Digital Learning R&D," accessed January 30, 2016, http://dlrd.davidson.edu.
k. Fiona M. Hollands and Devayani Tirthali, *MOOCs: Expectations and Reality—Full Report* (New York: Center for Benefit-Cost Studies of Education, Teachers College, Columbia University, May 2014), http://cbcse.org/wordpress/wp-content/uploads/2014/05/MOOCs_Expectations_and_Reality.pdf.
l. George Veletsianos, "Learner Experiences with Open Online Learning and MOOCs E-book," September 24, 2013, www.veletsianos.com/2013/09/24/learner-experiences-with-open-online-learning-and-moocs-e-book.

HUMAN-CENTERED DESIGN

Design, like data, can sometimes be primarily concerned with analysis and facts, while it is less focused on emotional components. As the goals of good design enhance purpose and improve efficiency while considering simplicity, what would make design centered on human use separate from another type of design? The history of user experience (UX) design and human-centered design (HCD) puts much more emphasis on the behavior and interaction of those who "interface" with what is designed than on the end product itself. A good source that reviews the history of design theory and traces the evolution of design methods leading to the current state of design thinking is the blog *I Think; I Design.*[32] In a post that leads up to human-centered design, Stefanie Di Russo relays, "It was also at this point that we found ourselves with a design methodology that was manifested as more of a mindset than a physical set of tools. . . . In its final (and current) phase of evolution, HCD is seen to hold potential for resolving wider societal issues."[33] Here again, we see an intent on a way to be more open and inclusive.

The popularity of design thinking in its many forms continues to gather steam. In the article "Is 'Design Thinking' the New Liberal Arts?" Peter N. Miller says it is the lack of looking back on the past that creates a "not yet" answer to the title question. Miller states, "[I]t is all conducted in the present tense, with no sense that the past matters to the present. Everything is ethnography. Libraries, archives, museums, the great repositories of the human past are rarely called upon for help. That puts a contradiction at the heart of design thinking, given the premise of a human-centered design practice, and the fact that we humans are all sedimentary beings in whom the past lives on and helps shape our experience of the present."[34]

As a way to emphasize collaboration and center on aspects of critical librarianship, human-centered design has an appeal for both academic librarians and instructional designers. Moving away from a concentration on content, both instructional designers and librarians are often concerned with prioritizing human interaction. At first glance, it seems a bit embarrassing or perhaps insulting that someone would consider a visit to a library anything but human-centered. Most librarians would potentially be aghast at the idea that someone partaking of a library experience would think that there was a lack of empathy or a distanced approach on the part of the librarian. Yet it is appropriate to take a short detour to explore once more how librarians are perceived and, a related and current topic, diversity in libraries. As a reminder, this look at librarians helps to form ideas on ways to achieve inclusiveness that were touched on in chapters 1 and 4. Critical librarianship is related to these themes, and gaining a fuller understanding of these topical issues can create dimensional insight into the current state of academic libraries and librarians. Understanding those with whom you team up is a fundamental principle of good collaboration.

At the core of this self-reflective need to evaluate what libraries and librarians do is the desire to improve an idea that was reflexively considered to be a core tenet of libraries: equal access to information. There is currently a backward-looking criticism of just how well equal access to information was achieved, and steps are being taken to correct this failure. Interesting criticisms of libraries and their history have been put forth recently by librarians themselves. Branching out of the idea of critical pedagogy and bolstered by certain connected aspects of ACRL's *Framework for Information Literacy for Higher Education* (particularly the frame titled "Authority Is Constructed and Contextual"[35]), librarians have begun to talk about aspects of libraries that were either hidden or brushed away in the past. It is revealing to see that one of the prompts for reviewing the place of the library in society and how the community is represented has corollaries in discussions about information literacy.

In an article from the blog *In the Library with the Lead Pipe*, "Locating the Library in Institutional Oppression," nina de jesus presents a self-critical look at libraries: "Libraries as institutions were created not only for a specific ideological purpose but for an ideology that is fundamentally oppressive in nature"[36] This oppressive nature, she says, is intertwined with the history of the library, as the overarching principles on which libraries were founded cannot be separated from a hierarchical place which posits that libraries are another institutional force that elevates the "uneducated" to a place of judged respectability. As in most cases with repressive behavior, especially when it is done unconsciously, the first step for those who desire to correct it is to gain an awareness of what is occurring. Understanding one's own biases can lead to a lifting of the veil that libraries do not contribute to exclusion and do not represent diversity. It does not generally take much more than a cursory walk through your own library's collection with the intent of trying to find a great deal of diverse materials to see what is lacking (and then imagining that someone who would be looking for materials that are not there for them would feel as though "your" library was not a place for them).

Probing further, other posts on the *In the Library with the Lead Pipe* blog, such as "Soliciting Performance, Hiding Bias: Whiteness and Librarianship," "White Librarianship in Blackface: Diversity Initiatives in LIS," and "The Quest for Diversity in Library Staffing: From Awareness to Action," point out the need for libraries and librarians to be more self-aware regarding their own field and to consider ways to act so that there is an accurate representation in libraries of those who may use them.[37] One way to define critical librarianship is "an international movement of library and information workers that consider the human condition and human rights above other professional concerns," and, therefore, "the ethos of critical librarianship is inextricably linked to the ethos of intellectual freedom."[38] Adding nuance to this definition is this reference from Kenny Garcia's "Keeping Up with . . . Critical Librarianship": "According to Elaine Harger, librarians that practice critical librarianship strive to communicate the ways in which libraries and librarians consciously and unconsciously support systems of oppression. Critical librarianship seeks to be transformative, empowering, and a direct challenge to power and privilege."[39] The key takeaway for librarians is the need to spend time exploring some of the preconceived notions about libraries and to examine how librarians can change the future so that it is one of inclusion. As a way to connect to the thread of these ideas in relation to a discussion on human-centered design, it is appropriate to analyze whether the library itself is centered on humans as part of its central design.

Where critical librarianship and human-centered design can intersect is in the concept of critical design. Although scant literature and research about critical design and librarianship exists, this idea of designing attempts to move beyond preconceived notions. "The term 'critical design' was first coined by design duo Anthony Dunne [and] Fiona Raby around the turn of the 21st century. It describes a design practice concerned with exploring the possibilities that new technologies and disciplines might bring to the field and how society as a whole might change in their wake. Critical design asks the questions 'what if?' and 'what else?'"[40] To extrapolate from the designers themselves, "Critical Design uses speculative design proposals to challenge narrow assumptions, preconceptions and givens about the role products play in everyday life. It is more of an attitude than anything else, a position rather than a method. Its opposite is affirmative design: design that reinforces the status quo."[41] One final quote about critical design serves to amplify its emphasis on inclusion: "It's worth noting that this process does not always immediately lead to functional objects, but rather, its use value is tied to the production of long-term thinking, empathy, and ultimately, more questions."[42] Once more, learning design can entail much more than the creation of products. It is the conceptual nature of related design thinking and learning that needs to be inferred from these ideas.

All of these ideas come together in the concept of critical instructional design, which is just beginning to gain currency. As conceived by Sean Michael Morris, Instructional Designer for the Office of the Associate Provost for Digital Learning at Middlebury College, and Jesse Stommel, Executive Director of the Division of Teaching and Learning Technologies at University of Mary Washington, this combination of critical pedagogy and instructional design is in an initial design phase as part of an online MOOC MOOC (a MOOC about MOOCs). Here, as part of the Online Digital Pedagogy Lab, they have begun discussion around a critical instructional design.[43]

Despite the fact that libraries have lost some hold as keepers of information, perhaps they have gained more understanding of how a library should be focused on developing people. As part of that goal, librarians have begun to think more about aspects such as how signage and acronyms are used; that is, there has been a spotlight shone on how libraries are experienced. In *Useful, Usable, Desirable*, Aaron Schmidt and Amanda Etches devote a chapter to signage and wayfinding, stating, "Think of the signs in your library as a form of customer service and an expression of your library's attitude towards its members. Are they as friendly and helpful as the people in your building?"[44] Another place in which the human-centered (and the interrelated student-centered) mindset takes hold is designing library space. In their recent book *Encoding Space: Shaping Learning Environments That Unlock Human Potential*, Brian Mathews and Leigh Ann Soistmann ask, "Can we create library environments that inspire people to be more creative, collaborative, reflective, or engaged?"[45]

Human-centered design looks to be a good fit for those libraries considering these issues. In fact, Ideo, a company that has been very involved with this type of outlook, first, created a human-centered design toolkit and, second, one for libraries. The website Design Thinking for Libraries, subtitled "A Toolkit for Patron-Centered Design," provides resources for librarians who are interested in design thinking.[46] The website also provides links to different Design Kits, one of which is for the Course for Human-Centered Design, which is designed to do the following:

- Equip you with the mindsets and methods of human-centered design so that you can be more intentional about facing and solving your current challenges
- Let you experiment with the power of human-centered design
- Teach you to identify patterns and opportunities for concept development
- Inspire you to approach challenges differently and experience how human-centered design can add new perspectives to your own work tackling poverty-related challenges
- Give you hands-on experience speaking to, prototyping for, and testing solutions with the people you're designing for[47]

Note the social justice connection here with the desire to solve a specific real-world problem.

There are so many good design resources available for the librarian that it would be remiss on our part not to include a few more here:

- "45 Design Thinking Resources for Educators," by Sara Briggs (www.opencolleges.edu.au/informed/features/45-design-thinking-resources-for-educators)
- *Designing Better Libraries* blog (http://dbl.lishost.org/blog/#.VrEZH_nigZw)
- The Virtual Crash Course in Design Thinking (http://dschool.stanford.edu/dgift)

A good review of case studies that apply to human-centered design can be found in the paper "The People in Digital Libraries: Multifaceted Approaches to Assessing Needs and Impact," by Gary Marchionini, Catherine Plaisant, and Anita Komlodi.[48] As can be seen when looking at all of these initiatives (digital humanities, MOOCs, human-centered design, and others), it is important to raise the bar on ways to improve technology skills but it is equally, if not more, important to keep people in mind as a focal point.

NOTES

1. Stephen Ramsey, "Who's In and Who's Out" (paper presented at the MLA conference, January 8, 2011), http://stephenramsay.us/text/2011/01/08/whos-in-and-whos-out.
2. R. David Lankes, *The Atlas of New Librarianship* (Cambridge, MA: MIT Press, 2011), 15.
3. Jason Heppler, "What Is Digital Humanities?," WhatIsDigitalHumanities.com, accessed January 29, 2016, http://whatisdigitalhumanities.com.
4. Day of DH 2016, "About: Welcome to Day of DH 2016," accessed April 14, 2016, http://dayofdh2016.linhd.es/about.
5. Matthew G. Kirschenbaum, "What Is Digital Humanities and What's It Doing in English Departments?," *ADE Bulletin*, no. 150 (2010): 55–63, doi:10.1632/ade.75.55.
6. Jonathan Senchyne, "An Introduction to the Digital Humanities for Librarians" (webcast), accessed January 29, 2016, http://ics.webcast.uwex.edu/Mediasite6/Play/3bdbc88895e54cd59265684550cd387c1d.
7. Anne Burdick, Johanna Drucker, Peter Lunenfeld, Todd Presner, and Jeffrey Schnapp, "A Short Guide to the Digital Humanities," in *Digital Humanities* (Cambridge, MA: MIT Press, 2012), 121–136, http://jeffreyschnapp.com/wp-content/uploads/2013/01/D_H_ShortGuide.pdf.
8. Korey Jackson and Aaron McCollough, "Introducing Digital Humanities (Full)," Prezi.com, August 7, 2014, https://prezi.com/r7rmqbxifpq9/introducing-digital-humanities-full.
9. Maureen Cech, "Digital Humanities: Home," University of Delaware Library, accessed January 29, 2016, http://guides.lib.udel.edu/c.php?g=85603&p=548790.
10. Association of College and Research Libraries, "dh+lib," accessed January 29, 2016, http://acrl.ala.org/dh.

11. CUNY Academic Commons, "Defining the Digital Humanities," accessed January 29, 2016, http://commons.gc.cuny.edu/wiki/index.php/Defining_the_Digital_Humanities.
12. Laurie Alexander, Beau D. Case, Karen E. Downing, Melissa Gomis, and Eric Maslowsk, "Librarians and Scholars: Partners in Digital Humanities," *EDUCAUSE Review*, June 4, 2014, http://er.educause.edu/articles/2014/6/librarians-and-scholars-partners-in-digital-humanities.
13. Janice M. Jaguszewski and Karen Williams, *New Roles for New Times: Transforming Liaison Roles in Research Libraries* (Washington, DC: Association of Research Libraries, 2013), 10, www.arl.org/storage/documents/publications/nrnt-liaison-roles-revised.pdf.
14. Stewart Varner, "What DH Could Be," *Scholarship, Libraries, Technology* (blog), January 10, 2016, http://stewartvarner.com/2016/01/10/what-dh-could-be.
15. Trevor Muñoz, "Digital Humanities in the Library Isn't a Service," *Notebook* (blog), August 19, 2012, http://trevormunoz.com/notebook/2012/08/19/doing-dh-in-the-library.html.
16. Mark Sample, Twitter post, January 9, 2016, 9:21 a.m., http://twitter.com/samplereality.
17. Alix Keener, "The Arrival Fallacy: Collaborative Research Relationships in the Digital Humanities." *DHQ: Digital Humanities Quarterly*, September 2, 2015, www.digitalhumanities.org/dhq/vol/9/2/000213/000213.html.
18. Ibid.
19. Jennifer Schaffner and Ricky Erway, *Does Every Research Library Need a Digital Humanities Center?* (Dublin, OH: OCLC Research, 2014), www.oclc.org/content/dam/research/publications/library/2014/oclcresearch-digital-humanities-center-2014.pdf.
20. Ibid., 14.
21. Ibid., 16.
22. Alexander et al., "Librarians and Scholars."
23. Kerry Wu, "Academic Libraries in the Age of MOOCs," *Reference Services Review* 41, no. 3 (2013): 577.
24. Ibid., 581.
25. Joseph Esposito, "MOOCs Rise from the Ashes," *The Scholarly Kitchen* (blog), November 23, 2015, http://scholarlykitchen.sspnet.org/2015/11/23/moocs-rise-from-the-ashes.
26. Curtis Kendrick and Irene Gashurov, "Libraries in the Time of MOOCs," *EDUCAUSE Review*, November 4, 2013, http://er.educause.edu/articles/2013/11/libraries-in-the-time-of-moocs.
27. Ibid.
28. Carmen Kazakoff-Lane, "Environmental Scan and Assessment of OERs, MOOCs and Libraries: What Effectiveness and Sustainability Means for Libraries' Impact on Open Education" (white paper), accessed January 30, 2016, www.ala.org/acrl/sites/ala.org.acrl/files/content/publications/whitepapers/Environmental%20Scan%20and%20Assessment.pdf.

29. Ibid., 41.
30. Joshua Kim, "Better Residential Learning Is the True Innovation of MOOCs," *Inside Higher Ed*, November 10, 2015, www.insidehighered.com/blogs/technology-and-learning/better-residential-learning-true-innovation-moocs.
31. Ibid.
32. Stefanie Di Russo, "About," *I Think; I Design*, October 1, 2011, https://ithinkidesign.wordpress.com/about.
33. Stefanie Di Russo, "A Brief History of Design Thinking: How Design Thinking Came to Be," *I Think; I Design* (blog), June 8, 2012, https://ithinkidesign.wordpress.com/2012/06/08/a-brief-history-of-design-thinking-how-design-thinking-came-to-be.
34. Peter N. Miller, "Is 'Design Thinking' the New Liberal Arts?" *The Chronicle of Higher Education*, March 26, 2015, http://chronicle.com/article/Is-Design-Thinking-the-New/228779.
35. Association of College and Research Libraries, *Framework for Information Literacy in Higher Education* (Chicago: American Library Association, 2016), www.ala.org/acrl/sites/ala.org.acrl/files/content/issues/infolit/Framework-ILHE.pdf.
36. nina de jesus, "Locating the Library in Institutional Oppression," *In the Library with the Lead Pipe* (blog), September 24, 2014, www.inthelibrarywiththeleadpipe.org/2014/locating-the-library-in-institutional-oppression.
37. Angela Galvan, "Soliciting Performance, Hiding Bias: Whiteness and Librarianship," *In the Library with the Lead Pipe* (blog), June 3, 2015, www.inthelibrarywiththeleadpipe.org/2015/soliciting-performance-hiding-bias-whiteness-and-librarianship; April Hathcock, "White Librarianship in Blackface: Diversity Initiatives in LIS," *In the Library with the Lead Pipe* (blog), October 7, 2015, www.inthelibrarywiththeleadpipe.org/2015/lis-diversity; Jennifer Vinopal, "The Quest for Diversity in Library Staffing: From Awareness to Action," *In the Library with the Lead Pipe* (blog), January 13, 2016, www.inthelibrarywiththeleadpipe.org/2016/quest-for-diversity.
38. Tara, "Critical Librarianship: An Interview with Toni Samek," *The (Unofficial) BCLA Intellectual Freedom Committee Blog*, November 13, 2007, https://bclaifc.wordpress.com/2007/11/13critical-librarianship-an-interview-with-toni-samek.
39. Kenny Garcia, "Keeping Up with . . . Critical Librarianship," American Library Association, accessed January 30, 2016, www.ala.org/acrl/publications/keeping_up_with/critlib.
40. Kristina Parsons, "In Defense of Critical Design," *Artsy*, Editorial, July 21, 2015, www.artsy.net/article/artsy-editorial-in-defense-of-critical-design.
41. Tobias Revell, "Critical Design/Design Fiction Lecture Finally Written Up," *Occasional Blog of Tobias Revell*, February 12, 2013, http://blog.tobiasrevell.com/2013/12/critical-design-design-fiction-lecture.html.
42. Parsons, "In Defense of Critical Design."

43. Sean Michael Morris, "MMID: Toward a Critical Instructional Design," *Digital Pedagogy Lab* (blog), January 31, 2016, www.digitalpedagogylab.com/toward-a-critical-instructional-design.
44. Aaron Schmidt and Amanda Etches, *Useful, Usable, Desirable: Applying User Experience Design to Your Library* (Chicago: ALA Editions, 2014), 71.
45. Brian Mathews and Leigh Ann Soistmann, *Encoding Space: Shaping Learning Environments That Unlock Human Potential* (Chicago: Association of College and Research Libraries, 2016).
46. Design Thinking for Libraries, accessed January 30, 2016, http://designthinkingforlibraries.com.
47. +Acumen, "Design Kit: The Course for Human-Centered Design," accessed January 30, 2016, http://plusacumen.org/courses/hcd-for-social-innovation.
48. Gary Marchionini, Catherine Plaisant, and Anita Komlodi, "The People in Digital Libraries: Multifaceted Approaches to Assessing Needs and Impact" (paper, University of North Carolina, School of Information and Library Science, Chapel Hill, NC), accessed January 30, 2016, http://ils.unc.edu/~march/revision.pdf.

BIBLIOGRAPHY

Alexander, Bryan, and Rebecca Frost Davis. "Should Liberal Arts Campuses Do Digital Humanities? Process and Products in the Small College World." In *Debates in the Digital Humanities*, edited by Matthew K. Gold and Lauren F. Klein. Minneapolis: University of Minnesota Press, 2012; 2013 digital edition. Accessed January 29, 2016. http://dhdebates.gc.cuny.edu/debates/text/25.

Alexander, Laurie, Beau D. Case, Karen E. Downing, Melissa Gomis, and Eric Maslowsk. "Librarians and Scholars: Partners in Digital Humanities." *EDUCAUSE Review*, June 4, 2014. http://er.educause.edu/articles/2014/6/librarians-and-scholars-partners-in-digital-humanities.

Blackwell, Christopher, and Thomas R. Martin. "Technology, Collaboration, and Undergraduate Research." *DHQ: Digital Humanities Quarterly* 3, no. 1 (2009). www.digitalhumanities.org/dhq/vol/3/1/000024/000024.html.

Burdick, Anne, Johanna Drucker, Peter Lunenfeld, Todd Presner, and Jeffrey Schnapp. "A Short Guide to the Digital Humanities." In *Digital Humanities*, 121–136. Cambridge, MA: MIT Press, 2012. http://jeffreyschnapp.com/wp-content/uploads/2013/01/D_H_ShortGuide.pdf.

Cech, Maureen. "Digital Humanities: Home." University of Delaware Library. Accessed January 29, 2016. http://guides.lib.udel.edu/c.php?g=85603&p=548790.

Churchill, Suzanne W., and Adam McKible, eds. *Little Magazines and Modernism: New Approaches*. Burlington, VT: Ashgate, 2007.

CUNY Academic Commons. "Defining the Digital Humanities." Accessed January 29, 2016. http://commons.gc.cuny.edu/wiki/index.php/Defining_the_Digital_Humanities.

Davidson, Cathy N., and David Theo Goldberg. *The Future of Learning Institutions in a Digital Age*. John D. and Catherine T. MacArthur Foundation Reports on Digital Media and Learning. Cambridge, MA: MIT Press, 2009.

de jesus, nina. "Locating the Library in Institutional Oppression." *In the Library with the Lead Pipe* (blog), September 24, 2014. www.inthelibrarywiththeleadpipe.org/2014/locating-the-library-in-institutional-oppression.

Esposito, Joseph. "MOOCs Rise from the Ashes." *The Scholarly Kitchen* (blog), November 23, 2015. https://scholarlykitchen.sspnet.org/2015/11/23/moocs-rise-from-the-ashes.

Garcia, Kenny. "Keeping Up with . . . Critical Librarianship." American Library Association. Accessed January 30, 2016. www.ala.org/acrl/publications/keeping_up_with/critlib.

Godin, Seth. "Embracing Constraints," *Seth's Blog*, July 20, 2011, http://sethgodin.typepad.com/seths_blog/2011/07/embracing-constraints.html.

Hepler, Jason. "What Is Digital Humanities?" WhatIsDigitalHumanities.com. Accessed January 29, 2016. http://whatisdigitalhumanities.com.

Hollands, Fiona M., and Devayani Tirthali. "MOOCs: Expectations and Reality—Full Report." New York: Center for Benefit-Cost Studies of Education, Teachers College, Columbia University, May 2014. http://cbcse.org/wordpress/wp-content/uploads/2014/05/MOOCs_Expectations_and_Reality.pdf.

Jackson, Korey, and Aaron McCollough. "Introducing Digital Humanities (Full)." Prezi.com, August 7, 2014. https://prezi.com/r7rmqbxifpq9/introducing-digital-humanities-full.

Jaguszewski, Janice M., and Karen Williams. *New Roles for New Times: Transforming Liaison Roles in Research Libraries*. Washington, DC: Association of Research Libraries, 2013. www.arl.org/storage/documents/publications/nrnt-liaison-roles-revised.pdf.

Kazakoff-Lane, Carmen. "Environmental Scan and Assessment of OERs, MOOCs and Libraries: What Effectiveness and Sustainability Means for Libraries' Impact on Open Education." White paper. Accessed January 30, 2016. www.ala.org/acrl/sites/ala.org.acrl/files/content/publications/whitepapers/Environmental%20Scan%20and%20Assessment.pdf.

Keener, Alix. "The Arrival Fallacy: Collaborative Research Relationships in the Digital Humanities." *DHQ: Digital Humanities Quarterly*, September 2, 2015. www.digitalhumanities.org/dhq/vol/9/2/000213/000213.html.

Kendrick, Curtis, and Irene Gashurov. "Libraries in the Time of MOOCs." *EDUCAUSE Review*, November 4, 2013. http://er.educause.edu/articles/2013/11/libraries-in-the-time-of-moocs.

Kim, Joshua. "Better Residential Learning Is the True Innovation of MOOCs." *Inside Higher Ed*, November 10, 2015. www.insidehighered.com/blogs/technology-and-learning/better-residential-learning-true-innovation-moocs.

Kirschenbaum, Matthew G. "What Is Digital Humanities and What's It Doing in English Departments?" *ADE Bulletin*, no. 150 (2010): 55–63. doi:10.1632/ade.75.55.

Langer, Ellen J. *Mindfulness*. Reading, MA: Addison-Wesley, 1989.

Lankes, R. David. *The Atlas of New Librarianship*. Cambridge, MA: MIT Press, 2011.

Marchionini, Gary, Catherine Plaisant, and Anita Komlodi. "The People in Digital Libraries: Multifaceted Approaches to Assessing Needs and Impact." Paper, University of North Carolina, School of Information and Library Science, Chapel Hill, NC. Accessed January 30, 2016. http://ils.unc.edu/~march/revision.pdf.

Mathews, Brian, and Leigh Ann Soistmann. *Encoding Space: Shaping Learning Environments That Unlock Human Potential*. Chicago: Association of College and Research Libraries, 2016.

McGann, Jerome. "Radiant Textuality." *Victorian Studies* 39, no. 3 (Spring 1996): 379–90.

Morrisson, Mark. "Preface." In *Little Magazines and Modernism: New Approaches*, edited by Suzanne W. Churchill and Adam McKible, x. Burlington, VT: Ashgate, 2007.

Muñoz, Trevor. "Digital Humanities in the Library Isn't a Service." *Notebook* (blog), August 19, 2012. http://trevormunoz.com/notebook/2012/08/19/doing-dh-in-the-library.html.

Nelson, Cary. *Repression and Recovery: Modern American Poetry and the Politics of Cultural Memory, 1910–1945*. Madison: University of Wisconsin Press, 1989.

Schaffner, Jennifer, and Ricky Erway. *Does Every Research Library Need a Digital Humanities Center?* Dublin, OH: OCLC Research, 2014. www.oclc.org/content/dam/research/publications/library/2014/oclcresearch-digital-humanities-center-2014.pdf.

Schmidt, Aaron, and Amanda Etches. *Useful, Usable, Desirable: Applying User Experience Design to Your Library*. Chicago: ALA Editions, 2014.

Senchyne, Jonathan. "An Introduction to the Digital Humanities for Librarians." Webcast. Accessed January 29, 2016. http://ics.webcast.uwex.edu/Mediasite6/Play/3bdbc88895e54cd59265684550cd387c1d.

Siemens, George. "Learning and Knowing in Networks: Changing Roles for Educators and Designers." Paper presented to the Instructional Technology Forum, Department of Instructional Technology, University of Georgia, January 27, 2008. www.ingedewaard.net/papers/connectivism/2008_siemens_Learning_Knowing_in_Networks_changingRolesForEducatorsAndDesigners.pdf.

Swanson, Sara. "Copyright Cop on the MOOC Beat." *DavidsonX* (blog), March 24, 2014. http://blogs.davidson.edu/davidsonx/2014/03/24/copyright-cop-on-the-mooc-beat.

Varner, Stewart. "What DH Could Be." *Scholarship, Libraries, Technology* (blog), January 10, 2016. http://stewartvarner.com/2016/01/10/what-dh-could-be.

Wu, Kerry. "Academic Libraries in the Age of MOOCs." *Reference Services Review* 41, no. 3 (2013): 576–87.

KAREN MANN

7
Digital Media in the Modern University

Integrating digital media into the curriculum is a good instructional strategy that can make a huge impact on student learning in higher education. This media format is growing exponentially, creating ample opportunity for university faculty to integrate these resources to increase student attention, engagement, and learning. All of us are exposed to a wide variety of digital media daily. One Google search can bring thousands, even millions, of results that can then be sorted by media types, including websites, images, videos, and more. A report by the Nellie Foundation asserts, "Computer technology and digital media have fundamentally transformed all aspects of our lives, and many education reformers agree that it can and must be an important part of our current efforts to personalize education."[1] Due to the digital media technologies that are now available to the educator, an opportunity has been created for librarians, instructional designers, and faculty to work together to build well-crafted and pedagogically sound courses, thereby meeting a critical need in higher education. With each department bringing its expertise to the table, a powerful pool of knowledge and skills can be used to improve student learning and enhance the student experience.

WHAT ARE DIGITAL MEDIA?

Wikipedia defines media as "collective communication outlets or tools that are used to store and deliver information or data."[2] Today, these communication outlets and tools are expanding, providing an overwhelming variety and abundance of resources for faculty to incorporate into classes. Many of these resources are now available in digital format and exist online, on DVDs, or on CDs, making it even easier for course integration. *Wikipedia* defines digital media as

> any media that are encoded in a machine-readable format. Digital media can be created, viewed, distributed, modified and preserved on computers. Computer programs and software; digital imagery, digital video; web pages and websites, including social media; data and databases; digital audio, such as mp3s; and e-books are examples of digital media.[3]

Think about the plethora of digital media resources that are now at our fingertips, especially when one considers the immense variety of media now available online. This wealth of digital media resources is definitely beneficial to education; however, it also creates a situation where filtering out the most appropriate resources for a particular curriculum can be difficult for faculty. Not only is filtering these resources an issue, but also determining the best method of delivery to the student. This is where the librarian and instructional designer can assist the instructor in making good choices. The librarian has the expertise to locate, collect, and recommend these resources to faculty. The instructional designer has the expertise to assist the instructor with embedding these digital media resources into the curriculum. Working together, the librarian and instructional designer can provide the prospect for faculty to use the most appropriate, interesting, unbiased, current, authoritative, and accurate digital media available today.

THE IMPORTANCE OF MULTIMODAL LEARNING

Multimodal learning is a term that has been discussed in education for years, but it still remains an important concept when creating engaging classes that meet the needs of all students. Providing multimodal learning opportunities is an instructional strategy that can cater to the diversity of students and their learning preferences. So what exactly is multimodal learning? The New London Group describes multimodal design as an interconnection between linguistic design, visual design, audio design, gestural design, and spatial design.[4] Michael Sankey, Dawn Birch, and Michael Gardiner state that "[m]ultimodal learning environments allow instructional elements to be presented in more than one sensory mode (visual, aural, written)."[5] Jeff Bezemer notes that

> multimodality assumes that representation and communication always draw on a multiplicity of modes, all of which contribute to meaning. It focuses on analyzing and describing the full repertoire of meaning-making resources that people use (visual, spoken, gestural, written, three-dimensional, and others, depending on the domain of representation) in different contexts, and on developing means that show how these are organized to make meaning.[6]

Whether we learn better through visual content, auditory content, textual content, or a combination thereof, providing multimodal options to students is a best practice that teachers can incorporate into their classes. This technique not only serves those with different learning preferences but also creates an embedded opportunity to reteach, support, or challenge a student using a variety of modes of learning. The Universal Design model encourages this approach to teaching:

> Student-centered learning models acknowledge that content can and must be presented in multiple ways in order to provide access for students who learn best in particular ways, as well as deepen learning for all students. Universal Design for Learning is an approach to curriculum design that aims to address the needs of the broadest range of learners by highlighting the importance of providing multiple means of representation, expression, and engagement.[7]

The availability of multimodal content is abundant and diverse, especially in the digital age. If faculty can incorporate multiple modes of content into their courses, this can be a very powerful tool to meet student needs. A white paper on multimodal learning, commissioned by Cisco, notes:

> Our brains are wired to process visual input very differently from text, auditory, and sound. Recent technological advances through functional Magnetic Resonance Imaging (fMRI) scans confirm a dual coding system through which visuals and text/auditory input are processed in separate channels, presenting the potential for simultaneous augmentation of learning. The bottom line is that students using well-designed combinations of visuals and text learn more than students who only use text.[8]

Sankey, Birch, and Gardiner state:

> In recent years, the use of multimedia in conjunction with hypermedia have been successfully applied to many e-learning environments in order to both enhance these environments and to cater for a wider

> variety of student learning styles (Birch & Gardiner, 2005; Sankey & St Hill, 2009; Sprague & Dahl, 2010). Neuroscience research has also revealed that "significant increases in learning can be accomplished through the informed use of visual and verbal multimodal learning" (Fadel, 2008, p. 12). In other words, students may feel more comfortable and perform better when learning in environments that cater for their predominant learning style (Cronin, 2009; Omrod, 2008). This is known as the "meshing hypothesis" (Pashler et al., 2008, p. 109). It has also been seen that presenting material in a variety of modes may also encourage students to develop a more versatile approach to their learning (Hazari, 2004).[9]

Teaching with multimodal content is a researched-based approach to student learning that can increase mastery and retention of information. Faculty, librarians, and instructional designers can work together to use digital media for that purpose.

MULTIMEDIA

Digital multimedia are a great way to satisfy the need for multiple modes in a class. By embedding these digital resources into the curriculum, students will have access to content communicated through audio, video, and even text. Sankey, Birch, and Gardiner state, "The innovative use of educational technologies provides higher education institutions valuable opportunities for their staff to design media enhanced, interactive, more inclusive and engaging learning environments. The key motivation for incorporating educational technologies into the curricula is unquestionably the desire to improve the engagement and learning of students."[10] They further suggest that "the increasing use of multimedia in teaching has provided many opportunities to present multiple representations of content (text, video, audio, images, interactive elements) to cater more effectively to the different learning styles and modal preferences of an increasingly diverse student body."[11]

In research conducted by Sankey, Birch, and Gardiner, they found that students preferred having content represented in multiple modes.[12] With that in mind, faculty who make it a priority to incorporate multimedia into their courses are posed to not only meet their students' learning preferences but also get them interested, excited, and engaged in the content. How often do students use digital media to meet personal needs? Most students of this generation and younger will go directly to the Internet and to websites such as YouTube to learn about something new. Why not harness that behavior to create inquiry-based learning opportunities in the classroom? Using technology that students are familiar with and interested in can gain their attention and increase student engagement. If faced with the choice of listening to faculty lecture for an hour or watching a video, simulation, or other media resource followed by the instructor discussing the highlights and extending the conversation, it is probable that the student would choose the latter.

Incorporating digital media into the class curriculum also provides the opportunity to incorporate relevant, authentic, and timely resources that demonstrate how the content being covered is pertinent to the real world. Students can be exposed to real-world issues in context through media resources. "Inquiry develops from a question or problem arising out of experience. Meaningful questions are inspired by genuine curiosity about real-world experiences and challenges."[13] Instructors can use that curiosity to their advantage. By choosing the right digital media resources, faculty can create an environment conducive to inquiry and enlightenment. That is a powerful learning tool. Collaboratively, librarians and instructional designers can encourage and facilitate the use of digital multimedia resources in the classroom. To ensure appropriate selections are made, it is essential that librarians offer their expertise to make certain that the digital multimedia resources chosen are relevant to course objectives and of good quality. The instructional designer can assist faculty with determining the best technology tools available to provide access to students. With both university departments involved in this mission, it is more likely that faculty will adopt this instructional strategy.

DIGITAL LITERACY

Digital media and other technology tools are widely used by college students on a daily basis; however, there is still a great need to educate students in order to make sure they are actually what one would consider digitally literate. By incorporating technologies into the classroom, instructors can expose students to the vast amount of valuable digital resources available and provide the opportunity to utilize them in a manner appropriate for higher education and their careers. "As is the case for literacy in general, digital literacy has a power dimension; in the last few decades, it has transformed from technical or specialist literacy into an everyday literacy. Teaching with digital technology has therefore also to do with preparation of pupils for future participation in an evolving society where new media practices are deeply embedded in the associated structures and processes."[14] Increased digital literacy increases lifelong learning and problem-solving skills. These are skills that can be called upon in students' current situations, future careers, and whatever life has in store for them. Librarians, instructional designers, and faculty are able to work together not only to incorporate information literacy into the college classroom but also to ensure students are aware of and prepared to use the digital skills they will need in the future.

DIGITAL MEDIA RESOURCES AVAILABLE IN ACADEMIC LIBRARIES

The plethora of digital media that librarians have access to today is quite diverse and includes both free and fee-based resources. The twenty-first-century librarian understands that he or she can no longer concentrate on only what is in the physical building but that the immense digital media resources available online must always be considered when collecting resources that can be useful for a particular program, class, or project. Librarians now think multimodally. Websites, LibGuides, media databases, article databases, digital archives, e-reserves, online simulations, instructional software, online periodicals, and the multitude of other resources can be considered when locating resources for courses. If instructional designers are informed of the digital resources being suggested by librarians, they can provide not only support to the instructors but also recommendations to those who seek assistance with their course design. This recommendation will hopefully result in the instructor working closely with the librarian to ensure that the ideal resource is chosen and incorporated into the course. In return, instructional designers can inform librarians of digital resources they are recommending to faculty and the options available to provide students ease of access. This exchange of information can make a huge impact on course design and enrichment. The more professors are exposed to these resources, the more likely they are to utilize them. Obtaining support and guidance from multiple departments provides another layer of comfort for faculty who are new to a particular digital media resource and decreases the fear of taking a "risk."

BUILDING RELATIONSHIPS

Building relationships between instructional designers and librarians is vital to developing a collaborative effort that serves both faculty and students. At many institutions, this may be more difficult if there is a separation of departments to the point where both feel proprietary toward their programs and the services they provide. Hopefully this is not the case at most universities, but if such a situation exists, it is worth the effort to build a bridge. The advantages of working together will benefit not only each department but also, and more importantly, faculty and students. Collectively, both departments have resources and areas of interest that can be combined to reach a common goal of providing access to and supporting the variety of digital, informational, media, and other technology tools that are currently available to university faculty and staff. Universities spend significant portions of their yearly budgets on both academic technologies and library resources. Working together, the librarian and instructional designer can ensure that information, training, and support are provided in the best manner possible, reaching many more users than possible if working separately. The collective support from both departments will provide faculty with an increased sense of comfort that is important when implementing new digital tools and resources into their curricula. For faculty, implementing these tools can be a risky endeavor, sometimes leaving them uncertain if the new approach is worth it. However, if a joint effort is made by both departments, the number of instructors utilizing these technologies will more than likely increase. It is advantageous to both university libraries and academic technology to team up to increase awareness, training, and support for these resources. Building relationships between the two departments is the key to developing this joint venture.

Sharing Information

The sharing of information between the instructional designer and the librarian is critical to ensuring that they are able to support each other and faculty when using the technology tools available. Think of the number of library resources that are technology based, many of which have the capability of being embedded in online course sites or learning management systems. A concerted effort can be made by both departments to share information about these resources in order to increase utilization by faculty. With this shared knowledge, the instructional designer and librarian can encourage usage when appropriate for the pedagogical needs of a particular course. One simple thing instructional designers can do is extend an invitation to librarians for training workshops. This creates an awareness of the technology tools available, and armed with that information, librarians can determine if those tools can be useful for improving access to digital resources. Workshops that pertain to LMS tools and digital media creation tools are definitely sessions that librarians may find relevant. Also, any training sessions that were developed with university initiatives in mind, such as active learning strategies, the flipped classroom model, multimodal learning, and simulation learning, to name only a few, may be of interest. Once the training session is complete, librarians and instructional designers can brainstorm on collaborative possibilities.

The benefits of sharing information between instructional designers and librarians were seen in a recent faculty training workshop conducted at Johnson & Wales University–Charlotte. The session presented ideas and techniques to add academic challenge and support options into the curriculum to differentiate learning based on the needs of the students. As part of the academic support component of the training, the instructional designer demonstrated several digital resources and how they can be embedded into Blackboard, the LMS available to all courses. Specific tools discussed included linking to specific LibGuides, embedding librarian contact information with images, embedding media from media databases, and embedding the library chat tool. The presentation of these digital library resources was well received by the faculty who attended, many of whom were not aware that these technologies could be embedded so easily into their classes. Without the library sharing this information with the instructional designer, the opportunity for faculty to discover these resources would have been decreased.

Sharing information can also provide the knowledge for both departments to be able to provide faculty and student technology support on certain digital tools. How many students are working right this moment in the library on an assignment that has some type of technology or digital media involved? If both departments share a known issue and its resolution, they can assist their students and decrease their frustration level. This process can be as simple as picking up the phone or sending an e-mail to mention an issue that occurred. Even if a resolution cannot be determined immediately, at least the issue has been discussed so the instructional designer or librarian can share that information with faculty or students when applicable.

A perfect example of this type of collaboration occurred a few years ago at a university when Blackboard was made available for traditional courses. The issue involved lost student assignment submissions. Blackboard assignments created by professors required students to submit their assignments online. Librarians had encountered a few cases in which students were unable to submit. In these cases, the students were typing an essay directly into a submission text box instead of creating and saving the document in another software program, such as Microsoft Word, and then submitting it as an attachment. If the entry took a tremendous amount of time to complete, students were timing out, resulting in the loss of the data typed. This data could not be recovered, causing a tremendous amount of frustration on the students' end. A call was made from the library to academic technology to discuss the issue, of which the instructional designer had been unaware. While there was not a fix to the time-out issue, there was a way to reduce the issue from occurring in the first place. Faculty were made aware of the problem by the instructional designer during consultations and training sessions and were encouraged to have their students create and save assignments in a word-processing program first and then submit them as attachments. This knowledge has significantly reduced the occurrence of cases such as these. Another example of the benefit of sharing information was found when difficulties arose in viewing digital media embedded in an LMS from Films on Demand. The instructional designer was notified by a student and instructor of the inability to view a video. The instructional designer informed the library of the incident and both departments worked together to ascertain the problem. The librarians were able to post information for students on the library website as well as within the LMS course to ensure that students understand how to access proprietary-based media databases when off campus. By sharing this information, a resolution was quickly found to reduce the number of students experiencing difficulties viewing Films on Demand media through the LMS.

All three of the cases just described are real examples of how sharing information between departments can increase resolution timeliness and reduce student and faculty frustrations when issues are encountered. This multidepartmental approach to technology resource support and guidance can encourage the adoption of digital resources, making the time spent well worth the effort.

Collaborative Faculty Consultations

Providing collaborative support sessions with faculty can provide a one-stop shop for those who are looking to enhance their curricula and teaching methods. The instructional designer and librarian can meet with an instructor to talk about current practices and instructional strategies and then brainstorm ideas on ways to integrate appropriate technologies, media, and other digital resources into the curriculum using sound pedagogical principles. Ideas that can be discussed during these consultations are wide and varied and fairly unique to each instructor. Here is a sample consultation: A professor is interested in adding more multimodal content into an upcoming unit. The librarian and instructional designer will review unit objectives with the professor and discuss the various digital resources that are available in multiple formats. The librarian can conduct a search of existing library resources as well as websites and other freeware available online to select the most appropriate resources. While evaluating the various content resources, the instructional designer can discuss ways in which the components can be provided to the students and the teaching strategies that can be applied, such as the flipped classroom concept or differentiated learning. If the decision is made to embed these digital resources into the course site, the instructional designer can discuss student assessment options as well as active learning techniques to increase knowledge retention and application.

At some universities, librarians are given access to online courses created in an LMS, such as Blackboard. Once this access is granted, the librarian can provide appropriate support and digital resources to students in a class for upcoming projects. At a consultation, the librarian and instructional designer can talk about this feature and what advantages it provides. If the instructor has an upcoming project, the librarian and instructional designer can discuss not only digital media integration into an LMS course but also the advantages of having an embedded librarian. The embedded librarian is typically well received by faculty because it reduces the time and training required by the instructor and increases student access and support. The instructional designer assists with this effort by facilitating the librarian implantation and by providing training to librarians on LMS tools. More about the embedded librarian is discussed in chapter 8.

Working together, a plan can be designed that incorporates the best ideas and tools from both departments, and once a strategy has been outlined, the instructor, librarian, and instructional designer can begin implementation. The positive effect that a collaborative session can have on enriching course curriculum is substantial and can be transformative.

Training for Library Staff

Instructional designers can extend an open invitation to librarians to all workshops offered. If this is not the current practice at your university, inquiring about the possibility of an invitation is a good first step in meeting this need. Attending these workshops will not only provide librarians with training on how to use specific tools that faculty and staff have access to but will also provide an opportunity for discussion about integrating digital media and other library resources. This knowledge can be very helpful during faculty consultations when recommendations are being made on the best digital resources available and options for integration.

Collaborative Faculty Training Workshops and Support

Collaborative faculty training workshops are a good way to integrate the services and resources of both departments to assist faculty with integrating digital technologies that are pedagogically appropriate. Faculty at all levels of technological savviness can benefit from training sessions that focus on best practices, digital tools, and techniques to incorporate these tools into their courses, especially into online course components such as an LMS course site. Several different training topics that are beneficial to instructors include digital media integration, database widget embeds, library chat window embeds, LibGuide training, information literacy module training, and the multitude of free tools that are available online. Academic Technology Services and the Academic Library at Johnson & Wales University–Denver collaborate on a multitude of workshops to make faculty aware of digital tools that are available and ways in which these resources can enhance their curricula (e.g., see figure 7.1). Some of their recent sessions included such presentations as "How to Make Assignments Visual," "Making Group Work Engaging," and "Making Finals Fun." These sessions include hands-on training on how to use specific technology tools and how these tools can be integrated into the LMS, if appropriate. Also included in the sessions is information concerning best practices. A LibGuide is created to provide resources to faculty after the session is completed, with librarians and academic technology continuing to provide guidance and support afterward. These types of collaborative training sessions can not only increase the digital literacy of students and faculty but also get the educator excited about trying something new. Activities such as these can also increase student interest and engagement.

University libraries and academic technology can also provide collaborative workshops on increasing student creativity through tools such as those

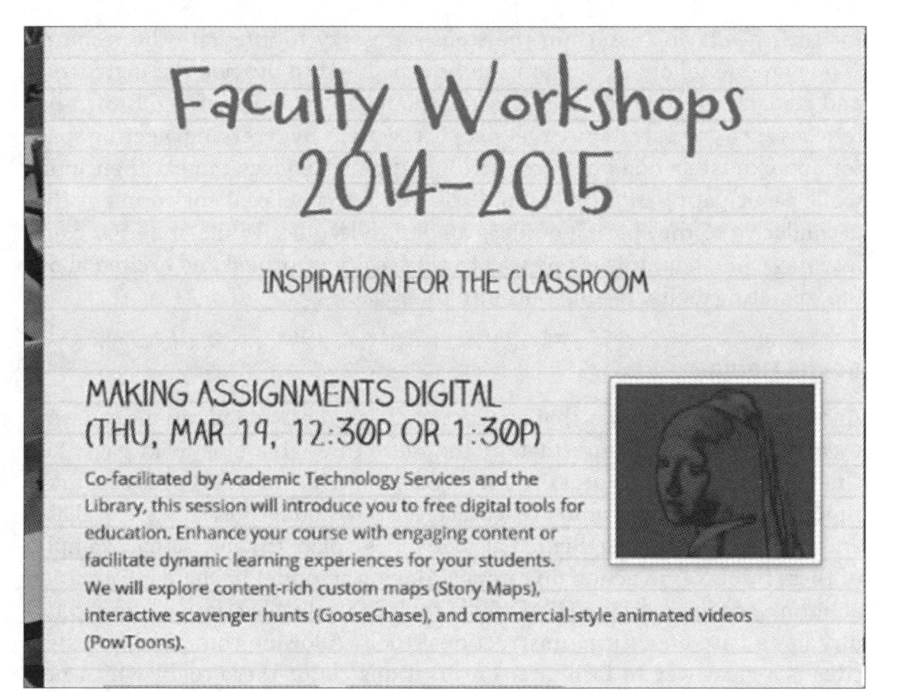

FIGURE 7.1
JWU–Denver LibGuide advertising collaborative workshops

found in the Adobe Creative Suite and other media applications. These software applications are typically found on university computers (including those in the library) and can provide an alternative format for synthesizing information. Digital media resources are available through installed or cloud applications that create visual representations of information, allowing students to express more creativity and increase their digital literacy. Additional ideas for collaborative workshops include student response systems, e-publications, and more. The possibilities here are immense.

Collaborative Small-Group Discussions

It is not always necessary to set up large formal training workshops to inform and assist faculty with digital resources. Small-group discussions, commonly conducted as brown-bag lunches, can be set up to allow for the free exchange of ideas and experiences between faculty, librarians, and instructional designers. Recruiting faculty who are already using digital media tools is a great way to share their experience with others and spark ideas. Attendees can ask questions of the librarian, instructional designer, or the professor who is utilizing the tool to determine if that digital media resource is appropriate for their needs and ascertain the steps necessary to integrate the resource. A one-on-one follow-up session can be scheduled to provide the instruction and guidance needed to get the faculty member up and running. Brown-bag lunches are a good strategy to get people together. By reserving meeting space for approximately one hour around lunchtime, attendees can eat their lunch while participating in the session. It creates a very relaxed environment that is conducive to the sharing of ideas among colleagues. While not a hands-on learning workshop, this is one way to get faculty informed and excited about incorporating digital media tools into their classes.

Social Media

Another collaborative way that instructional designers and librarians can work together is by sharing information and ideas through a blog, wiki page, LibGuide, Twitter, or some other social media platform. This form of communication provides the opportunity to let faculty know about tools that are available and to offer tips on using them. It also provides a place to share actual examples of these resources in action on campus. Having an outlet to share information about new or interesting digital media tools is a valuable strategy to keep faculty up-to-date on exciting instructional tools. Allowing comments on these sites is a great way to facilitate conversations about these tools, which may increase interest significantly. Word of mouth as a form of advertisement is an easy but effective way to motivate an instructor to try something new.

Open Houses

Conducting a collaborative open house is another good technique to market the digital media tools and resources that are available to faculty. The librarian and instructional designer can exhibit resources and answer questions as they arise. Demonstrating real examples of tool utilization is ideal. The open house can be on a large or small scale, depending on the time available to prepare for the event. It could be as simple as a show-and-tell type of occasion or much larger and include faculty who are manning stations where they present their digital tool integration and discuss its effect on student learning. Both are quite beneficial to faculty.

ISSUES TO CONSIDER

Digital media resources and tools are a great way for instructors to enhance how and what they are already teaching in the classroom. Nonetheless, as these tools become available to faculty, certain issues may arise.

Equipment Access

Incorporating digital media into the curriculum requires certain types of technological equipment to be readily available to faculty. If digital media resources are being used in a traditional classroom, the librarian and instructional designer must determine what equipment is needed to ensure not only the ability to view the media but also its ease of use. The instructional designer and librarian can be prepared to assist faculty by investigating the permanent classroom technologies available on campus by working with the IT department and mapping locations of technologically enhanced classrooms. Using this map when working with faculty will make determining equipment needs stress-free. We are in a day and age where most universities are installing computers and LCD (liquid crystal display) projectors into classrooms, making digital media integration a simple process. If the required equipment is not available in the classroom, however, the academic technology department, library, or IT department should have equipment available for checkout.

When integrating digital media into online course pages, equipment issues should not be as problematic. Typically, all that would be required is a computer and an Internet connection and perhaps a username and password in order to view the resource. One thing to keep in mind when using media online is the computer applications and plug-ins required to view certain media formats correctly. Also, applications such as antivirus software and other privacy settings can impact successful usage. If students and faculty are utilizing university computers, these types of issues should be less problematic; however, if students are using personal devices, especially mobile devices, these issues can become more significant. As these problems are reported, this information can be shared between the two departments so proactive measures can be taken to reduce user frustration.

Technology Support

Technology support is another area of concern when the use of digital equipment and resources is being encouraged. A technical support plan can be devised that contains just-in-time support resources such as user guides and video tutorials as well as information on who supports what. IT support contact information should also be readily available to faculty and students. Resources such as these can reduce user frustration, especially when the instructional designer or librarian is unavailable to provide assistance. In many situations, the user may be able to find the answer to his or her question or troubleshoot using the resources provided. Being proactive is beneficial and a time-saver for all parties involved.

Copyright Issues

When using digital media of any type, it is vital that copyright information be shared with faculty. It is important for both the instructional designer and the librarian to understand copyright law for digital media integration. In higher education, this can be a bit complicated due to the many formats in which media can be presented. Are the digital media going to be embedded in the LMS or within a LibGuide? Is a personal DVD going to be shared in a traditional classroom? Additional issues such as digitizing media for upload to online courses, use of streaming video sites such as Netflix and YouTube, embedding images and audio into presentations, and a plethora of others will come up at some point. Both departments need to understand copyright and assist faculty in utilizing digital media in a lawful way.

As this chapter has demonstrated, integrating digital media into university courses allows faculty to build more effective classes that ensure students have a variety of resources available to meet individual needs. All students are unique in the way they learn, and digital media can provide engaging multimodal content necessary to improve student learning. A campaign that includes collaborative marketing, training, communication, and support will encourage more faculty to take the risk and spend the time in an effort to enrich their curricula. With librarians and instructional designers working collectively to assist in the implementation of these resources, a transformation can take place that will have a positive effect on the students.

NOTES

1. Babette Moeller, Tim Reitzes, and Education Development Center, *Integrating Technology with Student-Centered Learning: A Report to the Nellie Mae Education Foundation* (Newton, MA: Education Development Center, 2011), 9.
2. *Wikipedia*, "Media (communication)," accessed April 18, 2016, https://en.wikipedia.org/w/index php?title=Media_(communication)&oldid=699182846.
3. *Wikipedia*, "Digital media," accessed April 18, 2016, https://en.wikipedia.org/w/index.php?title=Digital_media&oldid=700726440.
4. New London Group, "A Pedagogy of Multiliteracies: Designing Social Futures," *Harvard Educational Review* 66, no. 1 (1996): 60–92.
5. Michael Sankey, Dawn Birch, and Michael Gardiner, "Engaging Students through Multimodal Learning Environments: The Journey Continues," in *Curriculum, Technology and Transformation for an Unknown Future: Proceedings ASCILITE Sydney 2010*, ed. Caroline Steel, Mike Keppell, Phillipa Gerbic, and Simon Housego (Tugun QLD, Australia: ASCILITE, 2010), 853, www.ascilite.org/conferences/sydney10/procs/Sankey-full.pdf.
6. Jeff Bezemer, "What Is Multimodality?," MODE: Multimodal Methodologies, February 16, 2012, http://mode.ioe.ac.uk/2012/02/16/what-is-multimodality.

7. Moeller, Reitzes, and Education Development Center, *Integrating Technology with Student-Centered Learning*, 27.
8. Metiri Group, "Multimodal Learning through Media: What the Research Says" (white paper commissioned by Cisco Systems, 2008), 3, www.cisco.com/c/dam/en_us/solutions/industries/docs/education/Multimodal-Learning-Through-Media.pdf.
9. Sankey, Birch, and Gardiner, "Engaging Students through Multimodal Learning Environments," 853.
10. Ibid., 852.
11. Ibid., 852.
12. Ibid., 861.
13. Leo Casey and Bertram C. Bruce, "The Practice Profile of Inquiry: Connecting Digital Literacy and Pedagogy," *E-learning and Digital Media* 8, no. 1 (2011): 79.
14. Ibid., 77.

BIBLIOGRAPHY

Bezemer, Jeff. "What Is Multimodality?" MODE: Multimodal Methodologies. February 16, 2012. http://mode.ioe.ac.uk/2012/02/16/what-is-multimodality.

Casey, Leo, and Bertram C. Bruce. "The Practice Profile of Inquiry: Connecting Digital Literacy and Pedagogy." *E-learning and Digital Media* 8, no. 1 (2011): 76–85.

Metiri Group. "Multimodal Learning through Media: What the Research Says." White paper, commissioned by Cisco Systems, 2008. www.cisco.com/c/dam/en_us/solutions/industries/docs/education/Multimodal-Learning-Through-Media.pdf.

Moeller, Babette, Tim Reitzes, and Education Development Center. *Integrating Technology with Student-Centered Learning: A Report to the Nellie Mae Education Foundation*. Newton, MA: Education Development Center, 2011.

New London Group. "A Pedagogy of Multiliteracies: Designing Social Futures." *Harvard Educational Review* 66, no. 1 (1996): 60–92.

Sankey, Michael, Dawn Birch, and Michael Gardiner. "Engaging Students through Multimodal Learning Environments: The Journey Continues." In *Curriculum, Technology and Transformation for an Unknown Future: Proceedings ASCILITE SYDNEY 2010*, edited by Caroline Steel, Mike Keppell, Phillipa Gerbic, and Simon Housego, 852–863. Tugun QLD, Australia: ASCILITE, 2010. www.ascilite.org/conferences/sydney10/procs/Sankey-full.pdf.

Wikipedia. "Digital media." Accessed April 18, 2016. https://en.wikipedia.org/w/index.php?title=Digital_media&oldid=700726440.

Wikipedia. "Media (communication)." Accessed April 18, 2016. https://en.wikipedia.org/w/index.php?title=Media_(communication)&oldid=699182846.

KAREN MANN

8
Integrating the Library and the LMS

Librarians and instructional designers are natural allies in the effort to support the most ideal learning environments within the institutional learning management system. At most universities, the LMS course component can be considered the "hub" of the class, making it an ideal location to build a library presence and integrate library resources. The LMS is generally one of the most commonly utilized tools by the instructional technologist/designer in higher education. This individual often has the primary responsibility for preparing and supporting faculty to make the most of the multitude of features available, everything from creating engaging content to facilitating better online discussions to validating tests and quizzes. The librarian often interfaces with the LMS from the perspective of providing research support and over time has been able to significantly increase the librarian's presence in the LMS through integration of library resources and the embedding of librarians into courses.

The library's approach to LMS integration continues to evolve as more experience is gained in this area, especially as advances in the integration process expand, allowing for more automation. While both librarians and instructional designers often assist professors individually, a more focused partnership could be formed to promote the variety of ways in which library resources can be incorporated into individual LMS courses. Working together, the librarian and instructional designer can build a library presence in the LMS that increases awareness and provides the access and support needed to enhance the student experience and improve student learning.

LMS USAGE

The LMS has increasingly become an integral part of higher education, especially in the past decade. It would be surprising to find a university that did not provide faculty access to some type of LMS. The most common LMS platforms utilized in higher education today include Blackboard, Moodle, Canvas, Desire2Learn, eCollege, and Sakai, although there are many others. While access to these systems has become more common, the usage of the LMS still varies immensely from university to university and course to course. Much of this depends on the requirements of the institution, administrative oversight, and the training and support available to assist faculty with integrating this type of technology into their classes. While online and hybrid courses may require extensive guidance and support by the librarian and instructional designer because much or all of the content and resources must be in digital form, many traditional courses are now utilizing the LMS course as a central access point for all resources and content as well. This is a positive step for students in that the abundance and variety of multimodal resources that can now be integrated into their courses and accessed so easily can make a big difference in how well students learn and retain information.

What does this mean for the librarian? It means significant increases in time spent building, locating, and embedding resources into the LMS, as well as training, advising, and providing support, which are all essential components to encourage usage. A partnership between the librarian and instructional designer can provide some relief from the workload, ensure a well-crafted presence in the LMS, and promote the use of integration in order to increase student engagement and improve learning. Academic libraries are extremely interested in exploring methods to become more embedded in the LMS but must make well-informed decisions in order to ensure the process they choose meets the needs of the faculty and students at their universities.

In 2013 and 2014, EDUCAUSE surveyed 800 higher education institutions, 17,000 faculty, and more than 75,000 students to gather information on usage of learning management systems. The following statistics, which are quite interesting and pertinent to the instructional designer and librarian, should be considered as the library begins making decisions on an LMS integration strategy:

- 99 percent of institutions have an LMS in place.
- 85 percent of faculty use the LMS.
- 56 percent of faculty use the LMS daily.
- 83 percent of students use the LMS.
- 56 percent of students say they use the LMS in most or all courses.
- 56 percent of students say they wish their instructors used the LMS more.
- 74 percent of faculty say the LMS is a very useful tool to enhance teaching.
- 71 percent of faculty say the LMS is a very useful tool to enhance student learning.
- 47 percent of faculty make the LMS part of their daily digital routine.
- Faculty and students value the LMS as an enhancement to their teaching and learning experiences, but relatively few use the advanced features, and even fewer use these systems to their fullest capacity.
- Faculty say they could be more effective instructors—and students say they could be better students—if they were more skilled at using the LMS.
- Faculty are willing to receive more training to learn how to better use the LMS and are motivated mainly by evidence that suggests that what they do with the LMS will enhance student outcomes.[1]

These results indicate that the majority of faculty and students are using the LMS system quite frequently and would like to use it more if provided additional training. "Assisting faculty with the instructional integration of information technology" was found to be one of the top ten IT issues in higher education and an area that can be served by both the librarian and the instructional designer when implementing a library integration project.[2] Faculty want to use more technology in their courses, but the risk of trying to integrate new technologies can be an immense obstacle and minimize faculty use of tools that would benefit both the professors and the students. As the survey indicated, the LMS is accessed by many faculty and students on a daily basis and therefore is a prime spot for a library presence. However, it also demonstrates that certain areas such as guidance, training, and support need to be addressed in order to encourage more comprehensive usage. Librarians and instructional designers have the potential here to make a difference. As partners, they can develop a more in-depth library presence by building pathways to library resources within each course and providing the training and support needed, leading to increased library resource usage and LMS usage.

Figure 8.1 lists the top four motivators to integrate technology into teaching by institution type. It clearly demonstrates that a top area of concern found in all institution types is that before professors invest time into learning and implementing a new technology and resource into their courses, they need to see a clear indication that students will benefit in some way. As the librarian and instructional designer work with faculty, the effectiveness of specific system tools must be conveyed. This can be done by conducting technology demonstrations and eliciting feedback from other professors who have had successful implementations. Sharing other professors' experiences can be a powerful motivator and a source of encouragement for faculty who are looking for ideas to improve student learning in their classrooms. Three additional areas of concern discussed in figure 8.1 include (1) confidence in the system tool to work correctly; (2) the time it takes to redesign a course; and (3) a better understanding of appropriate tools available. As librarians and instructional designers work with faculty, these areas of concern should be kept in mind and addressed as early as possible to inspire usage and mitigate apprehension. Providing assistance with resource integration by embedding a librarian into a course will greatly minimize the time required by the professor and increase his or her comfort level.

Also, reassuring faculty that support and training will be provided is imperative in order to gain their confidence and provide them with the courage to try something new. "IT, educational technology, libraries, and centers for teaching and learning can use these findings to design (or redesign) professional development opportunities that allow faculty to experiment with underused LMS features."[3] To increase confidence and awareness of available technologies, the librarian and instructional designer can collaboratively provide the support and training required.

LIBRARY INTEGRATION INTO THE LMS

LMSs were initially adopted by higher education institutions due to the explosion of online learning classes, which have grown substantially over the past two decades. While the LMS still remains a constant and necessary tool for online courses, it is also now commonly used in blended and traditional courses as well. Most university systems automatically create an LMS course for each class in the registration system, encouraging more and more professors to use this component to post content and connect with their students. Thus, it is also an ideal location to provide student access to librarians and library resources. Rick Fisher and April Heany state, "Embedded practice enables librarians to become 'insiders' within faculties and courses."[4] Employing the LMS creates an opportunity to implant the library into the student's domain, allowing librarians to better serve their students by becoming "insiders" in the class. In a literature review conducted by Elizabeth L. Black and

	AA	BA pub.	BA priv.	MA pub.	MA priv.	DR pub.	DR priv.	Non-U.S.
Top interest	Clear indication/evidence that students would benefit							
2nd	Confidence that the technology would work the way I planned	Confidence that the technology would work the way I planned	Confidence that the technology would work the way I planned	Release time to design/redesign my courses	A better understanding of the types of technologies that are relevant to teaching and learning	Release time to design/redesign my courses	Release time to design/redesign my courses	Release time to design/redesign my courses
3rd	A better understanding of the types of technologies that are relevant to teaching and learning	Release time to design/redesign my courses	A better understanding of the types of technologies that are relevant to teaching and learning	Confidence that the technology would work the way I planned	Confidence that the technology would work the way I planned	A better understanding of the types of technologies that are relevant to teaching and learning	Confidence that the technology would work the way I planned	Confidence that the technology would work the way I planned

FIGURE 8.1

Faculty motivation to integrate more or better technology into teaching and curriculum by institution type

Betsy Blankenship, they note that most contributors "agree that the integration of library resources into learning management systems has the potential to significantly enrich the educational experience of students and increase student use of library materials."[5] They also state that students who are hard to reach, such as nontraditional students, those living off campus, and distance education students, find the LMS to be a convenient way to access and utilize library resources.[6] Considering that some students' campuses are actually only virtual, it is important that academic libraries have a presence online. As the survey mentioned earlier in the chapter indicates, students are already visiting the LMS course site quite frequently so it is the logical place for libraries to integrate their resources and to be "seen." "For academic libraries, incorporating library resources and services into an LMS offers the opportunity to improve library visibility, increase relevance with students, and strengthen relationships with faculty."[7] It is evident that the university library is discovering that the LMS is the "place to be"; however, the most difficult and vital part of the process, due to the complexities of university systems and the stakeholders involved, is the development and implementation of an integration strategy.

While there are many variations on how the library presence can be integrated in the LMS, the drawback is having the access and abilities needed to create the most effective and streamlined space:

> Despite the affordances of incorporating their services and resources, university libraries are rarely integrated into their institutions' LMS due to a number of institutional factors. Librarians are infrequently involved in the administration and management of courseware, must often negotiate with faculty to be given permission and access to a course website, and are often required to adapt pre-existing LMS roles such as instructor, graduate student instructor, curriculum support staff or administrator.[8]

Meredith Gorran Farkas traces the consideration of the role of librarians in LMSs:

> Cohen (2002) shared the results of a study which suggested that LMS developers were not considering the role libraries could play in the LMS nor how they could deliver content via the LMS. Unfortunately, even with Canvas, the newest LMS option, which is known for its flexibility, there is not a default librarian role, which suggests that libraries are still largely not being considered in LMS development (Perpich 2015). As a consequence, academic libraries have had to be creative in their approaches to embedding content, instruction, and librarians into the LMS environment.[9]

Although the librarian role may not be a default of the system, some institutions have created the "librarian" role to give appropriate and FERPA (Family

Educational Rights and Privacy Act)–compliant access. Typically, this role grants the ability to add content and integrate library resources into the course, which benefits both the students and the library. If libraries are represented in the LMS course, students will struggle less to locate the needed appropriate resources, reducing confusion, frustration, and the use of unscholarly sources.

Academic libraries have different ways in which they can utilize the LMS system to provide access and support for students. The idea of macrolevel and microlevel course integration of library resources, initially discussed by John D. Shank and Nancy H. Dewald,[10] is examined at great length in the literature when discussing different approaches to LMS course integration. Both integration levels are found throughout academic libraries, and in many cases, both are used in tandem.

Macrolevel Integration

The macrolevel method, which tends to be less time intensive in its implementation, is the integration of general library resources into LMS courses. Each LMS course is provided the same information. "The macro-level approach attains the goal of a library presence in the LMS in a scalable way that reaches many students with a single pathfinder. The downside is that the guides will need to be either very broad or too overwhelming a list to be useful as more specific resource guides might be."[11] The most common services or resources integrated at the macrolevel include pathways to access e-reserves, information literacy modules, library chat (instant messaging), and links acting as portals to library resources, such as webpages or LibGuides. While the macrolevel method may not be the most ideal implementation method for academic libraries, it does provide easy access to librarians and library resources, creating a library presence in the course that would not have been there otherwise. So, while not perfect, it is unquestionably a step in the right direction.

There are an abundance of examples of how universities are using the macrolevel integration method to extend a convenient access point for students. Northern Kentucky University uses both macrolevel and microlevel integration techniques in order to provide students with a gateway to library resources. The macrolevel method that was implemented includes a "My Library Tab" link that has been built into every Blackboard course in a prominent location.[12] It acts as a portal to general library resources. The University of Buffalo library developed a widget that is displayed in all online classes and provides catalog search boxes and commonly used links to library resources.[13] These components can be added by working with LMS administrators to build them into the general template of the LMS course.

Although these resources have not been customized for a particular course or department, the benefit gained is the easy access afforded to students with little or no labor required by the librarian or professor. In certain

LMSs, professors can choose to activate different types of library tools simply by enabling them. The way in which this is done is dependent on the system being utilized. One such component available is the learning object repository. This is an area where content can be placed and, if permission is granted, professors can enable access from within their courses. Libraries can use this component to build a spot for general resources or more specifically for resources such as e-reserves. It can also be a source of customized access if microlevel integration is being considered. The main benefit of the learning object repository is that it allows the librarian to update library resource information in one place. Although the learning object repository may cost an additional fee for the institution, since it could be considered an add-on, the ways in which it can benefit the library and other university departments make it an option worth exploring. If the "opt-in" procedure has been adopted by a university, librarians and instructional designers will need to engage in active marketing and training to ensure that faculty are aware of the tools and know how to activate them. Although there is probably an argument that supports the "opt-in" feature, especially if copyright issues for resources such as e-reserves are considered, the consistency of having the same library link found in every LMS course menu is ideal. Students, no matter the course in which they are enrolled, will know where to locate library resources when needed.

If the library is unable to incorporate library resources into the general LMS course template, librarians can work with their instructional designer to formulate ways to integrate their resources at the macrolevel one course at a time. The instructional designer can provide the training needed for the librarian or professor, dependent on the library's approach at integration. To make this tactic more scalable, it could perhaps be more realistic for librarians to focus on creating and updating a portal page and then instructing faculty on how to embed the link into their courses. The librarian and instructional designer can work together to provide the training, marketing, and support needed to increase this type of integration.

Microlevel Integration

A microlevel presence is defined as providing access to library resources at a course or departmental level. While this is certainly the most customized way to integrate resources into an LMS course, it is also the most time intensive if done manually course by course. Dependent on the size of the university, this type of integration may not be sustainable. There are a variety of factors that come into play when determining the type of process to use when individualizing library resources at the course or departmental level, with sustainability being at the forefront. If manual microlevel integration is not realistic for certain institutions, then exploring ways to automatically drive LMS users to more course-specific library resources is ideal. While this may involve a great deal of multidepartmental planning and collaboration, this streamlined process of integration can be a great enhancement to an LMS course if developed appropriately.

Many academic libraries begin resource integration by embedding chosen components into the LMS course manually, either by the librarian or by the faculty member. If librarians are expected to embed resources, an LMS access role must be assigned to them granting permissions to create content within the course. In many cases, as discussed throughout the literature, LMS administrators have created a role specifically for librarians providing the access level necessary. Although the "librarian" role may not be available at all universities, other existing access roles may be available that achieve the access needed without invading the privacy of the students (typically the grade center). The development of a librarian role is a good first step to microlevel library resource integration into an LMS course and may be worth a conversation with the university LMS administrator.

Once access has been granted, the content that can be added to courses is almost limitless. From hyperlinks to media to assessments to widgets, the multimodal components that can be added to a course can enhance the student experience, increase awareness of library resources, and improve the quality of final student products. Many institutions are providing links to resources found on the library website, such as LibGuides or research guides that are appropriate for the course as a whole or for specific research projects. "Research guides are becoming increasingly instructionally robust. In addition to providing useful resources, many librarians include search tips, tutorials, and videos in the guides they create for courses and subjects. Integrating research guides into the LMS makes librarians' instructional content more visible and accessible."[14] The inclusion of links to research guides or other webpages outside of the LMS can decrease the workload of the librarian by allowing the resource to be accessed by multiple courses and terms and by minimizing the labor involved in the updating of resource material since it can be accomplished in one location. Other components that can be embedded include discussion forums, instant messaging functions, and content—all of which provide easy access to information and library assistance. While these components can undoubtedly provide students with much-needed support and guidance, the main concern involved with this type of embedded librarian technique is the extent of the labor involved.

Johnson & Wales University–Charlotte has developed a program called the Personal Librarian. This program evolved from studying similar programs at other institutions. The librarian works with professors in assigned departments to provide not only information literacy training but also volunteers to be embedded into the Blackboard course in order to connect with students, add information about library resources, and add links to applicable resources, such as the library virtual chat tool. Professors also have the option to embed widgets into their courses such as catalog and database search mechanisms. To gain access to the course, the librarian is granted permission from the professor and then works with the instructional technologist to be assigned the "librarian" role. This role allows the librarian the ability to create, edit, and delete course components but keeps the grade center inaccessible. This ensures that the librarian can embed all of the needed resources but the course remains FERPA compliant. See figure 8.2 for one example of how librarians at JWU–Charlotte are embedding information and resource links into individual courses.

The librarians at Johnson & Wales University–Denver are not only adding content to Blackboard courses on their campus but also using the embedded role to determine training needs of faculty. Melissa Izzo, the instructional technologist at JWU–Denver, states, "Since our librarians are embedded in a large number of ulearn [Blackboard] sites, they have an in-depth knowledge of current assignments that faculty like to use. This helps tremendously with picking workshop topics and tools that will be relevant. As an instructional technologist, I'm able to provide the insight about how the tools we present can work with our LMS and what other technology we have available to facilitate the assignments or faculty content."[15] This collaborative strategy between the library and academic technology can certainly assist with meeting the training needs that are applicable to faculty.

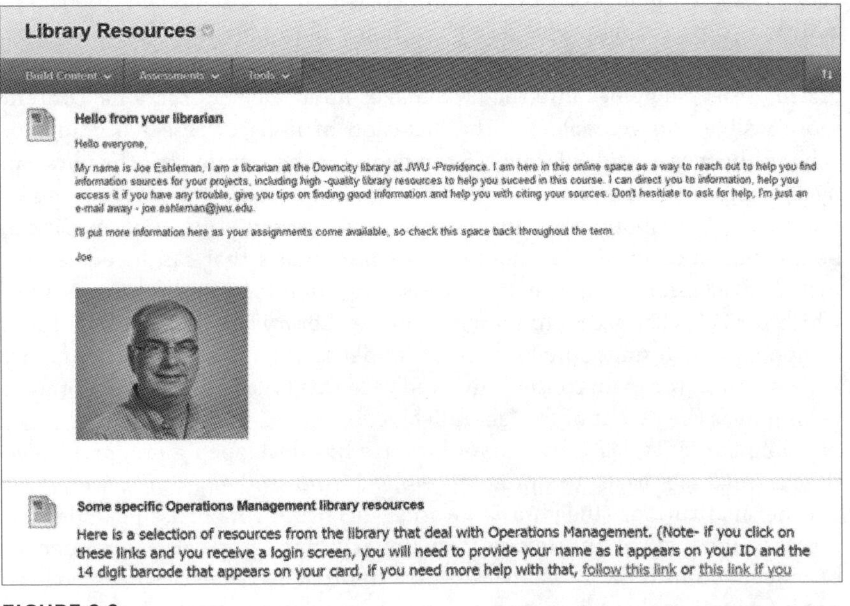

FIGURE 8.2
Example of microlevel integration at JWU–Charlotte

The library programs just discussed are excellent examples of manual microlevel integration and may work well for smaller universities or on a course-by-course basis. However, this technique is not a sustainable function at universities if the goal is to create a presence in all LMS courses. In order to overcome this obstacle, many academic libraries have been working with LMS administrators to develop automated processes that send specific courses to specific resources based on the course number. This automated process can increase not only the efficiency of microlevel integration but also its long-term sustainability.

At Duke University, programming has been developed so that with a click of a library hyperlink found in every LMS course menu, the user is sent to a LibGuide designed for the subject code of the course.[16] This dynamic process sends students to resources specifically chosen for their courses or departments and prevents librarians from having to access each individual course to embed tailored resources. Ohio State University uses a toolkit approach to integrate the library into each LMS course. The first component of the toolkit includes the creation of a learning object repository that contains all of the e-reserves for the library. The librarian has been granted privileges that provide access to the LMS course and the ability to enable course access to the e-reserves. The advantages of this component include providing access to specific courses that need information from e-reserves, the librarian's ability to enable e-reserves within the LMS course without bothering the professor, reducing copyright concerns since access is limited to students within the course, and finally, the ability of the librarian to update the e-reserves in one place.[17]

The next step in the toolkit includes using seamless authentication. This process allows the student's log-in credentials to be passed from the LMS to other proprietary resources that require authentication. It prevents the user from having to log in multiple times in one session to gain access to available resources. Other universities are using this process, including UNC–Chapel Hill, which developed an application that embeds library resources into its LMS courses and provides seamless access to proprietary library resources without multiple log-ins.[18] This type of back-end programming must be developed collaboratively with library technology and LMS administrators but once implemented will enhance the user experience. The third step in OSU's toolkit is the "librarian" role that was created by LMS administrators to provide appropriate course access to librarians. This role allows librarians to create content, post links, conduct assessments, and much more within the course. This microlevel integration provides the ability to customize development to meet specific course needs, though it also requires the most amount of development time. The final step in the toolkit at OSU includes automatically connecting courses to library resource pages that contain appropriate content for that specific course or department. Every LMS course contains a link titled "Library" found on the navigation menu. Once clicked, the system looks for a resource page at the course level. If one is not found, a resource page at the department level is located. If no page exists for the department, the user is sent to a generic library resource page.[19] This process is probably the best method to implement sustainable microlevel integration.

When this dynamic process is utilized, the librarian has to update information only on the resource page instead of in every LMS course that has integrated the resources. Although the time required in building the web resource page for each course or department may be substantial, the benefit is that the page can be used by multiple sections at the same time. Also, keep in mind that many libraries already have existing research guides or webpages that may require little or no change for specific courses or departments. This type of integration process is significantly more manageable than is building components into individual LMS courses, which for most universities would be impossible. OSU's toolkit involves both macrolevel and microlevel implementations that collectively have created a well-developed library presence for faculty and students with the flexibility needed for both informational needs and labor efficiency.

One thing that must be kept in mind with both macrolevel and microlevel library resource integration is the essential marketing and training that must accompany the process. This is where the collaborative effort of the instructional designer and librarian can make an impact. In a survey conducted by Chris Leeder and Steven Lonn on faculty usage of library tools in the LMS, results indicate the following:

- Both users and nonusers frequently reported that they were unaware of the existence of LMS library tools and roles.
- Nonusers reported that they were unaware of colleagues in their departments using the library tools and roles.
- Faculty groups reported a perceived lack of incentives to use the library tools and roles.
- Faculty groups reported positive perceptions of librarians.
- Faculty (users and nonusers combined) expressed significantly different expectations of the librarians' roles within the LMS than those expressed by librarians.
- Faculty groups reported that their LMS training needs were not being met.[20]

These findings are in line with the EDUCAUSE survey results discussed at the beginning of the chapter. So what does this mean for the librarian and instructional designer? It means that a campaign must be designed to make faculty aware of the library tools available to them within the LMS and the advantages of using them. How can using these tools enhance the student experience and increase learning? The answer to this question should be discussed in individual consultations, collaborative trainings, department meetings newsletter or discussion forum postings, show-and-tell sessions, and any other applicable settings. If both the librarian and instructional designer intentionally integrate examples of these resources into faculty consultations and structured training workshops, word will begin to spread, thus urging more professors to reach out for additional information and assistance. Faculty showcases and testimonials are also a *very powerful* tool to encourage and motivate others to try something new. If a professor recognizes that these resources have been successfully implemented in other courses and sees evidence of student benefits, then he or she will be more likely to reach out to the librarian to discuss integration and usage. Once the library components are embedded into the course, student usage will increase. Working in tandem, the instructional designer and librarian can ensure the needs of faculty are being met, increasing library resource integration awareness and student usage.

INFORMATION LITERACY IN THE LMS

The ACRL defines information literacy as when users have the ability to "recognize when information is needed and have the ability to locate, evaluate, and use effectively the needed information."[21] The ACRL further explains:

> Information literacy also is increasingly important in the contemporary environment of rapid technological change and proliferating information resources. Because of the escalating complexity of this environment, individuals are faced with diverse, abundant information choices—in their academic studies, in the workplace, and in their personal lives. Information is available through libraries, community resources, special interest organizations, media, and the Internet—and increasingly, information comes to individuals in unfiltered formats, raising questions about its authenticity, validity, and reliability. In addition, information is available through multiple media, including graphical, aural, and textual, and these pose new challenges for individuals in evaluating and understanding it. The uncertain quality and expanding quantity of information pose large challenges for society. The sheer abundance of information will not in itself create a more informed citizenry without a complementary cluster of abilities necessary to use information effectively.[22]

Information literacy has been a mission of the librarian throughout the ages, but due to the digital age, the explosion of information now available makes these skills more vital than ever, as indicated in the previous passage. "All types of libraries have championed the cause of information literacy, recognizing the need to support not only basic reading literacy skills development in their communities, but also to deliver computer and Internet literacy training programs to help their users 'locate, manage and use information effectively.'"[23] Libraries now provide access to information in a wide variety of formats, most of which require some form of technology. These informational resources necessitate technology skills and information literacy skills to locate and use the information effectively. The advantages that this generation has for meeting research needs are astounding, and educating students and faculty to use these tools successfully is a priority for librarians.

Integrating information literacy training into the LMS might be a solution that could work well for many universities. "In its online form a library can be less visible, difficult to access and confusing to navigate. The development of information literacy is too important to be left to chance encounters with the library—particularly students at risk. Embedded librarianship, through the LMS, provides an effective means for equitably facilitating these encounters."[24] Utilizing the LMS, information literacy training can be constructed in a variety of ways to reach more students, including the building of a stand-alone LMS course or the development of information literacy modules that are added to existing courses. LMS administrators and the instructional designer can help the library establish what their options are and what the best method of implementation for a specific university would be.

Some universities have chosen to create a stand-alone information literacy course within the LMS. This strategy allows libraries to have complete control over the course, providing them with the ability to add a variety of engaging components and activities to promote learning of information literacy skills. However, one thing to consider with this type of strategy is student enrollment and management. At Monmouth College in 2007, a library course was developed in Moodle that automatically enrolled all students. Once logged in to the system, students had only to click the course link to gain access to the course. The automatic enrollment functionality streamlined the enrollment process, reducing labor for the professor, the librarian, and the LMS administrator. Once students access the course, they are required by the professor to complete activities, including readings, videos, and worksheets, to prepare for the upcoming training with the librarian. All work is due before students come into the library for the traditional information literacy training, at which time resources completed in the LMS course are discussed.

In addition, the testing function in Moodle, as with most LMSs, allows librarians to assess student mastery by conducting pre-tests and post-tests.[25] Lauren A. Jensen, from Monmouth College, states, "Our use of Moodle has taught us that learning management software systems are multifunctional and easy to use. LMS features are conducive to inquiry, conversation, and feedback, making LMS a viable alternative to a course-specific resource guide on the library's website."[26] Using the LMS functionality also reduces class time required for information literacy training. It takes the approach of the "flipped classroom" in which students learn the content outside of the classroom and then actively use the content learned during class. This strategy leads to increased learning and retention, which is a benefit for the librarian, professor, and, especially, the student.

While the development of an information literacy course within the LMS is worth consideration, other issues must be contemplated before development occurs: How will students be enrolled in the course? How will students be separated into classes if multiple sections are enrolled? How will grading and monitoring of components such as assignment submission, testing, and discussion forums be handled? Finally, how will support be provided? All of these questions should be deliberated on before course development begins. Working collaboratively with an instructional designer throughout the development process can ensure a successful and streamlined course. There are many advantages to creating a course in the LMS, including the variety of functionalities available to present content and engage students, training consistency from instructor to instructor, multiple course enrollment, less in-class time required for training, and efficiency in updating content. Instructional designers can not only train the librarian on how to use the LMS tools available but also, and more importantly, help design an effective, well-organized course that integrates active learning techniques and appropriate assessments that lead to increased learning and retention. The instructional designer and librarian can work together to analyze the needs of the course, design and develop the activities and assessments needed, implement the course, and finally, evaluate the course once completed—all important components in designing and developing successful trainings. The collaborative effort between the librarian and instructional designer can be ongoing to ensure continuous improvement of the LMS course.

If a stand-alone LMS course is not the best strategy for a university, an information literacy module can be developed by the library and embedded into existing LMS courses. This can be done by creating a section within the LMS course and utilizing the variety of tools available to create the unit. Integrating third-party-vendor information literacy modules into the LMS is another option worth considering. The module content, activities, and assessments have been developed by experts in the field and can be customized to meet the needs of the university. Johnson & Wales University–Charlotte has integrated an information literacy module created by Credo. It functions as a stand-alone module in the cloud or can be embedded into Blackboard (see figure 8.3). The customizations allow faculty and librarians to select specific information literacy units that are appropriate for each class.

Libraries need to explore a bit to determine the most effective way to integrate information literacy into the LMSs on their campuses. LMSs provide a plethora of functionalities that can be used to create effective, engaging, multimodal information literacy courses that benefit all stakeholders. Although the development and integration process may require great effort, providing

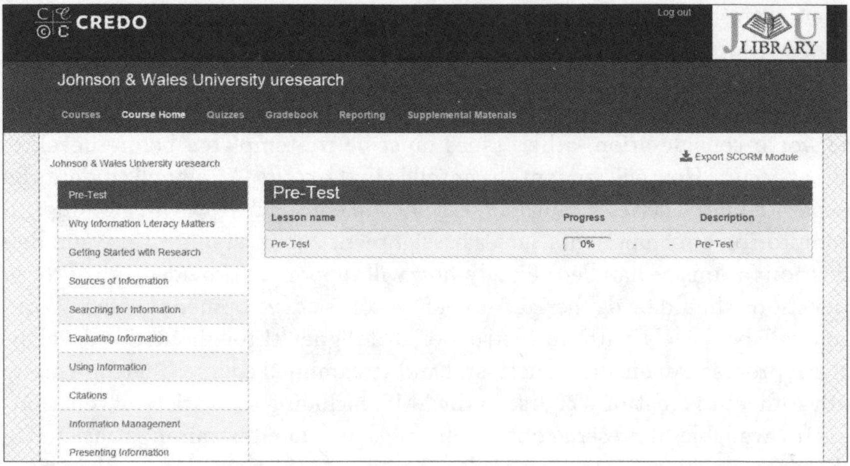

FIGURE 8.3
JWU-Charlotte's uresearch information literacy module developed by Credo

information literacy training in a prime location such as the LMS is ideal. Working with the instructional designer and LMS administrators, the library can formulate a plan to ensure that the outcome is streamlined and valuable.

HURDLES AND HOW TO GET STARTED

There are many hurdles for the academic library to overcome as it explores and expands upon the development of a library presence in the LMS; however, in the end, this is an effort that should prove beneficial to the library, professors, and students. Since building a library presence in the LMS will require customizations of some type, the first step should be talking with LMS administrators and the instructional designer to learn the possibilities. "The challenge for the Library is to develop strategic alliances and collaborative partnerships with key stakeholders in the organization."[27] This collaborative effort will ensure that all the information needed to make good decisions is on the table before development begins. Armed with this information, the library can then determine the level of access (microlevel or macrolevel) that is feasible at its institution and begin contemplating what that integration would entail. Developing a macrolevel presence may be a good first step because at least this presence creates student awareness and an easy access point to library resources and services. If that is the path chosen, decisions will need to be made concerning whether the integration will occur through manual or automatic placement in the LMS. While many universities are striving toward microlevel integration where back-end programming guides students to relevant resources automatically, this is a project that requires decisions to be made in multiple departments, which can make development and implementation a lengthier process. While that is most certainly a project worth taking on, in the interim, microlevel integration could begin with librarians being granted an access role in the LMS that provides permissions to build content to provide a gateway to the library resources needed. Although this approach is conducted course by course, it does increase awareness and interest in the library and could demonstrate a need for more automated microintegration.

Another hurdle and area to consider when getting started is library staff training. The librarian's technology skills play a vital part in how effective the library resource integration is. Most librarians will want to know what functionality options are available in the LMS in order to design appropriate components based on the needs of the class. Also, the more skilled librarians are with LMS tools, the more guidance and support they will be able to offer faculty and students. The instructional designer can provide the training needed to increase the library staff's comfort level with LMS tools and eventually can develop and collaborate on trainings with library staff, which is another component that is *extraordinarily* important.

Another idea to consider when getting started is initiating the implementation stage by creating a pilot. Working with a few professors, integration can be tested to allow time for adjustments to be made before integrating the masses. This step gives the librarian and instructional designer the ability to test the current integration strategy and make changes to content or process if necessary.

While there are many hurdles to overcome when integrating the library into the LMS, it is an approach that can make a significant impact on information literacy and student learning. Exploring the LMS to see what is possible is a challenge most librarians are excited about, and with the help of the instructional designer, the process can become somewhat less daunting. Working together for the good of the institution, an instrumental change in library access can take place and lead to great things.

NOTES

1. Eden Dahlstrom, D. Christopher Brooks, and Jacqueline Bichsel, "The Current Ecosystem of Learning Management Systems in Higher Education: Student, Faculty, and IT Perspectives" (Louisville, CO: EDUCAUSE Center for Analysis and Research, 2014), https://net.educause.edu/ir/library/pdf/ers1414.pdf.
2. Susan Grajek, "Top-Ten IT Issues, 2014: Be the Change You See," *EDUCAUSE Review*, March 24, 2014, http://er.educause.edu/articles/2014/3/topten-it-issues-2014-be-the-change-you-see.
3. Dahlstrom, Brooks, and Bichsel, *The Current Ecosystem of Learning Management Systems*, 4.

4. Rick Fisher and April Heaney, "A Faculty Perspective: Strengthening At-Risk Students' Transitions to Academic Research through Embedded Librarianship," in *Embedded Librarians: Moving beyond One-Shot Instruction*, eds. Cassandra Kvenild and Kaijsa Calkins (Chicago: Association of College and Research Libraries, 2011), 41.
5. Elizabeth L. Black and Betsy Blankenship, "Linking Students to Library Resources through the Learning Management System," *Journal of Library Administration* 50, no. 5/6 (2010): 459.
6. Ibid., 466.
7. Chris Leeder and Steven Lonn, "Faculty Usage of Library Tools in a Learning Management System," *College and Research Libraries* 75, no. 5 (2014): 1.
8. Amy C. York and Jason M. Vance, "Taking Library Instruction into the Online Classroom: Best Practices for Embedded Librarians," *Journal of Library Administration* 49, no. 1/2 (2009): 201.
9. Meredith Gorran Farkas, "Libraries in the Learning Management System," *Tips and Trends* (ACRL quarterly newsletter), Summer 2015: 1, http://acrl.ala.org/IS/wp-content/uploads/2014/05/summer2015.pdf.
10. John D. Shank and Nancy H. Dewald, "Establishing Our Presence in Courseware: Adding Library Services to the Virtual Classroom," *Information Technology and Libraries* 22, no. 1 (2003): 38.
11. Black and Blankenship, "Linking Students to Library Resources," 460.
12. Steely Library, "Blackboard and the Library," Northern Kentucky University, Greater Cincinnati Region, accessed April 19, 2016, http://steelylibrary.nku.edu/facultyandstaff/blackboardandlibrary.html.
13. Marianne Foley, "Putting the Library at Students' Fingertips," *Journal of Electronic Resources Librarianship* 24, no. 3 (2012): 167–76.
14. Farkas, "Libraries in the Learning Management System," 2.
15. Melissa Izzo, e-mail interview by author, September 22, 2015.
16. Emily Daly, "Embedding Library Resources into Learning Management Systems: A Way to Reach Duke Undergrads at Their Points of Need," *College and Research Libraries News* 71, no. 4 (2010): 208–12.
17. Black and Blankenship, "Linking Students to Library Resources," 499.
18. Keith Norbury, "The Library Has Left the Building, But . . . ," *Campus Technology*, December 5, 2013, https://campustechnology.com/articles/2013/12/05/the-library-has-left-the-building-but.aspx.
19. Black and Blankenship, "Linking Students to Library Resources," 500.
20. Leeder and Lonn, "Faculty Usage of Library Tools."
21. Association of College and Research Libraries, *Presidential Committee on Information Literacy: Final Report* (Chicago: American Library Association, 1989), www.ala.org/acrl/publications/whitepapers/presidential.
22. Association of College and Research Libraries, *Information Literacy Competency Standards for Higher Education* (Chicago: American Library Association, 2000), www.ala.org/acrl/sites/ala.org.acrl/files/content/standards/standards.pdf.

23. Ann Ritchie, "The Library's Role and Challenges in Implementing an E-learning Strategy: A Case Study from Northern Australia," *Health Information and Libraries Journal* 28, no. 1 (2011): 42.
24. Anne Horn, Alexia Maddox, Pauline Hagel, Michael Currie, and Sue Owen, "Embedded Library Services: Beyond Chance Encounters for Students from Low SES Backgrounds," *Australian Academic and Research Libraries* 44, no. 4 (2013): 248.
25. Lauren A. Jensen, "Extend Instruction outside the Classroom: Take Advantage of Your Learning Management System," *Computers in Libraries* 30, no. 6 (2010): 77.
26. Ibid., 78.
27. Ritchie, "The Library's Role and Challenges," 48.

BIBLIOGRAPHY

Association of College and Research Libraries. *Information Literacy Competency Standards for Higher Education*. Chicago: American Library Association, 2000. www.ala.org/acrl/sites/ala.org.acrl/files/content/standards/standards.pdf.

———. *Presidential Committee on Information Literacy: Final Report*. Chicago: American Library Association, 1989. www.ala.org/acrl/publications/whitepapers/presidential.

Black, Elizabeth L., and Betsy Blankenship. "Linking Students to Library Resources through the Learning Management System." *Journal of Library Administration* 50, no. 5/6 (2010): 458–67.

Dahlstrom, Eden, D. Christopher Brooks, and Jacqueline Bichsel. "The Current Ecosystem of Learning Management Systems in Higher Education: Student, Faculty, and IT Perspectives." Louisville, CO: EDUCAUSE Center for Analysis and Research, 2014. https://net.educause.edu/ir/library/pdf/ers1414.pdf.

Daly, Emily. "Embedding Library Resources into Learning Management Systems: A Way to Reach Duke Undergrads at Their Points of Need." *College and Research Libraries News* 71, no. 4 (2010): 208–12.

Farkas, Meredith Gorran. "Libraries in the Learning Management System." *Tips and Trends* (ACRL newsletter), Summer 2015. http://acrl.ala.org/IS/wp-content/uploads/2014/05/summer2015.pdf.

Fisher, Rick, and April Heaney. "A Faculty Perspective: Strengthening At-Risk Students' Transitions to Academic Research through Embedded Librarianship." In *Embedded Librarians: Moving beyond One-Shot Instruction*, edited by Cassandra Kvenild and Kaijsa Calkins, 35–45. Chicago: Association of College and Research Libraries, 2011.

Foley, Marianne. "Putting the Library at Students' Fingertips." *Journal of Electronic Resources Librarianship* 24, no. 3 (2012): 167–76.

Grajek, Susan. "Top-Ten IT Issues, 2014: Be the Change You See." *EDUCAUSE Review*, March 24, 2014. http://er.educause.edu/articles/2014/3/topten-it-issues-2014-be-the-change-you-see.

Horn, Anne, Alexia Maddox, Pauline Hagel, Michael Currie, and Sue Owen. "Embedded Library Services: Beyond Chance Encounters for Students from Low SES Backgrounds." *Australian Academic and Research Libraries* 44, no. 4 (2013): 235–50.

Jensen, Lauren A. "Extend Instruction outside the Classroom: Take Advantage of Your Learning Management System." *Computers in Libraries* 30, no. 6 (2010): 76–78.

Leeder, Chris, and Steven Lonn. "Faculty Usage of Library Tools in a Learning Management System." *College and Research Libraries* 75, no. 5 (2014): 650–63.

Norbury, Keith. "The Library Has Left the Building, But . . ." *Campus Technology*, December 5, 2013. https://campustechnology.com/articles/2013/12/05/the-library-has-left-the-building-but.aspx.

Ritchie, Ann. "The Library's Role and Challenges in Implementing an E-learning Strategy: A Case Study from Northern Australia." *Health Information and Libraries Journal* 28, no. 1 (2011): 41–49.

Shank, John D., and Nancy H. Dewald. "Establishing Our Presence in Courseware: Adding Library Services to the Virtual Classroom." *Information Technology and Libraries* 22, no. 1 (2003): 38–44.

Steely Library. "Blackboard and the Library." Northern Kentucky University, Greater Cincinnati Region. Accessed April 19, 2015. http://steelylibrary.nku.edu/facultyandstaff/blackboardandlibrary.html.

York, Amy C., and Jason M. Vance. "Taking Library Instruction into the Online Classroom: Best Practices for Embedded Librarians." *Journal of Library Administration* 49, no. 1/2 (2009): 197–209.

JOE ESHLEMAN

9
What's Next for Librarians and Instructional Designers?

As mentioned in the introduction, this book, as a combined effort between librarians and instructional designers, in some ways does more to represent the goals within it than simply what was written here. During the writing of this book and due to the collaboration it required, we contemplated specific areas where further partnership could be created. The decision to include outside images in the book of course forced us to collectively track down permissions for images, explore alternatives, and so on. At the same time, one of the librarians along with an instructional designer began fielding a higher volume of faculty questions about rights needed to use certain digital media in their presentations and publications. So this book is a prime example of how collaboration can lead to more chance encounters and need for support (which can lead to higher profiles within your institution). Collaboration leads to more collaboration. These examples are not intended to say that every librarian–instructional designer connection should produce a book (although we look forward to reading more collaborative writings in the future). It is obvious to us, however, from this and other examples that conversations and projects breed more opportunity. With this in mind, daily discussions inside and outside the library are a must. They should center on anticipating technological changes that impact higher education and libraries. Any librarian who is not talking about how technology will affect his or her job could be sideswiped or waylaid by the changes. At one point, it was prudent to think about how a library job would change in three years and prepare for that change. Now it seems wise to consider the changes we will see in less than a year. This is another clue we need to take from instructional designers, the need for continual planning and designing.

Instructional design librarian; user experience librarian; experience design librarian; technology planning, integration, and experience librarian; research/instruction design librarian; digital learning librarian—these and other similar librarian positions are making headway in academic libraries today. The importance placed on digital resources and design in libraries continues to grow, and the hope is that librarians will be ready to meet the challenges ahead and reinvent themselves if necessary. Reinvention is difficult to accomplish. And reinventing without any help, like all endeavors, can be even more difficult. There may even be a myth to reinvention. It often does not occur in the way in which we first consider it. Marc Freedman asks, "Isn't there something to be said for racking up decades of know-how and lessons, from failures as well as triumphs? Shouldn't we aspire to build on that wisdom and understanding?"[1] He questions what it means to reinvent yourself and wants us to ask what we are leaving behind if we make a radical transformation. He would like us to reconsider if the desire for reinvention creates a loss greater than the gain. It seems that these ideas are also relevant to libraries.

That libraries (and librarians) need to adapt to change is more than self-evident. And an accurate response to this claim is that this state of affairs has always been the case; that is, things are always changing. Yet the pervasiveness and rapidity of technological change do create a different situation. On occasion, a request for change due to technological impact can inspire a cynical response and some rankle. But what if librarians considered that they need to change because people are changing. They need to change because the students of even the recent past are now a much different and larger group who need help navigating through the information landscape. Perhaps that consideration would be easier to absorb or would create a more measured response. Most librarians appear to agree with the idea that academic libraries are currently in a position where they need to be able to respond proactively to change. As discussed in chapter 1, they also need to be proactive with regard to the turbulence that is affecting higher education. Surely, there is still some value in Ranganathan's fifth law, "The library is a growing organism."[2] At the risk of following a potentially pedantic course, what is meant by a "growing organism"?

Growth can at first imply a change in physical size (or shape). When libraries were at one time considered to be the "holders" of information for society (and institutions of higher education), an ever-growing collection of information was considered a worthwhile goal. Of course, what libraries (and, therefore, librarians) are considered to be has changed, primarily due to a diminished "hold" on information. But perhaps information is not what libraries need to collect, hold on to, or grow. Perhaps it is people (and their personal relationships with information) that librarians should be attempting to grow. The first indication of this importance has been a focus on information literacy and library instruction. As ways to access information continue to change, the trend appears to be a diminishing desire to point students to strictly "academic" information resources. Renewed focus is on experiential learning and the ever-changing information landscape. An increased priority on developing the aptitude to find information (the "why" of the ACRL *Framework* over the "how" of the ACRL *Standards*[3]) continues to gain momentum. We continue to move in a direction whereby authority must seek to understand the position of those who are the learners and the learners gain agency and divorce themselves from dependence on the authority.

Yet libraries seem to be stuck at a crossroads where they are not able to define their own future and often appear to be at the mercy of how others define them. Still worse, librarians are stereotyped when they are not being ignored. Is there something that librarians can do specifically to improve their perception in some instances from one of reactionaries to that of proactive solution finders? Yet another in a long list of conundrums that librarians must deal with in relation to their role is the idea that librarians should remain "off to the side." They should quietly accept how they are positioned within the campus, often for fear of drawing too much attention to themselves. But it would appear as if these types of librarian perceptions and pigeonholing may be coming to an end.

It is in the more politicized corners of the critical librarianship movement within the profession where a type of new future for librarians is being forged. The transformative impact of libraries is a main focus here. As mentioned in chapter 6, librarians are in the midst of creating exciting new environments in which all feel welcome. And this welcoming attitude extends into all facets of the library. Working toward librarians and collections that reflect the needs and desires of the community served is an admirable and reachable goal. Librarians are leading by example, and they are attempting to set a tone for their campuses that calls for openness, equal access, and a more representative reflection of the communities they serve.

One factor that may impact you, the librarian or instructional designer reading this book, could be your particular position in your career. You may be a new librarian who has already been exposed to the ideas presented here. Or you could be someone who has been in the field for some time. In either case, these ideas may either fall flat or resonate with you. The size of your institution is also a big factor in how you perceive changes in librarianship. As pointed out in the introduction, it's possible that no one has the title *instructional designer* at your school. Taking all of these factors into consideration, it is still worthwhile to contemplate the intersection of technology, instruction, design, and collaboration and how those forces, strategies, and responsibilities impact your job. As one example of the importance of refocusing our priorities, a way to illuminate the importance of design is to think about the recent history of librarianship. It may have developed differently if there had been a greater number of design thinkers and technologists in librarian positions in the 1980s and 1990s, or perhaps even further back. Would libraries have scooped Google and created the ultimate search algorithm and search engine? Might it have been design-savvy librarians who bypassed interlibrary loan procedure and designed something akin to Netflix's simple DVD exchange? Or might it have been librarians who invented the recommendation system of Amazon? Did the lack of librarian designers and technologists put us behind in the creation of a library-approved e-reader (one that doesn't use the reader as a surveillance opportunity)? What else might we be missing in the future if we do not capitalize on the potential opportunities available to us today? Will we refuse the spotlight because it is our lot in life to support those who design and invent the technologies that we end up paying for later?

There is an opening for those who are forward thinking, open to new ways for collaboration, and ready to take on this challenge. We think the time is right to work together as librarians and instructional designers and become pivotal players in the direction that higher education takes. We are interested in the move to digital and the way in which design is influencing our teaching. And we want to connect with all of our students, welcoming them whether they are in the library or in an online setting.

The time is right and the time is now to go and talk to those on your campus who are ready to work together to create an engaging and creative educational experience. The primary need is to design excellent instruction and library services supported with the best technology tools to help our growing number of students. This leads us to suggest collaborating with your instructional designer. But the overarching goal is to begin talking to coworkers in the library and outside of it as a way to raise the profile of the librarian on your campus. We need librarians who respond to the question, "Why did you become a librarian?" in a different way. The answer should not necessarily be, "Because I like books" or "Because I like information" or, even, "Because I like technology." It should be, "I became a librarian because I like collaborating and innovating with people."

NOTES

1. Marc Freedman, "The Dangerous Myth of Reinvention," *Harvard Business Review*, January 1, 2014, https://hbr.org/2014/01/the-dangerous-myth-of reinvention.
2. S. R. Ranganathan, *The Five Laws of Library Science* (London: Edward Goldston, 1931).
3. Association of College and Research Libraries, *Framework for Information Literacy for Higher Education* (Chicago: American Library Association, 2016), www.ala.org/acrl/sites/ala.org.acrl/files/content/issues/infolit/Framework -ILHE.pdf; Association of College and Research Libraries, *Information Literacy Competency Standards for Higher Education* (Chicago: American Library Association, 2000), www.ala.org/acrl/sites/ala.org.acrl/files/content/ standards/standards.pdf.

About the Authors

JOE ESHLEMAN received his Master of Library and Information Science degree from the University of North Carolina at Greensboro in 2007. He has been the Instruction Librarian at Johnson & Wales University Library–Charlotte since 2008. During this time, he has taught numerous library instruction sessions. Mr. Eshleman completed the Association of College and Research Libraries' Immersion Program, an intensive program of training and education for instruction librarians, in 2009. He is a coauthor of *Fundamentals for the Academic Liaison* (alongside Richard Moniz and Jo Henry) and a contributor to *The Personal Librarian: Enhancing the Student Experience*. He has presented on numerous occasions, including at the American Library Association Conference, the Lilly Conference on College and University Teaching, the Teaching Professor Technology Conference, and the First National Personal Librarian and First Year Experience Library Conference.

RICHARD MONIZ, EdD, has served as Director of Library Services for Johnson & Wales University's Miami campus from 1997–2004 and has been the Director of Library Services at Johnson & Wales University's Charlotte campus since 2004. He has also, in the past, simultaneously served as Head of Information Technology Services for Johnson & Wales in Miami and taught classes on subjects such as computer science, world history, US history, and American government. Additionally, since 2006, he has taught for the MLIS program at the University of North Carolina at Greensboro. Courses taught have included Information Sources and Services, Special Libraries, Library Administration, Information Sources in the Professions, and Online Bibliographic Information Retrieval. Dr. Moniz has published in numerous places. He is sole author of the 2010 textbook *Practical and Effective Management of Libraries*, coauthor of *Fundamentals for the Academic Liaison*, and coauthor and coeditor of *The Personal Librarian: Enhancing the Student Experience*. He is actively engaged in the profession and has held a number of committee and board responsibilities within the ALA, LLAMA (Library Leadership and Management Association), ACRL, CLS (College Libraries), and Metrolina Library Association (including serving as President of this organization) in addition to other nonprofit organizations such as Carolina Raptor Center, Charlotte Museum of History, and Charlotte's Arts and Science Council.

KAREN MANN received her Master of Library and Information Science degree from the University of North Carolina at Greensboro in 2007, a Graduate Certificate in Teaching, Training, and Educational Technology from North Carolina State University in 2015, and a Bachelor of Science degree in Secondary Education from Concord University in Athens, West Virginia. She earned her National Board Certification in Library Media in 2009. She has provided Instructional Technology and Design services in the department of Academic Technology Services at Johnson & Wales University–Charlotte since 2011. Her background also includes experience as a high school media specialist, technologist, and science teacher. Mann has presented at multiple conferences on best practices in teaching with technology and has provided a variety of training workshops that focus on creating exemplary courses and engaging the learner with technology.

KRISTEN ESHLEMAN is a graduate of the University of North Carolina at Chapel Hill, having received a Bachelor of Arts in Anthropology and in International Studies in 1992. She received her Master of Science in Social Anthropology from the London School of Economics in 1994. At Davidson, she serves as both practitioner for the humanities and Director of Instructional Technology, identifying current and emerging technologies and working with faculty in the humanities to determine whether they have pedagogical value in a small, residential liberal arts environment. She is also the lead instructional designer for DavidsonX, a cofounder of THATCamp Piedmont, and an active member of the EDUCAUSE Learning Initiative community. The anthropologist in her is drawn to the intersections between technology and culture. Her interests include digital scholarship, blended learning, educational research, and designing effective processes for institutional innovation.

Index

M